All Roads Lead To The Birchmere

America's Legendary Music Hall

GARY OELZE and
STEPHEN MOORE

Foreword by BUZZ McCLAIN

Afterword by BOB SCHIEFFER

BookLocker

Saint Petersburg, Florida

Dedications

To my wife, Susan, for her love, support and always reminding me to take the high road; and to my brothers and sister, and their families in Kentucky, who wonder where I've been these past 55 years.

Gary Oelze

To my children, Charles and Suzanna and my grand-daughter, Kona Sage, with love. And to Susan Oelze for friendship and support.

Stephen Moore

Foreword by Buzz McClain

A Few Words About Gary Oelze—
And He's Going to Hate Them All

"Don't make this about me," Gary Oelze says, over and over and over. "This isn't about me."

And he means it. But for once, and just for a few hundred words, we're going to make it about him. Because no matter how many times you've been to the Birchmere to see a show, no matter how many times the guy with the microphone thrilled you when he called your number for your turn to go into the theater (that's Gary), no matter how many beers he's silently signaled to the bartender for you to enjoy while you continue a pre-show conversation, you still have no idea who Gary Oelze is.

Before we get to the who, here's the why: In the history of regional performance promotion, Gary Oelze has been the club owner responsible for entertaining the Mid-Atlantic since 1975. That's over 3300 nights of music, across almost five decades. Top that, and if you can, I apologize, but I think I'm on firm ground here.

With the exception of the occasional dark night, when the club gets a well-earned rest, the hall brings to its humble stage touring and local performers every night of the week. Most of the times there's an opening act, so that's two performances each night. If the stars align, there's an opener for the opener. But rest assured, no matter how many artists will take the stage, plug in their gear, tune up, and play a set, you will be home in time to catch the news on TV. It's just the way it is.

When I was a music critic at the *Washington Post* from 2000 to 2010, I spent many a night gazing at the talent on the stage.

One night I noticed a digital clock off to stage right, in front of the sound board, and when the clock ticked 7:30 p.m., the first performer took the stage. Man, that's pretty precise, I thought to myself. A few weeks later, back in my favorite seat at Table 136, front and center. I watched again as the clock hit 7:30 p.m. and, right on time, the artist strolled out, all smiles, ready to rock. It happened again, and again. And that's when I realized, this was no accident or coincidence: Someone has told the talent that *there will be music at 7:30*. It's a promise Gary makes to his audience, and the artists—who, as you will see on the following pages—love and respect the venue and the owner and are all too happy to oblige by being timely.

Now here's more than Gary ever wanted you to know about him: Gary was born to S.V. Oelze and Carmelia Hagan on August 24, 1942. He was born and raised in Owensboro, Kentucky, a big little town on the banks of the Ohio River, as the third of seven children, six boys and a girl. His father ran a barbecue restaurant with a grocery store attached until he started a successful roofing company.

When Gary was 13, he got a job with a frozen food distributor so, as he says, "I could buy my own shirts and get my own haircut. Dad cut all our hair and he was no barber, that's for sure." It was the beginning of his entrepreneurial career.

Music of all sorts was all around the young Gary, on the radio and at school, where playing a musical instrument was not out of the norm. His instrument was acoustic guitar. With his brother on bass and a neighborhood friend, Floyd Stewart, as singer, 15-year-old Gary and his "band" (yes, Gary, it was a band, no matter how you want to downplay it) would play square dances around town—four 20-minute sets of country and rock 'n' roll a night. They also played off-the-beaten-path roadhouses that didn't open until after midnight, places even the sheriff avoided. "It was quite an experience for a kid," he says. I'll bet!

Gary downplays his musical ambitions, which were modest to begin with. "I had no desire to go to Nashville or anything like that. Just about everybody I knew played guitar, or tried to. It was hard for me, I was not a natural, I had to work at it."

Another thing you didn't know: Gary is an Air Force veteran. He enlisted at age 17, the year his mother died. He met his first wife and had a child as a serviceman and when his stint was over, he settled in the Washington area to be near his brother. "I really didn't want to go back to Kentucky after being in the military and traveling," he says. "I thought it was a little slower back there."

He wound up managing a People's Drug Store—vintage area folks will recall the growing chain of drug stores fondly—when a regular customer and friend offered him a position running a small restaurant. You'll get the details later, but the rest is music history.

So why do you need to know all this, especially since Gary never brings any of this up himself?

Gary's background made the Birchmere possible. Look at the evidence.

His father ran a barbecue restaurant, which showed him what was possible. Gary struggled to learn the guitar, giving him insight as to how hard it is to be an accomplished musician. He played unholy gigs with fellow teenagers in honky-tonks neither the Kentucky or Indiana police would have anything to do with, experiences that showed him the right way and the wrong way of accommodating talent and an audience. He learned discipline and routine in the military, two things any entrepreneur will tell you are essential for long-term success. He managed retail establishments and was hired away by someone who saw his potential in a risky new endeavor.

All of these experiences led him to devoting himself to creating and maintaining a venue people—artists as well as customers—could count on. The Birchmere.

An additional trait that contributes to the Birchmere being the Birchmere are the contributions of the theater's longtime in-house promoter, Michael Jaworek, who has been building relationships with artists and their managers since 1988. You'll hear more about him on these pages, too, as well as the others who have made careers catering to a loyal clientele for years.

A telling memory: Several years ago, during a pre-show chat with Gary, just before he took the microphone to call out numbers for folks to take their seats in the theater, Gary asked me how well I knew the work of songwriter Mickey Newbury, who had many songwriting successes including when Elvis Presley recorded a version of "American Trilogy." I admitted beyond that, I knew little. A few days later a boxed set of Mickey Newbury CDs arrived at my house in the mail, with a note to the effect of, "You really should know about Mickey." I've never forgotten that, although I'll wager good money Gary has. He must do those sorts of things all the time.

For years, I had a Birchmere mousepad leaning on the bookshelf across from my desk. I didn't need a mousepad, I just liked the look of it, with its montage of Fender guitars and acoustic instruments, the stylized script logo, and the slogan, "America's Legendary Music Hall." The sight of it comforted me, somehow, knowing there was a place I would be going soon—I always have a ticket for something—that I could count on for a decent meal, an assured professional performance, and spiritual sustenance.

What more can I say than thank you, Gary Oelze, for all those good times. I'm sorry you had to read this.

Buzz McClain

Table of Contents

Introduction

"Guy Clark had been trying to get me to come play the Birchmere. He kept saying 'you gotta go, you gotta go.' And then Rosanne Cash, Guy Clark, and me were booked there. We sat on stage and shot the shit and played songs together for almost four hours. It was an unrehearsed thing. Afterwards, we got paid in cash. Guy took the money and threw it in the air. He said, 'see, here's how it is.' Gary was standing there laughing. And I said, well, thank God all roads lead to the Birchmere."

Rodney Crowell

It is 5:00 pm on a Saturday night at the Birchmere. The roadside marquee at the entrance announces tonight's line-up, black letters against the lit white background. The soundcheck on the rectangular wooden stage wrapped up about an hour ago. The sound crew is huddling with the band's road manager, going over sound check details, and special requests from the performers one last time.

Backstage in the dressing rooms, tonight's act, roadies, and entourage are enjoying an early dinner selected from the customers' menu. In the kitchen maze, the smell of barbecue chicken, pulled-pork, and freshly made pizza fills the air as the cook staff preps appetizers, entrees, sandwiches, and desserts to fill the several hundred orders that will appear within the hour. Glassware gleams; the bar with its colorful bottles is stocked and ready, signed posters of Merle Haggard and Johnny Cash smile down with a glowing neon guitar hovering above on the wall. At the right is the Lofgren family player piano that Rock and Roll Hall of Famer Nils donated to the hall. A hundred tables that seat 500 people, each with an intimate view of the stage, are clean and set with menus. The waitstaff connects with the veteran—for over a quarter century—server and manager, Dawn Williams, to discuss table service for the night.

Friendly box office manager Stuart Wodlinger takes his usual place at the box office window connected to the merchandise store, arranges cash in the till, and prepares to welcome the crowd.

Down the hall, in a small office, the owner of the club, Gary Oelze ends a phone call, extinguishes his cigarette, and heads out to meet the crowd. Concert-goers continue arriving and line up outside the mural-adorned building. At 5:00, the doors will open, and the early comers will file by the box office, receive a line number and spend a little time socializing or relaxing with a drink from the bar while other patrons arrive to join them in one of the most famous musical spaces in America.

At 6:00, the inner doors will open. Gary himself will begin calling out their seating numbers for patient, orderly entry into the music hall. Anticipation mounts as people head toward their seats.

They pass through a hallway densely packed with framed posters of hundreds of legendary performers who have graced the stage of this also-legendary venue. In this case, the walls do, in fact, talk; each poster is personally inscribed: It's a visually stunning tribute to the place by bluegrass, country, folk, rock, blues, pop, jazz, funk, western, Celtic, Cajun, comedy, Latin, zydeco, and other entertainers from around the globe.

A small sample of celebrated artists would include Ray Charles, Pete Seeger, Kitty Wells, Chick Corea, Bill Monroe, Tony Rice, Peter Frampton, The Everly Brothers, Babyface Edmonds, The Seldom Scene, B.B. King, Leon Russell, The Whispers, and Isaac Hayes. Unexpected outliers include eccentric filmmaker John Waters, avant-garde artist, Laurie Anderson, actor Billy Bob Thornton, Bellydancer Superstars, the Beatles' producer, Sir George Martin, and both of John Lennon's sons.

An abridged list of affectionate photo inscriptions express allegiances:

"To the Birchmere - Loved My Stay."	Joan Baez
"To you beautiful cats at the swinging Birchmere."	Vince Gill
"Top of the world, Ma."	Chris Isaak
"A friend forever."	Richie Havens
"A lovely place to spend an evening."	Herb Alpert
"Thank You."	John Prine
"Fine Joint."	Ry Cooder
"I love you."	Judy Collins
"God cares for all of you. Remember that."	Little Richard
"Thanks for all the great times."	Shawn Colvin
"You are what artists dream a club will become!"	Janis Ian
"It's always wonderful to come home"	Mary Chapin Carpenter

This is the Birchmere, America's Legendary Music Hall, a venerable music and dining venue that occupies a unique and much-valued home in the Washington DC area. Beloved by patrons and artists alike for an astonishing sequence of shows, the internationally renowned club offers an atmosphere of comfort, excellent sound, respect, community, and rare intimacy.

Through decades, growing pains, and three different locations, the Birchmere has amassed an abundant history and wealth of great stories. This book is an invitation to explore and savor its legacy, with a thank you to the family of artists and friends who think of the Birchmere as their "home away from home."

One of many of Gary's signed guitars on display in the "merch" room. Signed by Nils Lofgren, Kris Kristofferson, Tommy Emmanuel, Dicky Betts, Marty Stuart, Guy Clark, and Lyle Lovett. © Oelze

Chapter 1 – Birth of The Birchmere

Ray Charles gave his final public performance at the Birchmere after secretly sitting in the tech room behind the stage while his sold-out-for-months crowd finished their dinner nearby. Singer-songwriters Guy Clark, Rodney Crowell, and Rosanne Cash once held a four-hour, impromptu "song swap," which *The Washington Post* proclaimed as the 1986 entertainment event of the year. And then there was the night when the father of bluegrass, Bill Monroe, showed up unannounced with his Blue Grass Boys, marched on to the stage, played for 45 minutes, and then strolled off.

After almost 50 years of music at the Birchmere, there are hundreds of beguiling stories like these to tell. Many moments stand out as markers that built the reputation of this durable music venue.

The name came from Dr. Frederick Kinsman, an Episcopal-turned-Catholic Bishop in Delaware in the early 1900's. Seeking to create a peaceful estate, Bishop Kinsman built a stately home on ten acres in Woodstock, Maine. He named it Birchmere in honor of the numerous birch trees on the property. He eventually resigned his religious ordinance and spent his remaining years as a professor of modern church history at Catholic University in DC.

In the 1940s, the Birchmere name found a second home at a summer camp in Milford, Maine about 140 miles south of Kinsman's Woodstock home. There the Birchmere Inn Dining Room and Cocktail Lounge featured live dinner music by local musicians and clambake and lobster specials galore.

1950s postcard of the Birchmere Hotel, Cabins and Cocktail Lounge.

It was the fond boyhood memories of those camp cabins and dining room that prompted the first owner of a Shirlington restaurant to adopt the name for his new business.

The modern Birchmere began as an unassuming suburban neighborhood restaurant, nestled between an A&P grocery and an aquarium store in the Claremont Plaza Shopping Center on 2721 South Wakefield St., Arlington, VA.

However, the true creative starting point of the modern Birchmere is literally gas in glass. It is the neon sign, designed by Richard Luxemburg, the late owner of the still-in-business Services Neon Signs Inc. in Springfield, VA. This now-distinctive glowing blue emblem has graced all three incarnations of the Birchmere and has served as an iconic memory for decades of grateful audiences. Technically, neon gas heats red when it is electrically charged. The Birchmere sign contains argon gas which produces its blue color. The gas is also original and has never been refreshed. It just keeps on glowing.

When the sign was refurbished 15 years ago, the seasoned serviceman who arrived was so impressed by the sign that he requested the attached small "Services Neon" name plaque as a keepsake when his work was completed.

Act One

Gary Oelze was managing a Peoples Drug store when he became friendly with a Baltimore native named William Hooper who helped direct the Maryland and Virginia Milk Producers Association. Gary recalls, "Mr. Hooper, a gentleman, would come in and have a cup of coffee with me. One day he told me his intention to buy this little restaurant as an investment and asked me if I would manage it for him. He knew I had an understanding of the restaurant biz from my father, owned a grocery store and barbeque restaurant. Hooper offered me a salary and stock options to be his 'operator and manager.' I eagerly accepted the position."

On April 4, 1966, Bill and Gary took over the Birchmere. Hooper later became the president of the Diners Club travel division, and his attention to the business waned.

On the corner near the Birchmere Restaurant was the Jack and Jill Cue Club, a famous pool room beneath a Drug Fair pharmacy. Open 24 hours a day for 14 years, all the major pool players then came through the 32-table billiards palace.

Jack & Jill's owner, Bill Staton, was a world-renowned pool player and high-stakes gambler, and founder of the Weenie Beenie chain of hot dog restaurants. "Weenie Beenie" became his nickname. It was Staton who gave pool player Rudolf Walderone his nickname, Minnesota Fats. Gary reminisced, "I met Minnesota Fats at J&Js once, at a time when allowing women in that pool hall was the big news on the block."

"Weenie Beenie" did the trick shots for the Martin Scorsese movie, *The Color of Money*, the sequel to the classic pool film *The Hustler*. Staton also once appeared on the TV show *I've Got A Secret*. Bill's secret trick was his ability to sink a full rack of balls on the table with one shot.

Hillbilly music clubs and other "honky-tonks," as Gary calls them, were ubiquitous in the DC area after World War II. People from Virginia, North Carolina, and other states came to the recession-proof Nation's Capital looking for jobs, and when they came, they brought their music with them. The music of the Stoneman Family, Buzz Busby, Mac Wiseman and many other like-minded musicians inspired by the likes of Bill Monroe, and his Bluegrass boys, fueled the rising popularity of this fast-paced new hillbilly music.

Ironically, Gary noted: "I was never a true bluegrass fan. I loved the country music of Hank Williams, but I took notice of an ever-growing taste for new kinds of bluegrass in DC when a radio program named *Bluegrass Unlimited* premiered on local public station WAMU in 1968." This show was hosted by Dick Spotswood and produced by engineer Gary Henderson, both bluegrass and old-time record collectors. The duo became beloved local radio legends for their knowledge and dedication to American roots music.

It was also at WAMU where Patricia Maloon, a government worker became the broadcaster, Katy Daley. "I wasn't going to use my maiden name of Maloon on the air, so Dick and I just looked at the turntable one day and saw the song "Katy Daley," recorded by Ralph Stanley and that's what we picked."

Daley began proselytizing bluegrass to her radio listeners and everyone else she met. Katy recalls, "There was a new publicity director who arrived at the station in the '70s named Nell Jackson. She made the big mistake of asking me to tell her, 'a little bit about bluegrass.' I gave her the full fire hose of history, beginning with Bill Monroe buying a mandolin and proceeding, through the Washington-area festivals, clubs, organizations, and DC bluegrass musicians, especially the popularity of the Seldom Scene playing weekly at the Red Fox Inn in Bethesda, Maryland.

"Her eyes glazed over," says Katy. "Nell responded, "So I guess you could say 'Washington DC is the capital of bluegrass.' It was her shorthand for 'I get what you're saying.' Before long, Katy and WAMU modified this slogan as "Bluegrass capital of the world," and added it to their on-air broadcasts, program guide, and fundraisers. The name stuck.

© *Oelze*

The Old Five and Dimers

Not far from the Pentagon, the restaurant's local area included enough government workers to guarantee a consistent lunch crowd. Gary changed the former German food menu to burgers and fries. About 60 customers a day kept the Birchmere's lights on. Evenings, it became a local bar scene with residents of the nearby Shirlington Estates apartments relaxing with their friends.

The first live music that appeared in the restaurant began on Sundays when local musician, "Stumpy" Brown, hauled his Hammond B3 organ and Leslie speaker in to play mellow jazz. In late 1974, Gary became friends with a young British man, John Longbottom, a regular customer at the Birchmere who worked in construction nearby, turning asphalt into new Alexandria roads. Discovering that each played guitar, they started practicing together. When club regulars, Phil Coopie and Don Fuller joined them on banjo, fiddle and bass, the Old Five and Dimers band was born. The name was borrowed from the "Old Five and Dimers Like Me" song by Texas country music singer and songwriter, Billy Joe Shaver. Thirty-five years later, Shaver, himself, would sing this song on the stage of the third Birchmere.

Fuller's widow, Wanda, and brother-in-law, Jimmy Maupin sums the band up: "Everybody loved them. We thought they were tremendous. As for presentation, Gary was a good

9

guitarist and vocalist but not a performer per se. Coopie played good banjo but he was really quiet.

(l to r) "Gary, Phil, John, and Don. Don lived in the nearby apartments and learned the bass to play. © *E. Fuller*

John Longbottom had the English accent, and he was a hell of a guitar player. Don had the jokes in between the songs and brought the humor and liveliness to the stage."

"Do you think they might have been biased?" Gary joked when he heard their assessment.

The band slogan was "Contemporary Country with a Blade of Grass." Early song list included Rod Stewart's "Maggie Mae" and "Mandolin Wind," John Prine's "Blue Umbrella," Dylan's "Nashville Skyline Rag," and bluegrass standards like "Foggy Mountain Breakdown." Longbottom began hosting nascent "open mic" evenings at the Birchmere. "Nobody became famous," he declares. Longbottom would later develop a following himself when he played the Irish bar, Murphy's, in nearby Old Town Alexandria.

Gary downplays the relevance of The Old Five and Dimers to this history. He was reluctant to even mention them. He states, "I don't want anyone to think that I started the Birchmere as some vanity project. Many club owners are motivated to hang with the stars to become a star, or to show how cool they are."

Only a few acts know that Gary played music. When informed of this fact, they generally agree that this is one reason he worked so well with acts over the years. Singer-songwriter Janis Ian agreed but commented, "I think Gary was very smart not to let artists know that he is a musician and was in a band. That's the kind of thing you should keep close to your chest. Very smart," said Ian.

Gary notes other DC area venues in the 1970s, commenting, "There were dozens of bars and clubs playing bluegrass back then. The Red Fox, Stricks, The Quonset Supper Club, Hunter's Lodge, William's Restaurant, Hillbilly Heaven, and the Shamrock on M Street in Georgetown were a few. The Country Gentlemen made the Shamrock renowned in the '60s.

"I considered most of them dives. And then when I started adding bluegrass music to the Birchmere, there were many bar owners, promoters, and even some players whose attitude was 'what the hell are you doing getting into *our* business?' At that time, there was the thinking that this bluegrass pie was only so big. There wasn't an idea of sharing or expanding the pie.'" Gary imagined that despite the beer-stained linoleum and scarred wooden paneled walls the Birchmere had the potential to attract a listening crowd. Gary reveals, "I thought 'The Cellar Door in Georgetown was the gold standard for a successful music club where respectful listening was expected. The Cellar Door, and its predecessor, The Shadows, were classy, listening rooms from the get-go."

More "dive" than "diva", the Birchmere "music club" could be the modest "start-up" with a hopeful future. While Gary continued in The Five and Dimers, he hired three local bluegrass groups: None of the Above, Hickory Wind —"the first group that sold out the place and raised my eyebrows," says Gary—and The Grass Menagerie.

Leading Grass Menagerie was an extraordinary mandolinist from Japan, Akira Otsuka, whose Bluegrass 45 band was discovered in Japan by *Rebel Records* owner Charles R. "Dick" Freeland. The band toured the United States in 1971 and were featured in the 1972 film *Bluegrass Country Soul.*

A rare photo of Akira Otsuka playing a Fender Stratocaster guitar instead of his mandolin.   © *Oelze*

Akira was enamored with the Seldom Scene, especially John Duffey. They were packing every Thursday night at the Red Fox Inn, were favorites on country radio stations in New York City and Washington, DC with five albums selling internationally including the 1975 double album, *Live at the Cellar Door.* Akira was also captivated by their innovative advancing musical style. By the mid-1970s, The Seldom Scene were also veterans of the bluegrass festival circuit.

Akira explains, "I was working at Rebel Records for Dick Freeland when Gary hired my band. One day Freeland asked me to take a box of records to Duffey's Arlington, Virginia home. I told Dick about playing at the Birchmere, and it was the first time he had ever heard of the place. When I got to Duffey's house that afternoon, I told John about the Birchmere. He too asked 'Where?'"

"Gary would eventually hire the Seldom Scene, but don't claim that the Scene *started* the Birchmere. It was None of The Above that began drawing people in. They launched the Birchmere," declares Akira.

None of The Above became the first band to earn a regular weekly slot from 8:00 pm to 12:30 am on Thursdays. By this time, they had played DC clubs and were one of the featured bands at WAMU's first bluegrass concert held September 22,

1974 in the New Lecture Hall on American University's campus. Mandolinist Dan Shipp built a long musical resume running in the same bluegrass circles as the Seldom Scene and Grass Menagerie.

None of the Above band (l to r) Carol Nethery, (fiddle), Dave Norman (banjo), Dan Shipp, (mandolin), Les McIntyre, (guitar), and Bob White (bass). Les went on to a prominent career on WAMU radio until his passing at age 69 in 2011. His music knowledge was only surpassed only by such folks as Pete Kuykendall of Bluegrass Unlimited and WSM's Eddie Stubbs. © D. Shipp

Shipp says, "None of the Above had played the Red Fox Inn; the manager was Walt Broderick. A nice guy but he wasn't particularly interested in music, especially the sound quality. And then Akira told us about the Birchmere. We went to see Gary and he hired us. It was immediately apparent that Gary was extremely interested in sound quality and investing his profits into improvements. He didn't want a noisy bar with the band in the corner."

Gary investigated the Red Fox a few times and wasn't impressed. "You couldn't get a seat because all the friends of the bands had them."

After those visits Gary bought a Bose sound system and professional lighting for the Birchmere. The once-unassuming restaurant began its tradition of continuous improvement and Gary's attention to sonic quality became an Oelze trademark.

Many of the earliest Birchmere music club staff were essential in the club's musical start-up success. This included the indispensable early support and encouragement from Gary's future wife, Linda Hodge. It was head waitress Linda who hand-sewed the original red checkered tablecloths. Part-time waitress Teresa O'Brien arrived from Dublin, Ireland and came on board. Along with his fellow players in the Old Five and Dimers they shared Gary's goal to advance the Birchmere.

And then came the rules! Gary's quest to provide the best quality sound led the Birchmere to become the first bluegrass club to enforce a "Quiet—Please!" policy so you could really hear the music. Gary looks back: "Forcing order on a bluegrass music club was a challenge. I stole the wording on my "Quiet—Please!" in deference to the artists…" cards from the Cellar Door. I had to look up what the phrase "in deference" meant."

Gary's friend Marlise Mason did the early graphic art for the club. She designed the cards which adorned each table, politely requesting people to shut up. Marlise remembers that Gary wasn't confident that these cards would actually work to silence anybody.

It turned out that the rule cards were effective but required enforcement. "Either Moose, our doorman and bouncer, or I would ask people who broke this rule to leave. Once I evicted 12 out of 24 customers." Asked if anybody objected to the policy Gary, responded, "I always found that it would usually be just one guy who was entertaining his group at a table. Then I'd go over a few times and ask the talker to be quiet. Finally, when I made him leave, the people at his table would thank me afterward. And I always thought, 'Then why did you invite this asshole to begin with?'"

It was not always the audience who broke this 'Silence is golden" rule. When Commander Cody (George Frayne) and the Lost Planet Airmen played, "Cody would start his rowdy country rock show by ripping up one of the cards on stage with his fans cheering," says Gary.

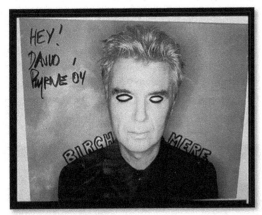

The Talking Heads' David Byrne.   © Oelze

For the record, perhaps the liveliest violation to the "Quiet, please" policy occurred in 2004, when Talking Head's David Byrne gave a solo concert named "Finite=Alright." His two encores, "Psycho Killer" and "Once in a Lifetime" had the crowd singing and dancing, some atop their chairs. "It was a disco party," Gary recalls.

BeauSoleil, performing music rooted in the music of the Cajuns and Creoles of Louisiana, also preferred their audience loud, partying, and dancing. The band told Gary that they felt intimidated if their audience wasn't animated.

One standout early band, The Rosslyn Mountain Boys, began playing the Birchmere every Wednesday night in 1975, generating lines around the strip mall block. "We often had to turn people away," confirms Gary. Their "bluegrassy" name was an inside joke. Rosslyn is an urbanized Virginia city on the edge of DC known for its high-rise buildings, with no mountains in sight. The joke continued to the cover of their 1977 debut album on Adelphi Records, posing the band in front of a tongue-in-cheek pastoral rendition of Rosslyn's skyline. The band's co-founders Joe Triplett and Happy Acosta began as a country-rock duo, later recruiting Bob Laramie on drums, Peter Bonta, the early Nighthawks pianist (who fibbed when he told them he played bass) and Tommy Hannum on pedal steel. Hannum today plays with Wynonna Judd and was Ricky Van Shelton's steel player and band leader for 17 years until Ricky retired.

Bonta switched to piano when bassist Jay Sprague came on board." Nils Lofgren's drummer Bob Berberich replaced Laramie when Lofgren's first band, Grin, broke up. The Rosslyn Mountain Boys deserve huge credit for helping establish the Birchmere as a regular go-to music venue.

Tommy Hannum holds first album. Cover photo by Mike Oberman. Album design by Dick Bangham. © *T. Hannum*

Lead singer Triplett's celebrity began as a 12-year-old when he played trumpet in his Bethesda, Maryland junior high school band, the Flat Tops, appearing on the local Milt Grant

TV teen show. He's also the vocalist on The Hangmen's popular 1966 hit record, "What a Girl Can't Do." Before the Rosslyn Mountain Boys, Joe, Happy, and Jay were members of DC's "communal band" Claude Jones, regulars around town, and at The Emergency club in Georgetown.

It was booking agent Tom Carrico, later the manager of the Nighthawks and Mary Chapin Carpenter, who first got the Rosslyn Mountain Boys a Birchmere gig. Carrico heard of the music club through Akira Otsuka. Peter Bonta remembers: "It was like stepping back through a time warp to an early '60s honky-tonk bar. Gary had already broken through the wall of the next-door aquarium shop to expand the place. We played every Wednesday for three years. After the show we'd play small stakes poker—sometimes until dawn—with the Birchmere staff, including "Moose" and Don Pricer, another musician. It was a family."

Their first album received nice airplay on local alternative radio station, WHFS, selling over 10,000 copies. One theory of

(l to r) Tommy Hannum - pedal steel guitar/vocals, Joe Triplett – lead vocals/ rhythm guitar, Bob Berberich – drums/vocals, Barry Foley, bass, Peter Bonta - keyboards/lead guitar/vocals.   *© Oelze*

why they didn't break big is offered by their first manager, Michael Oberman. He believes that disco music heralded by the *Saturday Night Fever* album made country music less desirable, the country rock of the RMB included.

However, "promotional timing" is often the excuse for bands that don't succeed. Gary asserts, "Many good bands don't make it. Lesser bands do because they have a song. You need a tune like "Mr. Bojangles" or "Gentle on My Mind." Another problem is they were on the smaller Adelphi records label."

The Rosslyn Mountain Boys were lured away from the Birchmere by another club and officially disbanded in 1981. But before that happened, Peter Bonta swiped one of the Birchmere's checkered tablecloths on the last night the band played. He keeps small swatches of that tablecloth in the cases of all of his instruments to this day. The Rosslyn Mountain Boys have occasionally reformed to play outstanding reunion shows at the Birchmere. Gary added the band Yellow Rose to play every Tuesday nights in these early years.

Many thought another early Birchmere favorite, The Star-Spangled Washboard Band, was a local group due to their high popularity in the DC area, especially at the Childe Harold bar in Dupont Circle. In fact, they were an up-and-coming national act from New York. A 1977 *New York Times* profile called them a blend of Earl Scruggs Revue and the Three Stooges. "They spend at least as much time cracking one-liners and running through elaborate skits and sight gags as singing and playing," wrote *Times* music critic Robert Palmer.

When Gary booked the Star-Spangled Washboard Band, Bill Heard, the eccentric Childe Harold owner, took some offense. "Wild Bill" was already in competition with the Cellar Door booking-up-and-coming acts, and suddenly there was comparable great talent playing at the Birchmere as well.

One evening Heard drove over to the club to check out his new rival. Gary recalls the encounter: "I'd been to his place but had never met him. He sat down next to a couple and soon he was in an argument with them. He hurled a lit candle at the guy, getting hot wax on his leather jacket. I threw him out, but I learned later from other acts that Wild Bill thought the Birchmere was going to be a great success."

Autoharpist Hall of Famer Bryan Bowers in 1977. © Oelze

Autoharpist Bryan Bowers played for both Gary and Wild Bill. "I once asked Bill why he thought the Birchmere would be so successful," said Bowers. Bill replied, "Because he threw *me* out of his club."

Bowers played solo shows at the first and second Birchmere locations. He also opened for the club's later headliners including The Seldom Scene, The Dillards, and The Red Clay Ramblers. He shared memories from his Seattle farm: "From my perception, the Birchmere has always been about the music. It stunned me how great the bluegrass groups were and are.

"I was pretty star-struck back then. I was trying not to step on anybody's toes. I was astounded that anyone would pay me to play, especially in a "listening" room. If I were in town and wasn't working, then I'd be at the Birchmere. Gary would welcome me in and would never charge me. I'd stand in the back with a beer watching a show, sharing jokes with Gary."

1977 and 1978 Unicorn Times newspaper print ads.
Courtesy of Richard Harrington

Chapter 2 – National Calls

Other local bluegrass bands in the pioneering days were: Country Gazette, Coup de Grass, Foggy Bottom, Fireside, Garris Brothers, Hickory Wind, Home Brew, Lost and Found, Plum Hollow, and Southgate. Gary hired the Northstar Band, with Paul Goldstein on drums, to become the third band to hold a regular Wednesday night every week. Other bands like singer-songwriter Joanna Dodd band, Charlie Waller's Country Gentlemen band—minus John Duffey, who left the band in 1969—and ex-Country Gent Eddie Adcock and his wife Martha in their group. Generation II, were early draws. Another was Bill Harrell and the Virginians.

William Harrell (b. Sept. 14, 1934, Marion, VA)

Bill Harrell grew up in Maryland, and first played in bands while attending the University of Maryland, mostly in local bars. In 1961 Bill and the Virginians, with fiddler Buck Ryan, banjoist Smitty Irvin, and bassist Stoney Edwards, began their recording career.

Banjoist Bill Emerson, who with Charlie Waller and John Duffey co-founded the Country Gentlemen in 1959, also played with Harrell. IBMA Bluegrass Hall of Famer Emerson reminisced about Harrell: "Bill Harrell was one of the first bluegrass guys of any major consequence around here. He got a Starday recording contract and he, with Buzz Busby and the Stoneman family, playing as the Bluegrass Champs, were the three major bluegrass acts of prominence in the DC area. Bill played the Birchmere with some of the great players who came through his band, including fiddle player, Carl Nelson and mandolinist Larry Stephenson, later with the Bluegrass Cardinals.

"And then there was also banjoist, Donnie Bryant who filled in with Lester Flatt when Earl Scruggs was laid up following a 1955 car accident. Donnie later became a part-time musician and a full-time Metropolitan DC police captain."

Harrell joined skilled banjoist Don Reno briefly as lead singer and guitarist in Reno's group the Tennessee Cut-Ups. All played the Birchmere.

Gary was impressed: "Bill did not have that high lonesome sound' of bluegrass, but rather he had a warm country crooner style like Eddy Arnold. When they played the Birchmere they had already appeared on Jimmy Dean's network TV show." Harrell was inducted into the Bluegrass Music Hall of Fame in 2008. Recommended Bill Harrell Record Albums: *The Wonderful World of Bluegrass Music* (UA, 1963); *Bluegrass and Ballads* (Adelphi,1978); *Bluegrass Gospel, Pure and* Simple (Leather,1980).

Buck White & The Down-Home Folks were also early players at the club beginning in 1977. White's daughters, Sharon and Cheryl, sang in the band with their dad. They would become The Whites after catching their big break in 1979, recording with Emmylou Harris on her album, *Blue Kentucky Girl*, and then touring with her. Sharon White would marry Ricky Skaggs in 1981.

Ricky Lee Skaggs (b. July 18, 1954, Cordell, KY)

A child prodigy, Ricky received his first mandolin at the age of five after his father recognized his interest in music. By the age of seven he was such a local music phenomenon that his hometown crowd urged the father of bluegrass, Bill Monroe, to let him up on stage to play a song with him. Following his beginnings in The Stanley Brothers, Emmylou Harris and the Hot Band, and with J.D. Crowe and New South, Skaggs became an acclaimed country and bluegrass singer, musician, producer, and composer.

Lineup at first show in 1977: (l to r) Wes Golding, Terry Baucom, Ricky Skaggs, and Jerry Douglas.

However, it was during Ricky's first stint as a bandleader in Boone Creek when Gary Oelze regularly booked him. With fleet-fingered dobro player Jerry Douglas (also from New South) and later Steve Bryant on bass, their sound wasn't appreciated by some bluegrass purists. Still, the progressive bluegrass sound of Boone Creek was a must-see Birchmere act.

"I've played every Birchmere since the late '70s. With Boone Creek, J.D. Crowe, Keith Whitley, the Whites, John Starling, and others." says Skaggs. "The clientele that comes here sees everyone because the Birchmere has everybody. It's a unique place in the center of bluegrass heaven in northern Virginia. It's always a cool place, and I've always loved Gary. He's been a great friend.

Ricky Skaggs   © *Oelze*

"Every January I play my first shows of the year there with Kentucky Thunder. We work on new songs to see how they fly, and that helps us set the tone for the rest of the year." says Ricky. "The Birchmere has a great crowd that's willing to let us showcase new things."

It was customary for Associate Supreme Court Justice Antonin Scalia and his wife, Maureen, to attend Skagg's first show each year. Wearing a large cowboy hat, Scalia would sit at a close table. When he passed away, Skaggs requested a lit candle at the empty table.

With Boone Creek, Ricky Skaggs said he didn't want to just sound like Stanley, Monroe, Flatt, and Scruggs. Birchmere crowds loved the new sounds they were bringing to bluegrass. Ricky thinks of himself as the heir to Bill Monroe. He wrote in his 2014 book, *Kentucky Traveler,* how Monroe passed the baton to him before he died.

About Vince Gill, Ricky said, "He was the youngest in Boone Creek. And he could already do it all! Hiring Vince worked out great and not just because of his talent. He had a van too, so he hauled the sound system and his instruments: electric guitar, pedal steel, electric bass, and fiddle. He could play just about anything with strings and he sang like a bird." Both Skaggs and Gill are exalted members of the Birchmere family, with scores of special performances over the years.

One special Boone Creek performance was their last one in 1977. Gary: "The band was stranded in New York City on the day they were booked for the hall. A serious snow storm had hit and Ricky called me up to report the roads were closed. I told him to catch a shuttle flight and I'd pay for it. It was snowing outside the hall also, but that didn't stop a long line gathering outside in the snow hoping to get in even though we were already at capacity. I took the microphone and announced that Boone Creek were on their way and the crowd waited for them to arrive. When they did, we decided to let everyone in. I'd estimate 350 folks piled in the old Birchmere. People were sitting on the bar, the cigarette machine, and in people's laps. It was wild, and wonderful."

Vince Gill   © *Oelze*

Vincent Grant Gill (b. April 12, 1957, Norman, OK).

After Boone Creek, Vince Gill returned to the Birchmere as a band member in Bluegrass Alliance, led by co-founder and fiddler Lonnie Peerce. The Alliance was a springboard for numerous musicians early in their careers including Tony Rice, Sam Bush, Courtney Johnson, Dan McCrary, and Ebo Walker.

Gill's first fame came in 1978 with a four-year stint in country rock band Pure Prairie League. He replaced lead singer and guitarist, Craig Fuller, who sang "Amie." Since then, Gill has done 20-plus studio albums and won 21 Grammy awards. He estimates he's played on a thousand others' recordings, and wanted to be a session player when he began in music.

Vince was inducted into the Country Music Hall of Fame in 2007 and was hired by the Eagles in 2017 to replace the late Glenn Frey.

In 2020 Vince called it a "treat" to discuss his affection for the Birchmere and memories for this book: "When you're a gypsy like me, you look forward to being around a crew of people that are like-minded. The Birchmere has the feel of a family. You know what the food's going to taste like. How nice the people who bring you the food are going to be. It all kind of goes from the top down. It's exactly a mirror of what Gary is. It's a continuation of him. And a lot of times the same thing holds true in a band and a crew. They'll be similar to who they're representing and who they work with. People go to the Birchmere because of the people that are associated with it.

"Yeah, I just smile when I see the Birchmere booking on my calendar. 'Oh, good. I get to see old friends. I get to go see familiar faces. A lot of times I'm backstage in a big place and I don't know anything or anybody. There's nothing to connect me to it, you know?

"Woo Hoo. I finally made it to the Birchmere!" wrote Amy Grant on her wall poster in 2013. She's returned many times to the hall, including in 2021. Fans hope she and husband Vince will do a show together.

"There were other great venues back in my early days. One was in Calhoun, Georgia. You knew how much fun it was going to be because of the people who were going to cook the meals. The meals were probably more legendary than the music. You knew you were going to get great fried chicken. And that's the spirit that the Birchmere has. The people all care about the place. you can kind of depend on that."

Vince on Sound

"The key to any venue is to play *to it,*" Vince says. "If a venue can take volume so then it's okay. But if it can't take a certain level of volume, then it will let you know pretty quick. I've always felt like you have to play to a room, just like you play an instrument the way it wants to be played more so than the way *you* want to play it. Whether it's the tension of the strings or the action of the instrument, the sound of it. You play a little harder to get the sound out of it or a little lighter. I feel like I want to honor that in the Birchmere."

Gill has been doing full band as well as solo shows for over four decades at the club. He appreciates the superior quality of the audience too: "I love the open mind that's willing to have all kinds of music that are great in their own ways. Going in the Birchmere, your audience is very, very well educated in their love for music. They wouldn't be there if they weren't just a cut above. It's going to be a different audience than what you might normally get. You know the Birchmere crowd are students of great music or they wouldn't be supporting the different kinds of music that they have at the Birchmere."

***

Gary recalls the early days of building that special audience: "We did well with the local bands, but the Birchmere name and logo just wasn't out there yet. Today you'd use social media to get broader recognition. We do that now with a website and an email blast to over 150,000 followers.

"I had the idea then to book one national act every month and add a cover charge. I knew that breaking even at the door was the best I could do on these performers. But I figured people would notice these famous acts that we'd publicize in our *Unicorn Times* newspaper ads and folks would say 'Wow. Look who's playing somewhere called the Birchmere. Let's go check out that place!'"

Donald Ray Williams (b. May 27, 1939, Floydada, TX).

In 1966, the Pozo-Seco Singers released a smooth version of Bob Dylan's "Tomorrow Is a Long Time," and a more successful later tune "Time." This group helped launch the solo career of founding member Don Williams. His straight-yet-suave low, baritone voice, subtle tones, and imposing six-foot build earned him the nickname "Gentle Giant." He had a 1972 hit record with "We Should Be Together."

Williams was just the kind of performer Gary was hoping to book at the Birchmere. He had several Top 40 songs, including his most famous hit, "I Believe in You" when Gary discovered that Williams was playing a nearby Richmond, Virginia club. Gary contacted Don's agent and got him booked.

(l to r) Billy Sanford, Don Williams and David Pomeroy returning to the club in 1980.   © *Oelze*

Don arrived a month later with his first bass player, Dave Williamson, and guitarist, Danny Flowers on guitar and harmonica. Williamson, now retired in St. Petersburg, Florida, remembers they were all surprised by the humble exterior of the restaurant.

At the time, these big-named music acts could give Oelze a little trepidation. "Don was no music rookie on the road," says Gary. "He met me at the door and strolled in. He looked around, turned to me, and asked, 'Have you ever done a show here before?'

"His question kind of floored me. I laughed, but it scared me a little. Fortunately, the show sold out. One of the reasons this gig was memorable to all of us was a Don Williams fan in attendance named Mike.

Michael Dennis Auldridge (b. Dec. 30, 1938, Washington, DC)

Mike was a multi-instrumentalist playing dobro regularly at the Red Fox Inn with the Seldom Scene bluegrass band when he and his wife, Elise, came to see Don Williams. He greatly admired William's use of the dobro on his early recordings. This was the first time Gary met the Auldridges.

"Before Don's sets, Mike and Don went into the back room, sat down, and started playing face-to-face together. Elise, Danny Flowers watched, and I pulled me up a chair, too. They played for an hour. I would give a million dollars for a tape of that private concert. It was brilliant. Mike learned the dobro from his hero, Josh Graves, and even then, had mastered a special technique on this instrument as Earl Scruggs had demonstrated with his banjo, and Doc Watson could do flat-picking his guitar. Beautiful, powerful, unforgettable." Gary also recalled Auldridge's reaction to the club "He told me he liked what I was doing."

Flowers later blossomed as a songwriter with a catalog of stellar tunes like "Tulsa Time," hits for both Williams and Eric Clapton, and "Before Believing" by Emmylou Harris, from which her album title, *Pieces of the Sky*, was drawn.

In a 2020 interview, Flowers agreed that it was a significant musical event: "I remember this well. I was a friend of Mike's through Emmylou, who I'd known since college. Being a fan, Mike knew almost all of Don's songs. The first they played was "Amanda," which has a significant dobro intro and also wouldn't be the song without the dobro instrumentation.

"They did "Come Early Morning," "In the Shelter of Her Eyes," and others. Mike had most of them down. If he didn't know one of them completely, it sounded like he did. But I had to know them note-for-note because that was my job description in the band: to cover every fill and make my Stratocaster sound like a dobro, a guitar, and a piano.

"They were both huge admirers of one of Nashville's premiere steel players, Lloyd Green, who recorded with Johnny Cash, Bob Dylan, Alan Jackson, and the list goes on. Mike just fit right in because every great musician is a good listener. After their playing, Don asked Mike Auldridge if he wanted to join the band."

There were drawbacks to that offer. Mike would have to quit his graphic arts job at the *Evening Star* newspaper, abandon his spot in the already successful Seldom Scene band, and make the big move to Nashville. The late Mike Auldridge's wife,

"I particularly dislike this rare picture of Mike Auldridge wearing a hat because he was extremely fussy about his hair," says Gary. "But I'm glad he's happy here playing pedal steel." © *Oelze*

Elise said in a 2020 interview that "Don's offer was peanuts, about $13,000 a year as I recall."

Williams declined a counter-offer because he was not touring regularly, and he wasn't even paying his own players that much.

Mike later called Lloyd Green to ask if there really was a demand for Nashville session guys playing dobro. Green claimed there was absolutely no need for dobro session work, leaving Mike disappointed. Later, Mike reported Green's lousy news to Gary who laughed out loud and shot back, "Mike! He's trying to fool you. He doesn't want you in Nashville as his competition!"

Nevertheless, Elise urged Mike to go with her to look at Nashville houses. "I thought it might be good for Mike and the family to relocate. We found a house we liked and were about to put an offer down. But the real estate agent had made a mistake and raised the price considerably. We declined and Mike seemed happy about not moving. But I do agree that the move would have changed our lives and Mike's music. I was willing but Mike obviously wasn't ready to move."

Dave Williamson confirmed that Williams enjoyed playing that first Birchmere show, "There was a lot of energy in the room, and we all had a good time." On the cost of booking Williams as his first prominent national act, Gary says, "It wasn't that much. He only had one album at that time and it was hard to find." Williams continued to play the Birchmere until 2014. He died from emphysema in 2017, leaving a legacy of 17 number one hit songs.

Gary would recruit another band in 1976 that not only changed his life, but also advanced the popularity and evolution of bluegrass music.

Chapter 3 – Thursdays Scene

I always say this: There wouldn't have been a Birchmere if it weren't for The Seldom Scene. They made me a legitimate club. In return, I made a decent club for them, too.   Gary Oelze

In 1976 The Seldom Scene was the most exciting act in bluegrass music. The Washington DC-based group was the driving force for modern bluegrass and considered among the best bands in the country. The Bicentennial year would begin a deep relationship between The Seldom Scene and Gary Oelze that would establish both the Birchmere and the group as national treasures.

John Humbird Duffey, Jr (b. March 4, 1934, Washington DC)

John Duffey was a gregarious, iconoclastic, and self-confident musician. He was the foremost leader of the second generation of bluegrass and the phenomenal 12-year veteran of the acclaimed Country Gentlemen. They successfully transformed bluegrass music for America by reworking popular material outside the tradition of Bill Monroe, and infusing a performance style on stage that put the "show" into bluegrass show business.

The Country Gentlemen's bass player, Tom Gray, says, "John's creative influence is heard and felt in the two main bands that he fronted, The Country Gentlemen and The Seldom Scene. These bands created the Washington sound, a newer, more cosmopolitan approach to a genre that had been invented by rural southern and Appalachian musicians in the 1940s."

John co-founded The Country Gentlemen with Charlie Waller and Bill Emerson in 1957. Eddie Adcock replaced Emerson and this classic Country Gentlemen line-up revolutionized bluegrass. Duffey stayed with them until he left the group on his 35th birthday in 1969.

John Duffey, Eddie Adcock, Charlie Waller, and Tom Gray: "Classic" Country Gentlemen reunion in 1989. © *Penny Parsons*

In a 1984 interview with Stephen Moore, Duffey explained the reasons why he left: "I was tired of traveling these tremendous distances. It was like we were saving up to go on tour. We had already beat around the bars. We had paid our dues and I didn't think we really needed to do that. I began to realize that we don't have to play out on the roof of the men's room at the Drive-In Theatres, you know? "

"So, I just said, the hell with this. I'll just stay at home and glue my guitars together (work in his instrument repair shop). I was out of the business, I guess, for almost three years."

Then, in 1971, Washington DC bluegrass players Ben Eldridge, John Starling, and Mike Auldridge invited Duffey to Ben's house for an informal "pickin' party." A rumor began that Duffey was returning to show business. The "basement band" kept waiting for a call from Duffey, but it never came. Mike and John started thinking: "This band idea is pretty good. What can we do? Should we go over to John's house and kidnap him and bring him over to Ben's house?" Finally, they got up the nerve to call him.

"Yeah, I heard that rumor, too," said John.

"Well, do you want to get together some night and see what we sound like?" Ben asked.

"Yes, I might like to do that," said John.

He was coaxed back into performing and so began the Seldom Scene. Duffey possessed a beautiful and powerful high tenor voice, distinctive mandolin dexterity, and an outrageous personality. He would proudly agree, "I don't mind that," when Richard Harrington called him the "father of modern bluegrass" in 1986. Harrington added that "the band was pickers and friends coming together for a weekly game in which songs and instruments were dealt out instead of cards."

The other Scene members had day jobs: Mike Auldridge, a commercial artist with the *Evening Star*, Tom Gray, a cartographer with *National Geographic*, Ben Eldridge, a mathematician with the Johns Hopkins University Applied Physics Lab, and Dr. John Starling, an "Ear, Nose, and Wallet" physician (Duffey's characterization).

Dr. John Starling   *© Oelze*

The Seldom Scene became radio favorites, especially on WAMU-FM, were a main draw on the bluegrass festival circuit, released popular albums, and packed the Red Fox Inn in Bethesda, MD every Thursday night.

Gary was intent on making the Scene a Birchmere attraction. Gary says, "I had never heard a band that sounded so good. It's hard to describe their stage presence, their harmonies, and showmanship. Both musically and personally, I loved this band."

Mike Auldridge and Akira Otsuka began encouraging Duffey to let Gary book them. Gary: "I also began lobbying John Starling and Ben Eldridge for their support and I got it. Starling was the first to vote "yes" on the move, but I also knew he was planning to leave the group soon and concentrate on his medical practice."

Through his experiences in the Country Gentlemen, John had developed ideas about what he was looking for in a music club to anchor The Seldom Scene. Duffey felt a loyalty to the Red Fox Inn and owner Walt Broderick, so it was with some reluctance that Duffey accepted Gary's invitation, "OK, I'll go over there and see the Birchmere."

(l to r) Ben Eldridge, Tom Gray, Gary, John Duffey, and Mike Auldridge.
© *Oelze*

Gary remembers John's first visit well: "I was still open in the daytime. Duff came in the door and walked around the place and looked at things. He scared the hell out of me. It was the first time I had met him one-on-one. Duffey intimidated a lot of people. He was big and he had built this wall around himself. I don't mean to exaggerate this, but Duffey was the kind of guy you took notice of when he walked in the door. After we talked, he agreed to play one Saturday night. That show produced a line around the block."

John and Gary were both impressed by the success and convinced they were on to something. The Seldom Scene did three successful Saturday shows that year and then Gary made his proposal: "I told Duffey I had talked with the band, and I wanted them to play on Thursday nights." John replied, 'But we play the Red Fox on Thursday nights,' and I said 'I want you to quit the Red Fox and play the Birchmere.' They were making $400 a night. I offered $800."

"How are you going to do that?" John asked.

"The Red Fox charges $2.00 at the door. I intend to charge $4.00."

"You'll never get that."

"Well, that's my problem," Gary finished.

First Seldom Scene promo picture hangs on the wall of the hall.

As a professional musician, John knew the Birchmere could be a good fit, "OK, then let's try every other Thursday."

John admitted he didn't want to simply abandon Red Fox owner Walt, and say 'The hell with you" so he agreed to start alternating every other week at both clubs. Duffey appreciated the many dedicated fans the Scene had across the Washington area's tightknit bluegrass scene.

However, their show lost money the very first Thursday the group played. John was distraught that Gary didn't make the door, thinking that it had been a mistake moving to the Alexandria club. Gary repeatedly assured Duffey that the Birchmere was a great opportunity for everyone involved. The next Thursday when the Seldom Scene played, they completely sold out, beginning a tradition of the music club as a home for the second generation of bluegrass. "And we sold out every week they played for the next 20 years," says Gary today with satisfaction.

Gary at the soundboard.   © *C. Fleischhauer*

Gary installed an improved sound system that all the bands appreciated. Equipped with a new mixing board and house speakers, Oelze developed a special rapport with the group. Gary: "I ran the sound for The Seldom Scene for over 1,000 hours. I was a good sound guy for them because I knew what they were going to do before they did it. Sometimes—and I wish they had done this more often—they might start with an old song and then move to another impromptu old song, and then bassist Tom Gray would suggest yet another earlier old song and it was astonishing to watch and listen to them. They knew this music history so well. I'm sure that there wasn't a bluegrass song that had ever been written that Duffey didn't know."

Gary adds, 'I don't know if John Duffey is the highest tenor singer I ever heard, but he is by far the loudest."

Duffey deeply respected the classic bluegrass of Bill Monroe, but the Seldom Scene never stuck to a traditional repertoire. Crowd-pleasing attractions of the Thursday shows included an eclectic mix of songs the Scene "bluegrassified," ranging from Dean Martin's "A Small Exception of Me," to Eric Clapton's "Lay Down Sally," to the local football fight song "Hail to the Redskins." Guitarist John Starling brought contemporary tunes in like "Sweet Baby James" and "I Know You, Rider," a traditional blues song dating back to 1927. "Rider" was a favorite Scene closing song.

The rainbow harmonies on songs like Herb Pedersen's "Wait a Minute" became an addictive request for fans. The band excelled in rich folk-like vocals, but like the Country Gentlemen, the Scene never tried to replicate the "high lonesome" nasal sound that many traditional bluegrass bands honored.

Mike would sometime play guitar and John would play dobro on songs like "She's Gone, Gone, Gone," "Crying Won't Bring Her Back," and "Bottom Dollar." © *Oelze*

(l to r) Bill Monroe, John Duffey, Phil Rosenthal, and Mike Auldridge.   © Oelze

Singer-songwriter Phil Rosenthal joined the Scene as lead singer in 1976 when John Starling went back to his medical practice full-time.

"Phil did a great job stepping up to replace Starling," says Gary. "He never got the credit he deserved. After almost ten years, Mike Auldridge persuaded The Seldom Scene to abruptly fire Rosenthal because 'the band wished to go in a different direction. They let Phil know he was fired in the Birchmere dressing room after their regular Thursday night sets."

Phil was devastated by the news. It was Tony Rice who phoned Rosenthal to comfort him. Rice let him know that he, too, was abruptly fired by bandmate David Grisman so he knew how Phil was feeling. WAMU broadcaster Lee Michael Demsey also called Phil with condolences. Gary thought this firing was unfair.

Moreover, Gary was told a lie by the group that Phil didn't want to participate in the 15th anniversary Kennedy Center celebration. Phil didn't know anything about it. Gary made sure Rosenthal was invited to the Seldom Scene's 20th Anniversary concert at the Birchmere.

By then, Auldridge and Rosenthal had renewed their friendship. Phil's long-distance phone calls were comforting when Mike was later diagnosed with cancer. Mike Auldridge passed away a day before his 74th birthday on December 29, 2012. The Birchmere has held tribute shows to honor one of the great dobro players.

The Birchmere attracted a suburban audience often unfamiliar with bluegrass music traditions. The transformative modern style of the Seldom Scene made it easy to become a fan. Gary agrees it was sometimes an unusual audience for this modern blend. "Many people who came to hear them told me they didn't like bluegrass," says Gary.

They also played on special occasions like New Year's Eve and with major guest stars like Bill Monroe and Jethro Burns. "They were always full of energy. And everybody in the audience seemed to know that the band was having a good time. They were enjoying what they did which was a main reason for their success," Gary remembers.

Elise Auldridge   © *Oelze*

Baby Huey

Mike Auldridge's wife Elise called John Duffey "Baby Huey" after the cartoon character. "He was a baby about many things. He was an only child and used to getting his own way," she says today.

"We got along fine. I was outspoken, which sometimes horrified Mike. But Duffey didn't care about that. My take on John is that he was a bit of a control freak. It was his way or the highway. And he didn't like taking a lot of chances. It was

John Starling who was so good at bringing those new songs into the Seldom Scene and recording them. With Duffey it was like pulling teeth. But it was John Starling who called Duffey 'a great man.'"

Adding to their music, nobody could ever guess what the incorrigible Duffey might do or say on stage. Audiences loved the group's stage banter, and John was politically incorrect before that term existed. "May your gynecologist keep his rubber gloves in the freezer," was bandmate Dr. John Starling's favorite Duffey quip. Song breaks and tune-ups for Duffey were filled with one-liners like, "Bless your heart and all your vital organs." Or "We'll pause a minute and let Ben change his 7-day deodorant pad." Duffey often critiqued his own band on stage: "That was adequate," when a song was just OK and when a song had serious hiccups, "Thanks for suffering through that with us."

Gary: "John was always ready with a joke. But some of that was a defense mechanism. He never discussed politics or much of anything else except music and cars, and even then, he never went very deep. Sometimes I think he didn't want people to know his lack of knowledge on some things."

Bob Dylan's Dream

The Birchmere's national reputation grew alongside the Seldom Scene. Mary Beth Aungier, later Mary Chapin Carpenter's road manager, and now a live-event executive in Charlottesville, Virginia, worked as a Birchmere waitress from 1985 through 1990. She recalled a shock after answering the kitchen phone one night.

"Are the Seldom Scene playing?" a hushed voice asked.

"They just finished their last set," answered Mary Beth.

The man replied, "Well, Bob Dylan just did a concert, and he's in the car, and we are driving to your place. Can the band do another set so Bob can hear them?"

Mary Beth said, "Hold on." It was the end of the night and everyone was preparing to close. Gary breezed past Mary Beth, and she said to him, "It's Dylan, and he wants the Scene to play another set."

"I could always get John to listen to me," says Gary.
© *C. Fleischhauer*

"That's not going to happen," Gary replied as he rushed by. Aungier then went to John Duffey who always called the shots on these special requests.

Duffey calmly told Mary Beth, "Please tell Mr. Dylan that I have some cold beverages waiting for me at home, and if he's ever in the neighborhood early on a Thursday night, then he's welcome to drop in."

Mary Beth never spoke to the other members of the band that night, and only told the story about their near-brush with greatness in 2010. "It was the first time they had heard this story. Ben yelled, "What?" says Aungier. Gary Oelze thinks had *he* answered the phone that night, he might have talked John into staying around to sing for Bob Dylan.

Duffey liked Dylan's music. Both the Country Gentlemen and the Scene recorded "It's All Over, Baby Blue," so, it was curious, but not unexpected, for Duffey to blow off a musician he so admired.

The close personal and professional relationship that Gary developed with the Seldom Scene extended beyond the Birchmere walls. Gary recalls, "People would always ask Duff if he had a sound guy, and he'd say, 'Yeah, we have Gary.'"

On the road, Gary traveled with the Scene as their friend and sound guy in Europe and on California tours every winter. "Touring with the Seldom Scene was never dull. I did the sound. And I helped the guys. For example, Mike would call me when his hair dryer wouldn't work overseas, and I'd help him get electrical adapters. Always impeccably dressed, Mike was very fussy about his hair."

Gary concluded, "I didn't get many opportunities to get away from the Birchmere for the most part and I loved traveling with them and road managing. All the members of the Seldom Scene were part of my family, part of my life."

Regular backstage warm-up for the Scene.   © *C. Fleischhauer*

Good Friends

The 1970s Washington bluegrass scene became a well-worn crossroads for musicians. Byrds bassist Chris Hillman was responsible for introducing singer Linda Ronstadt to Washington, DC music veteran Emmylou Harris. He presciently told them, "You two could be good friends." And it was Emmylou who brought Ronstadt to her first Seldom Scene show at the Red Fox Inn with her then-boyfriend, Lowell George of Little Feat. "It's the only time in my life I've ever become an instant fan," Ronstadt told the *Baltimore Sun* in 2001. Afterwards, they all went to John Starling's house and sang for most of the night. While the professional musicians, Linda, Emmylou, and Lowell could sleep in, Doctor Starling had to get up early the next morning for his hospital duties.

John, Ben, Linda, Dr. John, and Mike.　　　© *C. Fleischhauer*

That night began Linda Ronstadt's long musical and professional relationship with Starling. On an otherwise typical Thursday evening in 1976, an early bird crowd was surprised when Starling strolled in with Ronstadt. The Scene's banjo master Ben Eldridge noted that she had flown into nearby Dulles Airport on the supersonic Concorde.

A Paul Craft tune that the Scene played regularly at the Birchmere and put on their 1972 album *Act II*, "Keep Me from Blowing Away" was also a track on her 1974 multi-platinum album, *Heart Like a Wheel*. This was the only song she had casually rehearsed with Starling and the band prior to this surprise Birchmere sit in. A stunned, appreciative crowd glowed when Ronstadt took the stage with the Scene to perform lead vocals on "Blowing Away," and then added powerful harmonies on a few more of the Scene's other setlist favorites.

When Gary Oelze recognized Ronstadt walking into the Birchmere, he headed outside to find somebody (anybody) with a camera. Fortunately, he spotted a young bluegrass devotee named Carl Fleischhauer standing in line. Carl, a Fulbright scholar, had just moved to the Washington area to work at the American Folklife Center division at the Library of Congress.

"Gary asked me to take some photos and escorted my ex and I to a much better table than we could have got standing in line. That's how I was able to take those Ronstadt pictures."

John Duffey talked about playing with Linda Ronstadt in the 1984 interview: "She was going with Lowell George and staying at Starling's house for two weeks. The Scene was recording *Old Train* [their fourth album that also features Ricky Skaggs on fiddle] and going over some of the numbers. Linda asked if she could sing on a couple of songs with us.

"She was getting pretty hot then, you know, a pretty hot item. I said, 'sure, if you want to sing then fine.' Linda asked, 'are you going to do any gospel songs?' because she loves to sing gospel tunes. She knows that's not where the money is but that's one of the things she likes to do.

"So, we had her sing "Old Crossroads" and "Bottom of the Glass." We also did "In the Pines," which never came out because it just didn't sound good. It's long gone now.

"Afterwards, we let her dub the high baritone on "California Earthquake." It's funny because on the back of *Old Train* are some pictures of Linda. I had dubbed in a faint high part and everyone thought that was Linda. But it was me."

"And then she tottered in to the Birchmere and listened for a while. Then we asked her if she wanted to sing a few, and she got up on stage."

Linda Maria Ronstadt (b. July 15, 1946, Tucson, AZ)

Linda was inducted into the Rock and Roll Hall of Fame by the Eagle's Glen Frey in 2014.

Linda Ronstadt was on the cover of *Rolling Stone* magazine the night she sang with the Scene. A bluegrass fan in the audience that night, Sandy Fenner, also recognized Linda. Fenner works today for Joe Barden, who fabricated the dual-blade T-style guitar pickups co-designed by another Birchmere favorite, Danny Gatton. Immediately after Linda's impromptu stage jam, Fenner ran to a nearby 7-Eleven convenience store to grab a *Rolling Stone* for her to sign. She inscribed it, "Please don't tell anyone I don't look like this."

Both Linda and Emmylou would join Charlie Waller, Tony Rice, Ricky Skaggs, Jonathan Edwards, Paul Craft, and band members John Duffey, John Starling, Lou Reid, Ben Eldridge, and Tom Gray to celebrate The Seldom Scene's 15th Anniversary concert at the Kennedy Center in 1986. "It was 3

½ hours of "singing and playing to the very limits of its members' imposing abilities," reported Geoffrey Himes in the *Washington Post.*

15th Anniversary Kennedy Center. (l to r) top: Duffey, Auldridge, Ronstadt, Starling. 2nd row: Charlie Waller, Emmylou Harris, Jonathan Edwards. row 3; Tony Rice, Harris. Bottom: Duffey, Paul Craft, Ricky Skaggs, Lou Reid, and Paul Craft. © Oelze

Gary produced this event—and won a Washington Area Music Association award for Best Live Sound Engineer— with John Starling directing and staging the show. "It is one of the finest bluegrass concerts ever," Gary exclaims. "It's also one of the few times Duffey followed a set list."

THE WHITE HOUSE

WASHINGTON

November 10, 1986

I am pleased to join my Press Secretary, Jim Brady, and fans of bluegrass everywhere in offering warm congratulations to the Seldom Scene on your 15th anniversary as a group.

Your origins in a basement and your modest ambitions inspired your name, but now your influence can be seen, and especially heard, throughout the world of bluegrass. Your love of music and your superior musicianship have been heard in every song you've played.

As members of the Seldom Scene, each of you has helped continue and enhance one of the richest traditions of American music. I hope you'll keep up the good work. God bless you.

Ronald Reagan

Presidential letter celebrating the band's 15th anniversary.

Gary won a Washington Area Music Association award for producing the Kennedy Center double concert album, which has been a best-selling record for 35 years. "I'm still waiting for a royalty check," says Gary without a grin.

John Duffey passed away from a heart attack at age 62 on December 10, 1996. Ben Eldridge retired from the group in

2015. With Lou Reid on mandolin and high tenor vocals and Ron Stewart on banjo and fiddle, the Seldom Scene remain Birchmere favorites, appearing several times each year.

A 20th anniversary Seldom Scene concert was held at the Birchmere in 1991. In the back row above is (l to r) Sally Gray, Tom Gray, Barbara Eldridge. Ben Eldridge, John Duffey, Nancy Duffey, Amy Rosenthal, Phil Rosenthal, Lou Reid, Billy Wolf, and Mike Auldridge. Sitting on the floor is Gary and Linda Oelze with John Starling. Other anniversaries followed with Katy Daley organizing their 40th anniversary celebration.

© Oelze

Duffey silences Monroe.   *© Becky Johnson*

Chapter 4 – Presidential Visits

Jerry Jeff   © *C.B. Smith*

Country music singer-songwriter Jerry Jeff Walker's debut Birchmere show was in 1983. His last was 2017, with his Lost Gonzo band, the same year he was diagnosed with throat cancer. In 34 years, he did 133 shows. Jerry Jeff was beloved and the first club veteran contacted to participate in this history. However, his wife of 46 years, Susan, sent regrets because his throat cancer made it impossible for him to speak. He passed away on October 23, 2020. "He went very peacefully, which we were extremely grateful for," said Susan.

It was the evergreen popularity of Jerry Jeff that kept crowds returning to the hall. And he sparked the Birchmere's first Presidential visit.

Ronald Clyde Crosby (b. March 16, 1942, Oneonta, NY)

His first stage name was Jeff Farris. Then he adopted Jerry Walker. He finally became Jerry Jeff Walker and is best remembered for the 1968's "Mr. Bojangles" song about a tap-dancing drifter he shared a New Orleans prison cell with after he was pinched for drunkenness.

(l to r) Jerry Jeff with Mike, solo, and with Doc Watson. © *Oelze*

Walker was one of the first pioneer "outlaw" singer-songwriters and an early champion of a loosely-defined group troop that included Willie Nelson, Waylon Jennings, Kris Kristofferson, Steve Earle, Joe Ely, and many other Birchmere players. Jerry Jeff's version of Ray Wylie Hubbard's "Up Against the Wall Redneck Mothers" became an outlaw anthem.

In the early '80s, Senator Al Gore lived close to the club and was a faithful fan of Jerry Jeff. Gary remembers, "On many nights with Jerry Jeff and other country acts and even some bluegrass shows, I would see Al Gore sitting alone in the back wearing a pair of Levi's and a flannel shirt. I'd sit with him for a few minutes. We'd talk about the old country music. We had this plan to get some money from the government to bring up some of the older musicians that nobody wanted to hire. We'd bring them up from Nashville and showcase them at the Birchmere. We had fun talking about doing this. We knew this was just BS and an excuse to talk about the old Nashville stars we both loved. I never got any of that government money.

"There were times he would call me and say, 'Tipper and the girls are coming down tonight, and would you keep an eye on them?' I knew Al Gore before he was Al Gore."

When Al and Tipper came together, they'd sit in a front row. Former waitress Sesi Warnock Miller remembers serving them. "They were super nice. I didn't know he was a Senator for a long time."

In 1993, a few months after Bill Clinton was elected President, he asked his new vice-president Al Gore what his plans were for a Thursday evening. The way Gore explained this to Gary was "I told Bill that Tipper and I were headed to the Birchmere to see Jerry Jeff Walker."

"Well, hell, Hillary and I will go with you," said Clinton.

Gary paints this picture of the visit: "While we were accustomed to senators, congressional leaders, and various VIPs, a Presidential visit was exceptional. However, the Secret Service detail was the Vice-President's, not Clinton's. Friendly agents arrived in the afternoon. They checked every door and closet.

"They then mapped out exactly where the Presidential party would enter and exit. One agent mentioned Senator Robert Kennedy's assassination as the reason there'd be no travel through the kitchen.

"I reserved one table for the special guests. The plan was they would come in through the back door and take their seats after the show had started. A couple of our regular early customers came asked, 'Who's coming tonight? You don't reserve tables.' I answered, 'Well, the President's coming.' They all laughed, 'Yeah, sure.'

"And then here comes Bill, Hillary, Al, and Tipper taking their seats. Bill wore a leather bomber jacket, with Hillary in slacks. They were having fun and enjoying the show. Right behind the President's table was a group of six. One person had a ponytail. They all looked like regular Birchmere patrons, except they turned out to be a fully armed Secret Service detail. They showed me their weapons. To this day, I have no idea how they got that table.

"The Clintons and Gores hung out in the dressing room with Jerry Jeff, Billy Wolf, and me. They invited Jerry Jeff to visit them at the White House in the morning."

Bill Clinton, Jerry Jeff, Al and Tipper Gore, Freddy Steady Krc (Jerry Jeff's drummer), Hillary Clinton, Jon Inman, and Billy Wolf. © Oelze

In 1997, the Prez and Veep returned to the hall in its third location to see country singer Kim Richey. Playing guitar for Richey was Kenny Vaughan, longtime member of Marty Stuart's Superlative band. Clinton signed his Les Paul guitar. This time it was the President's entire security detail with his motorcade, complete with an ambulance and a fire truck.

"How long you been here in this location?" asked Clinton when he arrived.

"We've been here for three months, Mr. President," Gary replied.

"Well, let's go and inaugurate this place," Bill quipped.

(l to r front) Kenny Vaughan (with guitar), Tipper, Al, Kim Richey, Bill, Gary, Linda, and Hillary.   © *White House*

Kenny Vaughan remembers being in the dressing room when a doctor arrived with a stretcher and medical equipment and set that up. He thought, 'Oh, wow. This is for real. And then I'm tuning my guitar and I hear one of the Secret Service guys start counting down: 'The President will be here in 3 minutes, 32 seconds, the President will be here in 1 minute, 45 seconds, etc. Right on cue, in walks the Presidential party. Bill with a big smile on his face, shaking hands and looking really casual and cool, with cowboy boots.'" And when the show started, the Clintons' and Gores' table was right in front of Kenny's position on stage during the show.

Kenny has returned a dozen times with Marty Stuart and The Superlatives. "Marty and all the Superlatives love the Birchmere. It is our clubhouse. Gary and all the staff are friends. I know the neighborhood and nearby Latin food stores and just feel at home. We always look forward to playing the Birchmere."

When Gary was asked how the late Jerry Jeff reacted to playing for the President on that first visit and whether it was a big deal for him, Gary laughed. "Nothing was a big deal for Jerry Jeff.

***

Gary with Birchmere partner and friend, Jimmy Mathews, were invited to the White House in 2002. Gary: "Marvin Bush asked us if we wanted to see his older brother, George, fly in on Marine One helicopter. This was a big deal for visitors. Marvin had a business in Tysons Corner. He and his wife, Margaret, came to see shows, especially by fellow Texan Lyle Lovett. We were on the White House porch when "W" flew in. The President waved to a group of visitors behind a rope on the lawn.

"Marvin invited us to meet his brother. We saw Vice President Cheney as we strolled through the White House hall to the Oval Office. Cheney smiled and simply said, "Hello Virginia," as he passed us by.

"We talked with President Bush for about 30 minutes. He was chatty about the office, decorations made at the White House, things he had bought, and the then-in-progress Iraq war. What he said about the war was what we had already heard in his TV speeches. He was amiable. We took pictures."

President Bush, Gary, Marvin Bush, and Jimmy Mathews. © Oelze

"The Oval Office is quite an experience regardless of your politics. You can't help getting a kick from standing in that place," states Gary. place," states Gary.

Birchmere friend, Jonathan Edwards, in rare jam with President Ronald Reagan. Gary adds, "Jonathan is important to the Birchmere, but we can't remember who was in the Reagan mask." © Oelze

Chapter 5 – Gypsy Songsmiths (Side 1)

Gary Oelze's beloved performers are the singer-songwriters who came out of Texas. "People like Guy Clark, Townes Van Zandt, Kris Kristofferson, Rodney Crowell and others, especially Mickey Newbury, who is my favorite. Mickey played often at the Birchmere. Most of these Texas songwriters came from prominent families. Yet, they wanted to be nonconformist.

"They turned their back on their inherited wealth and privilege. They were inspired by Hank Williams and Buddy Holly. They'd rather be artists who expressed their feelings. This book is an opportunity to introduce them to people who may not be aware of their talent, and one of the main reasons I wanted to write it."

Mickey was beat up very badly as a kid in his rough Texas neighborhood. He spent nearly a year recuperating in his bedroom. While he was disabled, he learned the guitar and began songwriting. He used to say "Music has never been anything but an escape from depression for me. I write my sadness. I call it robbing the dragon."

Milton Sims Newbury, Jr (b. May 19, 1940, Houston, TX)

As a teen, Mickey enjoyed R&B vocal groups like the Penguins and Flamingos. He sang tenor harmonies in his first band, The Embers, opening for future stars like Sam Cooke and Johnny Cash. After his enlistment in the Air Force, Mickey moved to Nashville to focus on songwriting. "Funny Familiar Forgotten Feelings," recorded by both Don Gibson and Tom Jones became his first hit composition in 1966.

Two years later, Newbury was an unprecedented success with four top-five songs on different charts at the same time: Andy Williams' "Sweet Memories," #1 on the Easy Listening chart; "Here Comes the Rain, Baby," by Eddy Arnold at #1 on the Country chart; "Time Is a Thief," #1 by Solomon Burke on the R&B chart; and "Just Dropped in (To See What Condition

My Condition Was In)" by Kenny Rogers and The First Edition,"
which reached #5 on the Pop/Rock chart. No other songwriter
has ever repeated this feat.

Mickey   © *Oelze*

Gary deeply admired Newbury's songwriting: "Mickey wrote
lovely, touching, sad, and sometimes dark music. His songs
almost work as well as poetry as they do musically."

Lyrics from "A Long Road Home"

*How I long to feel the salty wind off Galveston Bay in my face
once again.*

*A warm southern wind on my weather worn skin
Perhaps I would not feel so old,*

Now I long to hold the golden sand in the hollow of my hand.

*Stand for a while there and fill in the hole left in the heart of a
wounded old soul.*

Gary notes that "Mickey's songwriting royalties enabled him to live on a Nashville houseboat where fellow songwriter friends like Guy Clark and Kris Kristofferson would socialize."

Kris once said, "God, I learned more about songwriting from Mickey than I did any other single human being. To me, he was a songbird. He came out with amazing words and music. I'm sure that I would never have written "Bobby McGee" or "Sunday Morning Coming Down" if I had never known Mickey. He was my hero and still is."

Nashville singer Larry Gatlin says he once woke up on Mickey's houseboat about 5 am to hear Mickey working on a version of the confederate anthem, "Dixie." Although modern-day reactions to Southern Civil War-era songs are divided and increasingly adverse, this was not Newbury's intention when his medley version called "An American Trilogy" debuted at NYC's Bitter End coffee house in 1970. In attendance that night at the famed club were Joan Baez, Kris Kristofferson, and Odetta, considered by Dr. Martin Luther King, Jr. to be "The Voice of the Civil Rights Movement."

"Dixie" had been the 1968 campaign song for segregationist third-party candidate Governor George Wallace. President Richard Nixon was also planning to use the song for his 1972 reelection campaign as part of his "Southern Strategy." There were already calls to ban the song on the radio outright in some states because of its racial insensitivity.

But with his soft guitar accompaniment Newbury's mournful, sensitive rendition of "Dixie" as a ballad brought Odetta to tears that night at the Bitter End. Mickey mixed in "All My Trials," a popular gospel song during the Civil Rights movement of the '60s, and "Battle Hymn of the Republic." Some accounts of the "Trilogy" debut claim Mickey improvised this song mix. Newbury later said his desire was "'to take the Klan's marching song "Dixie" away from them and return it to the land and its people." He recorded the powerful medley for his 1971 album *Frisco Mabel Joy*.

The reworked song became a huge success and he played it often at the Birchmere," Gary says, "By the time I got to know Mickey, his "Trilogy" had become a showstopper for Elvis

A small piano sat in a corner of the first Birchmere. Mickey would play it alone when customers weren't there. © Oelze

Presley's tours. He told me that Elvis 'saved the song.' Mickey had warned Elvis that the song might be controversial. 'Elvis said, 'Don't worry. If I record it then it will be fine.' Mickey said the Elvis recording alone earned him $120,000 a year in royalties for twenty years."

Joan Baez and Glen Campbell did their own cover versions of "Trilogy," as did about 150 other artists from Meat Loaf to the London Symphony Orchestra.

Gary recalls an incident after one of Mickey's shows that speaks to his compassion: "Mick and I were standing outside in front of the place. A car pulls up, the passenger door swings open, and a man shoves a young woman out to the street and drives off. She appeared to have been beaten up and was hurt.

"Mickey goes to the woman lying on the curb. He kneels, helps her up, and starts whispering to her. I could sense he knew just the right words that would help her at that moment just as he found the right lyrics for his songs. I could feel his emotion and empathy. Mickey came from the rough side of East Houston and knew what it was like to get beat up. For me, the way he comforted the woman was spiritual."

Texas songwriter Rodney Crowell, who was inspired by Newbury and knew him well recalls, "I can believe Gary's story.

Mickey was ten years older than me. I'm from a section of Houston called Jacinto City. You had some street cred if you grew up in Jacinto City. You were to be respected. But if you were from the area of Denver Harbor, which is where Mickey was from, you were to be feared. When I was around Mickey, I behaved myself."

Crowell offers another little-known side of Newbury: "In day-to-day life, he was very affable. A sweetheart, you know. But Mickey was also very skittish, or could be, especially before a show. I remember Guy Clark, Townes and me together asking 'where's Mickey?' 'Oh, he's in the bathroom puking. His pregame nerves. He was throwing up because he would get really nervous before a performance."

Newbury accompanied by violinist Marie Rhines in 1999. He politely serves her a glass of wine to begin their performances. With the exception of Marie, Mickey performed solo with his guitar. © *Oelze*

In a 1988 show review, *Washington Post* writer Mike Joyce wrote, "Newbury proved that he knows how to separate true emotion from mere sentimentality, how to explore a man's dashed dreams, fractured romances and lost youth by making the experience seem universal, not self-indulgent."

Newbury, who chain-smoked cigarettes on stage, died at age 62 from emphysema on September 29, 2002.

Guy Charles Clark (b. Nov. 6, 1941, Monahans, TX)

A signed 1988 album, Old Friend. In dressing room in 2009, his last appearance. © *Oelze*

Guy Clark used an economy of language to write brilliant songs, often simply about the beauty of daily life. His compositions became chart-topping hits by others, including: "Desperados Waiting for a Train" (The Highwaymen, Willie Nelson), "Heartbroken" (Ricky Skaggs), "Oklahoma Borderline" (Vince Gill), "Homegrown Tomatoes" (John Denver), "She's Crazy for Leaving" (co-written with Rodney Crowell), "Baby I'm Yours" (Steve Wariner), "Out in the Parking Lot," (Brad Paisley, Alan Jackson), and "Boats to Build" (Jimmy Buffet, John Denver.

Guy Clark trained for the Peace Corps but ultimately did not go on to dig wells in India. Instead, he found work at a Dobro factory and repairing guitars in Houston, Texas.

Someone once told him that the only reason he played music was as an excuse to drink. Guy said, "I don't need no reason to drink." His first musical recognition came playing in the Houston area bars and clubs with fellow struggling songwriters and musicians Mickey Newbury, Jerry Jeff Walker, Kay, (later Kay T.) Oslin, Frank Davis, Gary White, Crow

Johnson, and Townes Van Zandt. He married his first wife, folksinger Susan Spaw, and they had a son Travis in 1966.

After moving to Nashville in 1971, Guy spent much time on Mickey Newbury's boat, and mentored future Birchmere regulars Rodney Crowell and Steve Earle. Just when the songs Clark wrote began charting for other artists, Nashville booking agent Keith Case sent Guy on a solo acoustic tour in 1984 and the Birchmere turned out to be his first stop.

Gary recalls, "Guy came and introduced himself, and before the show asked me to get him a cab to go back to his hotel to get ready. I threw him my car keys and said, 'Use my car.' The next times he played the hall he'd always come to me when he needed a ride and ask, 'Can I have the car keys, *Dad*?'"

Washington Post writer Joe Sasfy reviewed that first show favorably, writing "Clark's songs bring to life remembrances of his childhood in a small Texas town. His storytelling—wry, naturalistic and powerfully evocative in its real-life detail—conjured dramatic images of the same kind of small-town Westerners who inhabited the movie, *The Last Picture Show.*" A second tour teamed Guy with his best friend, Townes Van Zandt, who often stayed with Guy and his second wife, artist Susanna Talley, in their Nashville home.

On another occasion in 1987, Clark appeared with Mickey Newbury. After the show. Mickey, Guy, and Gary settled into what became an all-night discussion—with topics fueled by substantial wine and beer.

Gary recalls, "At some point, Mickey began to get preachy on religion. Guy wasn't impressed and dismissed Newbury's observations with a 'Who gives a shit?' comment.

"When this happened a second time, Mickey jumped up from his chair, and I had to get between them to calm Mickey down. A few minutes later, they laughed together, and I think we all left the building at sunrise. I only wish I could remember more of what we talked about all night," laughs Gary.

Clark returned a year later to promote *Old Friends*, this time with Robert Earl Keen as his opener. He also came back

Mickey, Gary, and Guy.   © Oelze

with Joe Ely, Lyle Lovett, and John Hiatt for an acoustic story and song swap tour.

"The Songwriters Showcase" toured together, in different configurations, for over a decade, with the Birchmere one of their favorite stops.

Vince Gill had a hit song, "Oklahoma Borderline," co-written with Guy Clark and Rodney Crowell when Guy was just beginning as a songwriter.

In Tamara Saviano's 2016 Clark biography, *Without Getting Caught or Killed*, Vince explained Clark's lyrical artistry: "To me, Guy Clark is a painter. His lyrics are familiar to me because I came from that part of the country, too. I can see oyster shell roads... all of those things are so real. Every word matters, and you don't waste words. They're bound for the Mexican bay of Campeche. And the deckhands are singing 'Adios Jole Blon.' That is poetic. God, it just rolls off so well. There are no words that are uncomfortable. One of the greatest lessons to try to learn from Guy is how to find a common sense yet elegant way to say it. The visual side of those songs is what completely annihilates me."

"The finest songwriter that the state of Texas ever gave us," said Nanci Griffith. © C. B. Smith

John Townes Van Zandt (b. March 7, 1944, Fort Worth, TX)

A connecting thread of the Texas contingent was Townes Van Zandt. "Every songwriter who knew Van Zandt would tell me that he was the greatest of them all," Gary Oelze says, adding "Newbury once stressed that Van Zandt had the greatest one-to-one influence on him." It was Mickey who introduced Townes to the legendary Nashville producer "Cowboy" Jack Clement, who began producing Townes. Clement was a flamboyant and inexhaustible character, who during his Marine duty had played bluegrass with Buzz Busby and Scotty Stoneman in Washington, DC.

At Sun Records, "Cowboy" Jack worked with Johnny Cash and oversaw the first records by Jerry Lee Lewis. It was Clement who had the foresight to turn the Sun studio recorder on to capture Presley, Cash, Lewis, and Carl Perkins—The Million Dollar Quartet—in their impromptu singing jam session.

Over the next 50 years, he produced and wrote songs for Waylon Jennings, George Jones, Charley Pride, and dozens of other artists from Louis Armstrong to U2.

One time when folk, country, and bluegrass composer John Hartford appeared, Gary got a big surprise, "I couldn't believe my eyes when I saw 'Cowboy' Jack quietly backing him up on guitar. But I didn't realize how truly important he was in the music business when I met him that night."

In his recollections of Van Zandt, Oelze says: "Townes came from a family of prominent Texans. His father was an oil executive and saw Townes as having an important future. But Townes chose music after seeing Elvis on the *Ed Sullivan* TV show."

Gary tells this story: "From a fourth story balcony during a party at college, Townes wondered what it would feel like to fall, so he let himself fall backward. He landed square on his back but wasn't hurt badly. His worried parents had him examined"

Schizophrenic–reactionary manic depressive was the diagnosis. Insulin shock therapy was prescribed. "This procedure erased his childhood memories, and Townes' mother deeply regretted that therapy decision," says Gary.

"Townes often joked on stage about his schizophrenia. He introduced his song "Two Girls," by explaining his split mental condition required them both."

The lyrical refrain of this song is:

"I got two girls
Ones in heaven and ones below
Oh, one I love with all my heart
And one I do not know.

Townes unpacked his experience with mental illness more directly with his tune "Sanitarium Blues."

Townes would joke that his next selection was a *medley* of his "hit" "Pancho and Lefty," often hailed as the ultimate outlaw song. In an oft-told tale, ten years after "Pancho" was written, Willie Nelson noticed it on an Emmylou Harris album. Haggard had a hazy recollection of recording the tune one late night with Willie and apologizing the next morning for being so drunk.

"We'll have to try it again," Merle told Willie.

"What do you mean?" Nelson replied. "I sent it to New York already. That's our next record." Their version became a number one hit song in July of 1983.

Towne's song lyrics from "Pancho and Lefty" embodied the "outlaw country" music of Waylon, Willie, and others and reached a wide audience. Townes recounted in the PBS series *Austin Pickers* in 1984: "I realize that I wrote it, but it's hard to take credit for the writing, because it came from out of the blue. It came through me."

***

Lyle Lovett on Townes: "I was playing "Pancho and Lefty" and "If I Needed Someone" when I was 17. On the last tour that Guy Clark and I did with Joe Ely and John Hiatt in 2008, I asked Guy if he had seen the movie that Margaret Brown did on Townes [*Be Here to Love Me,* 2004] and Guy said 'I tried to watch it but all everybody wants to do is talk about the dark stuff about Townes. He wasn't dark. He was lighthearted and funny.'

"That was my experience, too," says Lyle. "A typical Townes line is 'I may be a lowly schizophrenic but at least I have each other.' He was so good at telling those kind of jokes.

"I met him when I did my first 1984 set at the Kerrville Festival. I walked off stage and when I saw him, I thought 'Oh, my God.' Townes said 'Hello. I just got here and didn't hear your set, but people whose opinion I respect say you're all right.' It was such a compliment. That was everything to me. And everything he said, including his humor, made you think about it later."

Bob Dylan once told the *New York Times,* "Townes is like a philosopher poet. He gets to the heart of it in a quick way. He gets it out. It's over, and he leaves the listener to think about it."

Lyle adds, "He had what I think of as a wonderful Texas sense of humor, the way he would sort of say something just to see if you were paying attention or if you were smart enough to get his meaning. He would kind of throw things out. And it reminded me of the way my uncle treated us kids when I was growing up."

On Townes, Rodney Crowell says, "He was possessed of an other-worldliness and his songs were just so poetic and seemed so effortless. Sadly, he was bipolar and was constantly kicking heroin in those early days.

"It was so breathtaking having known him and being really close when he was at his absolute peak. When it got really bad, I just shut myself down. It was painful and I pulled away and in some ways, so did Guy Clark. His wife Susanna didn't. She stayed present. He was kind of in recovery mode using alcohol. I know that the alcohol overtook the gift. It killed the gift."

Townes' infamous bouts with alcohol, drugs, and depression were mainly overlooked by Gary and his staff. "To know and love Townes you almost had to just accept his self-destruction," Gary admitted. "He also never lost his sense of humor."

The club's no-talking policy seemed made for singer-songwriters like Townes Van Zandt. When asked in 1986 by writer Holger Petersen if it was difficult to sing his deeply personal songs to an audience, Townes said "Not really. Once they are written I can just close my eyes and sing them. The two or three fan letters I get a year are usually from mental hospitals. They tell me, 'Wow, you saved my life. I didn't realize there was anybody else in the world who is as miserable as me.' Sometimes I get halfway through writing a song and then just throw it out thinking that nobody needs to listen to this."

Geoffrey Himes wrote in his 1987 *Washington Post* review that Townes "reasserted his claim of being the best wordsmith in the Texas school of cowboy writing he helped launch... his best songs seemed suspended between yearning and a fatalistic realism."

Many of Townes' songs—"Pancho and Lefty," "For the Sake of the Song," "Tecumseh Valley," "Rex's Blues," and "To Live Is

To Fly"—were successfully recorded by others. It's a sad fact of Van Zandt's career that his own records didn't sell very well.

Unfortunately, Van Zandt's relationship with Gary would become strained. The effects of drinking and drugs debilitated Townes toward the end of his career, prompting Gary to quit booking him. "And then his agent called and swore that Townes had cleaned up his act, had been to rehab, was off drugs, and needed money." So, Gary reluctantly said, "What the hell, let's get him back."

In what would be his last Birchmere show in 1996 before his passing, Van Zandt arrived and gave Gary a hug. "He was very calm, but the first thing he asked me was where he could get some heroin. Otherwise, he was Townes. He never changed."

Gary ignored his request. Fortunately, Townes got through a charming yet meandering at times performance. The board tape of this show provides his song introductions:

- "This next song is "Buckskin Stallion Blue." It's about a girl and a horse. The girl didn't like it much. I still miss the horse."
- "If you like this next song, then you better get some professional help in the morning."
- "This song, "Rex's Blues" is about my friend, Rex. He had it legally changed to "W-R-E-C-K-S.""
- "Here's a song about Janis Joplin. A good friend of mine. It's called "You Are Not Needed Now.""
- My Dad asked me what I was doing and I said I was playing joints as a folk singer. He said, 'Didn't your Mom tell you to stay out of joints?' I said, 'Yeah, but I'm playing on the stage where it's the safest place to be.' I invited him and the family to a show. So, they all come down, and about halfway through the show this big brawl breaks out. My brother joins in and it is pandemonium. And when it's all over I get home, and my Dad says, "I see what you mean. Nice folks, Nice place."
- "I got some records and CDs downstairs on sale. I'll sign the records but I left my CD laser pen at the hotel. That's a joke, but I'll sign anything but the Bible."

However, one audience member came to Oelze afterward and griped about how awful he was. An annoyed Gary dismissed the complaint with, "Listen, one of these days you'll be boasting to your friends how you got to see the legendary Townes Van Zandt at the Birchmere."

Van Zandt died the following New Year's Day 1997, 44 years to the day after the passing of another songwriting genius, Hank Williams, who also suffered alcohol and opiate abuse.

Alternative country group, The Cowboy Junkies have played the third Birchmere nine times since 2006. They were friends with Townes, toured with him in 1990 on their bus, and credit him as their greatest songwriting influence.

At Van Zandt's funeral, Guy Clark prefaced a tuneful eulogy to his old friend by saying, "I guess I booked this gig 30-some years ago." Lyle Lovett, another who opened many times for Van Zandt, spoke at his funeral and performed a heartrending version of Townes' "Flying Shoes." Good friend Steve Earle also offered his tribute at the funeral.

Stephen Fain Earle (b. Jan. 17, 1955, Ft. Monroe, VA)

"It was Steve's record, Copperhead Road, that led me to think he's right down our alley. Let's book him."   Gary Oelze

Born in Virginia, Earle moved to Texas with his parents when he was two years old. He was mastering the guitar at age 11, and was a big Townes Van Zandt fan, meeting him in Houston, when he was 14. Ultimately, it was Van Zandt's' endorsement that led to Earle becoming the bass player in Guy Clark's band in 1975.

Clark also helped him get him his first publishing deal in Nashville in the early 1980s. Earle's songwriting success began with "A Far Cry from You," the hit song recorded by country music's beloved Connie Smith. Many have recorded Earle's well-crafted, poignant songs, including Emmylou Harris, Johnny Cash, Patty Loveless, Kathy Mattea, Del McCoury, Ricky Skaggs, and The Seldom Scene.

Steve Earle in 1986 © Oelze and 2021.   © *S. Moore*

Earle has been candid over the years about conquering the drinking and drug problems that landed him in prison. Veteran Birchmere staff still remember the night that Steve delayed his show waiting for a "package" to arrive at the side door. In 1993, Earle was arrested for weapons possession. After serving 60 days of his sentence, Earle completed an outpatient drug treatment in Hendersonville, Tennessee.

Steve Earle recalls his first headlining gigs in in Washington, DC in 1986 at the old 9:30 Club one night and the second Birchmere the next night. "Two songs in at the 9:30 Club, my guitarist Mark McAdam who grew up playing the DC bars and was a Danny Gatton disciple, told me it was a punk club. But I thought it was the smart thing to play both clubs because I knew country music was going to abandon me. I was a singer-songwriter folkie from Texas—and not a new country traditionalist—who also grew up on really high-quality musicianship-level country music. That's what there was in South Texas. I used to go see Willie Nelson at the Floors Country Store venue in Helotes, Texas along with Ray Price and Johnny Bush. But I played in coffee houses because I was too young when I started to play in places that served liquor. And I didn't know a lot about bluegrass until I moved to Nashville when I was 19.

"The other people that smoked pot besides me and some of the Texas and North Carolina songwriters I hung out with, were the people that were hanging out at John Hartford's house. He had just moved from the West coast. And so that was the other sort of salon that was going on: the long hair bluegrass guys.

"And I knew the Whites who were next door neighbors to Guy and Suzanna Clark, and the Newburys. I heard all about the Birchmere from them. So, playing the Birchmere was a big deal to me."

With his band, the Dukes, he earned his national success with his first two albums, *Guitar Town* and *Copperhead Road*. "When I got out of jail in the '90s, my M.O. became playing the Birchmere on my solo tours and playing the 9:30 Club with my 4-piece, very-vigorously-loud band. After a few years my audience got older and Gary opened up the third place. We got offers from both places but when I did the bluegrass album with Del McCoury, that sort of cemented me playing the Birchmere. I surrendered to it. And I'm 67 and my audience is too old to stand up."

Steve's son, **Justin Townes Earle** (b. Jan. 4, 1982, Nashville, TN) became a successful performer of American roots music and a frequent act at the hall. He was known for his inward-looking and evocative style. Justin was a singer, musician, entertainer, and music historian. He played keyboard in his father's band, the Dukes, when he began professional music.

But the job title that meant the most to him was *songwriter*. He released eight-full length albums and one E.P. during his lifetime. His 'Harlem River Blues" won "Song of the Year" award in 2011 by the Americana Music Association. *Rolling Stone* magazine described Justin in 2012: "The son of country-rock renegade Steve Earle has grown into a songwriter to rival his dad."

JUSTIN TOWNES EARLE

© *Oelze*

Justin died in 2020. The cause of death was an accidental overdose of fentanyl-laced cocaine. Steve said his favorite picture of his son was from the Birchmere.

In 2010 Steve Earle released *Townes*, a tribute album of fifteen of his friend's songs, winning the Texas songwriter his third Grammy award for Best Contemporary Folk/Americana Album. He returned to Alexandria in 2019 for the "The Guy Tour," performing songs from *Guy*, a tribute album to his mentor Guy Clark.

At this show, Earle spoke quietly about the last time he saw Guy Clark, cancer-ridden and hospitalized. Steve had sent barbecue over, but Guy was sleeping when he arrived. As Earle began to leave, Guy's eyes opened and quietly said, "Stephen." Clark was the only person who ever called him Stephen. When asked how he liked the barbecue, Guy answered with a single word, "pork." Earle smiled, explaining Texan cuisine to the Birchmere audience, "Despite 40 years in Nashville, Guy had never come to accept pork as a legitimate barbecue meat."

Earle returned to the Birchmere in July 2021 and announced his next recording project would be a collection of Jerry Jeff Walker tunes.

It's hard to pinpoint exactly what a large, diverse group of Texas singer-songwriters might have in common, other than to say that it is something uniquely American and deeply personal, and somehow bonded to the land and the people who inhabit it. A list of Texas-born songwriters who have played the Birchmere:

Alejandro Escovedo
Amanda Shires
Billy Joe Shaver
Boz Scaggs
Buck Owens
Butch Hancock
Carolyn Hester
Darden Smith
Doug Sahm
Freddy Fender
James McMurtry
Jimmie Dale Gilmore
Joe Ely
Katy Moffatt
Kinky Friedman
Kris Kristofferson
Lee Ann Womack

Lyle Lovett
Mark Chesnutt
Michael Martin Murphey
Michael Nesmith
Michael Tomlinson
Michelle Shocked
Nanci Griffith
Ray Price
Robert Earl Keen
Rodney Crowell
Roger Miller
Shawn Colvin
Shawn Phillips
Stephen Stills
Tanya Tucker
Waylon Jennings
Rockin' Dave Allen

Tanya Tucker on stage in 2019. © Oelze

Chapter 6 ~ Gypsy Songsmiths (Side 2)

© *Oelze*

John Cowan Hartford (b. Dec. 30, 1937, New York, NY)

John Hartford was a bluegrass, folk and country singer-songwriter who mastered the banjo and fiddle. "I remember how excited I was when John Hartford came to the Birchmere," says Gary. "Chet Atkins discovered him in 1966. Hartford was never a major act, but his song "Gentle on My Mind," earned him a fortune."

"John told people that he wrote his best-selling composition the night he saw the film, *Dr. Zhivago*, and he kind of thought it would be a hit when he finished it. I first heard his version about a year before Glen Campbell's version. It was one of the most played-on-radio songs at that time."

With the song royalties he and his wife, Marie bought a VW bus, and travelled around with their dog, playing solo shows.

"All of his gig contracts specified that venues provide him with a new plywood board, which he'd amplify with little pickups, play the fiddle or guitar, with harmonica, and keep rhythm with his clogging feet while he sang and played. It was amazing. It was almost like having a bass player with your feet.

At some point we had the idea to just sand the same board, so it would look new every time. The board would look new every time he came.

"The last thing he'd do was yell: 'C'mon everyone, 'let's he let's move the tables out of the way and square dance.' I had always thought this offended the waitresses because it disrupted their tips," said Gary.

But when asked in 2020, former waitresses Neva Warnock, Sesi Warnock, Perrie Allen, Connie Brandt Smith, and Teresa O'Brien disagreed, saying, "What bothered us was that we were the ones who had to move the tables out of the way and put them back before we left for the night. We had already closed out our tables by then and we had our tips."

Gary continues: "John played the bluegrass festivals and with Roger McGuinn and Chris Hillman on the pioneering album, *Sweethearts of the Rodeo,* fiddle on "I am a Pilgrim" and banjo on "Pretty Boy Floyd." Our bluegrass audience knew who he was, but I don't think the Cellar Door hired him as much as we did."

In 2019, the Birchmere produced the 50th anniversary *Sweethearts of the Rodeo* concert held at the Strathmore music center in Bethesda, Maryland. Roger McGuinn, Chris Hillman, with Marty Stuart and The Superlatives performed this classic album adding commentary on its production.

***

"John Hartford was very undemanding," Gary adds. "After the show we always got them Peking Duck, which he loved. We'd sit around and talk about the Civil War. He knew much about that and did some narration for the Ken Burn's documentary. And he'd talk about his riverboat. He was a licensed riverboat captain."

During later years, Hartford had apparently beaten throat cancer. "Then one day he came to the club and I walked up to him. I was going to give him a hug like I always did. But he stepped back and said, "Gary, I'm on chemo.""

When John Hartford died on June 4, 2001 at the age of 63, the *New York Times* described his beginnings: "He became fascinated with local bluegrass pickers like Marvin and Clifford Hawthorne and with the riverboats he saw on the Missouri and Mississippi Rivers. He took up the fiddle, performing at barn dances when he was 13 and sneaking out at night to perform in rough-and-tumble honky-tonks. After hearing Earl Scruggs, he decided to turn to the banjo."

Inscribed photo to waitress and photographer Connie Brandt Smith.

Do Good Work

Bryan Bowers contributed this Hartford story: "Once John took a group of us to dinner. When we finished, John napkinned his mouth and looked me in the eye and said, 'Bryan, now comes the reason I invited you to dinner with us. I have a gift for you. I like what you are doing with the harp, your songs, stories, and how you entertain. I think you're doing good. You remind me of a Grandpa Jones, only a little more musical.'"

They both laughed and Bryan thanked him. Then Hartford said, 'But that's the last time you'll hear that kind of praise coming out my mouth. I'm not much for that. But here's the deal. The musical traveling path is a very strange thing. It's like when you go to an amusement park and try to get on the rollycoaster. You pay your money, get your ticket. You go up, and you go down, and after five minutes, you know where the scary parts are. If you ever want to go again, then you already know when it's scary.

"The life of a traveling, committed, making-music-for-the-rest-of-your-life musician is much like riding the rollycoaster, except you never know when the turns are going to be scary, or funny, or weird. So here is how you stay sane on the rollycoaster of making music your whole life: You do good work."

"What do you mean, good work?" asked Bryan.

Hartford answered, "Every day, without fail, you get up and work on something that relates to your craft. You work on a song. You learn a fiddle tune. You learn the Mother Maybelle G chord run. You read a book about a musician you want to learn more about their music. You work on your craft."

Meanwhile, John hadn't noticed as he shared his "gift" with Bryan, but the entire restaurant of about 20 people had slowly hushed down to stone silence, trying to hear his every word.

John concluded his advice by stretching his legs out, rearing his head back, folding his arms, closing his eyes and smiling as he said these final words:

"And if you do all that, Bryan, then every night just before you close your eyes and go to sleep, you can say to yourself, "I've done good work today. ""

Buddy Gene Emmons (b. Jan. 27, 1937, Mishawaka, IN)

John Hartford gave one of his trademark bowler hats to pedal steel master Buddy Emmons. Buddy started wearing it on stage. Emmons started in 1957 playing with Ernest Tubb, known as the Texas Troubadour, credited as an early honky-tonk music pioneer. Buddy Charlton, Tubb's original steel guitarist, also played the hall in 1982.

Tubb's biggest hit song was "Walking the Floor Over You." Buddy Emmons is considered as one of the foremost pedal steel players. He won the Academy of Country Music "Best Steel Guitarist" award nine times.

Buddy Emmons was an important musician with a long Birchmere association.   *© Oelze*

During the afternoons when he toured, he taught pedal steel students who came with their instrument. Gary watched his lessons: "He'd have everyone wear earphones and he'd draw diagrams on a blackboard. They called him "Big E" and one of the reasons his students loved him was because he was an innovator of the instrument, adding strings and special pedals. They'd play their instruments that were connected to the stage monitoring system. You would need earphones to hear what was happening.

"Buddy also played bass with Roger Miller when Danny Gatton was also in the Miller band. And Buddy Emmons would later play pedal steel in Danny's Redneck Jazz band, as well as for Gatton's tribute show after he passed away," says Gary.

Lyle Pearce Lovett (b. Nov. 1, 1957, Houston, TX)

While initially categorized as country, Lyle Lovett is not easily confined to a single genre. Firmly rooted, like the musician himself, in his Texas roots, it is an amalgam of country, R&B, swing, big-band, bluegrass, jazz and gospel, with a sprinkling of wry observational humor.

Whether he's performing with the expert ensembles that have made up the various iterations of his own band, or partnering with other legendary contemporaries, Lyle's live shows are known for their polish and generosity to both his collaborators and the audience.

"Guy Clark would bring someone along to surprise the audience every time he played the hall," says Gary. Steve Earle joked that "Guy whitewashes the fence a lot. You'd come with him to his gigs, and he got you to work for him."

In 1985, Guy introduced Gary to a tall, then-unknown Texan with a "clump of hair piled on his head like so much loose-leaf lettuce," as the *Baltimore Sun* would later opine.

"This is my friend, Lyle Lovett. He's going to be putting an album out soon. Can he open the show?" asked Guy. Gary always agreed to whatever Guy requested.

Lyle had attended Texas A&M University, majoring in journalism. Lyle describes his musical beginnings: "I started playing in a Houston pizza parlor and later in hamburger joints in 1967. I was background music. Later Eric Gale and Nanci Griffith introduced me to the owner of the Anderson Fair Retail restaurant. It was a no-talking listening room that's still open. National acts would come in like Ramblin' Jack Elliott and Odetta. I opened for all of them." says Lyle. "So, when Guy brought me to the Birchmere in 1986, I was right at home with the ethic of the place. I found myself on stage and thinking, 'Oh, my God, everyone's listening to me. Now what do I do?' Both Anderson Fair and the Birchmere teach you to have some intent to what you're doing in your music and how to perform."

"Lyle Lovett represents a new voice in Nashville. proclaimed *Musician* magazine in 1988: "The quirky country songwriter who believes that even cowboys get the blues. Consequently, this Texan's viewpoint can pique listeners whose affection for country music is nonexistent, along with ardent fans."

Guy, Perrie Allen, and Lyle.   © *C. B. Smith*

Lyle's First Night

Gary recalls his first show: "Lyle played songs that later appeared on his first self-titled debut record and his next two albums for MCA. That's how many songs he had in his pocket. And just the nicest person you'd ever meet. He hasn't changed a bit over the years. Gentlemanly, generous, kind, and charming." says Gary.

Lyle has always been beholden to his early benefactor Guy Clark, who even penned liner notes for the debut album, which ultimately made *Rolling Stone's* Best Albums of the 1980s: Says Lyle: "Guy was a real big help to my career before I even knew him. He got hold of a tape of my songs and shared them with Nashville guys. He was passing my tape around town and telling people they needed to listen to it. He was helping me get a contract. Guy certainly understood his own value but didn't see helping me and helping himself as two things incompatible. And I think that there's a real lesson in that, you know helping someone else doesn't take away from what you do.

"I've always been appreciative of playing the Birchmere over the years. The very first gig I ever played in 1988 with the version of our band that we called the Large Band was there."

First show and later with his Large Band. © Oelze

"We started the Large Band tour in March of 1988. We could actually hear each other through the air and not through our monitors and that made it a really fun way to play."

Lyle told the packed room that night: "I'm not used to getting so much help."

"That was a tight squeeze on our small stage, but we managed to fit them all," confirms Gary.

Lyle says, "Gary's personal support of the people that he booked in the Birchmere meant the world to us. He would lift you up and give you confidence that you could do it. And when you're first starting out, that's a huge thing. I mean, that's what Guy Clark did for me. We don't always have that kind of confidence in ourselves and getting that kind of reinforcement from Gary Oelze was important to my career. He was already an icon to me by the time I walked into the Birchmere."

Lyle became a member of Gary's family of performers, playing numerous times with different band line-ups. In 2005, he joined fellow songwriters Guy Clark, Joe Ely, and John Hiatt for a three-night run. With no advance setlist planned, Guy warned the audience that they would be surprised with the music that would follow, and the evening became an intimate session of shared songs and stories.

Signed poster and backstage.   © *Oelze*

Fun quote: When Gary first heard that Lyle had married actress Julia Roberts in 1993, the press dubbed this news as "Beauty Marries the Beast." Gary asked, "I wonder how Julia Roberts is going to feel about being called the Beast'?"

Steven Benjamin Goodman (b. July 25, 1948, Chicago, IL)

Gary: "When Steve Goodman died of complications from a bone marrow transplant in his attempt to beat leukemia in 1984, I read some of his obituaries about how he had a small audience, and had he lived maybe he'd be a Nashville songwriter. It sounded like he never really made it in show business. That's not how I see it." Many critics, fellow artists, and steadfast fans would agree.

Steve Goodman had big songwriting success when Arlo Guthrie recorded his best-known song, "City of New Orleans." Willie Nelson's version won a Best Country Song Grammy in 1985. He mentored and became the life-long friend of another rising Chicago musician, John Prine. Goodman and Prine co-wrote, "You Never Even Call Me By My Name" a hit recording for David Allen Coe. His song, "Go Cubs Go" became the Chicago Cubs baseball team's anthem.

In Steve's early performing days, he had opened for Steve Martin when the "wild and crazy" guy was at his stand-up peak. Goodman's humor, warm and whimsical stage presence, and a catalog of great songs earned him bookings at the Cellar Door and other top venues.

Steve Goodman   © *C. B. Smith*

Unbeknownst to many in the audience, Goodman was diagnosed with leukemia in 1969 early in his musical career, and pursued his passion through both remissions and recurrences. "The main reason I could hire him is partly because of the leukemia," explains Gary. "During and after chemo, he went into remission and liked to play our place because he could perform early, be done around 10 pm, and take care of himself. We all loved him dearly. And he continued to play for us when his disease returned and he went back on chemo."

Guitarist Al Petteway often opened for him, Al says "What impressed me most of all is that he went out on stage and you would never know he was feeling bad. He did his whole set with a big smile on his face. Everybody laughed and had a great time.

"When he left the stage, he collapsed in the dressing room. The audience wasn't aware as he did this show that he was literally dying. That really made an impression on me as a young player."

The Visit

Steve Goodman came to town to play a Johnny Cash concert at the Kennedy Center in 1982. It was a benefit concert for the

Vince Lombardi Cancer Research Foundation. And was shown on August 21, 1982 as an HBO TV Special.

Gary remembers "After rehearsal for this show, Steve called me up and asked who's playing tonight at the Birchmere? I told him, The Seldom Scene."

Steve replied, "Can we come?"

"Who's 'we?' Gary asked.

"John Prine, Vince Gill, and Rodney Crowell. Johnny Cash might come, but he's got something wrong with his leg," Steve answered.

The Scene took a break. Gary told the band that they were coming over. Duffey was unimpressed. They showed up just as the band started their second set.

Prine wrote a note for the band, "I'd sure like to get up and sing with you' swellows." Gary passed it to Mike, who gave it to John, who just continued with the show. Then Gary wrote another note: "Look, all these guys are here." John still ignored them.

Mike started quietly getting on John about this snub, and finally, Duffey invited Prine up on stage. Gary thought, "I don't think Duffey knew who he was. He respected Monroe and those older musicians but didn't know who the younger players were." Phil Rosenthal left the stage and sat in the audience when the guests came on.

According to Gary, "When Prine started to sing, Duffey gave him a look like, 'What in the world? This guy can't sing.' But then Prine began to rag on him, and Duffey always loved that."

On that same night, Duffey, Vince Gill, and Peter Rowan attempted to out-high note each other on the Dillards song "Little Cabin Home On the Hill." Rowan just happened to be at the Birchmere that night.

Duffey stood three feet from the mic, hit the highest notes, and blew them off the stage.

John Prine would become friends with Duffey and asked the Scene to open for him when he played Wolf Trap a few years later.

In 2020, Vince Gill offered his version of Gary's memories:

"I remember it well, and I'll tell you *exactly* what happened. I was the "bluegrasser" of the group. So, I said, yeah, let's go to the Birchmere. That'd be fun. Rodney didn't join us.

"We arrived, and Duffey's up there, holding court like he usually did. So, he eventually says, 'Ladies and gentlemen. I just got some great news. We got some really amazing people here tonight. One of the greatest songwriters that ever lived, John Prine. He wrote, "Paradise." The place goes nuts. And not only that but the great Steve Goodman, who wrote "City of New Orleans," and the place goes nuts. And here we also have..." [pause] "Who? Someone named Vince Gill. I've never heard of him. Let's get them all up here."

"Duffey wasn't kidding," Gill continues, "because there's no reason he should have heard of me. But, I'm like beyond embarrassed, you know? And, so we all go up there, John and Steve and me. There were two extra guitars, and they grabbed them. I walked up there, and there were no instruments. And I was embarrassed again.

"I started to leave the stage, and this Japanese gentleman comes up to me and holds up his mandolin case. He says, 'I know exactly who you are. Here's my mandolin.'

Then John sings "Paradise" and Steve does "City of New Orleans." Duffey asks me, "Would you like to sing one" and I say, 'Sure," and I just rip "Molly and Tenbrooks" by Bill Monroe. Duffey's eyes got as big as bowling balls.

"That's also the night I met Mike Auldridge. What's really cool is not too long after that night, Mike called and asked me if I would consider coming to join The Seldom Scene. And I said, 'Man. I can't. That's a flattering thing because I always adored that band. But it's so funny that it went from 'I've never heard of you' to 'I want you be in our band in one week.'

"You know, I had been playing with Pure Prairie League. We were on television shows, and I was the front man. I quit to be a sideman with one of my favorite singer-songwriters and musicians, Rodney Crowell. Just to be his guitar player and sing harmony. And I sure didn't want to move from Southern California to DC. I had to decline."

In 2020, Akira Otsuka, the "Japanese gentlemen" in Vince's story, offered his own take the two versions of the tale. Akira says, "I remember that John Duffey not only didn't know who Vince was, but he also mispronounced his last name, rhyming it with "Jill." And Vince actually left the stage and was standing nearby when I offered to get my mandolin from my car, and Vince thanked me."

Akira added, "I also heard that night that Johnny Cash indeed wanted to join them at the Birchmere, but he and Rodney Crowell couldn't easily get a cab."

However, Rodney corrected Akira's account. "My guess is that Roseanne was pregnant with our daughter Carrie so we didn't go out and stayed in the hotel that night." He added that the 'not being able to get a cab' didn't sound right for Johnny Cash "who could have signaled for a limousine that night if he wished to visit the Birchmere."

Ten years later Johnny Cash arrived to play his only show at the Birchmere in 1992.

Goodman and Burns.   © *C.B. Smith*

Kenneth Charles Burns (b. March 10, 1920, Conasauga, TN)

It was Steve Goodman who introduced Jethro Burns to the Birchmere. Goodman and Burns were frequent collaborators, touring and recording together. Gary explains, "Steve encouraged Jethro to come out of retirement after his musical partner, Henry D. 'Homer" Haynes died in 1971. They were popular for their "corny" song parodies like "The Battle of Kookamonga" (Johnny Horton's "Battle of New Orleans") and "Baby, It's Cold Outside." (The composer allowed them to parody this song as long as "With apologies to Frank Loesser" disclaimer was printed on the record.)

In reality, both Homer and Jethro were accomplished jazz musicians influenced by gypsy guitar genius, Django Reinhardt. A beautiful video of Jethro leading the Mike Douglas TV show band on "Take the A Train" is available on YouTube. Jethro would tell Gary stories about touring with Abbott and Costello and their many 1940's-style risqué jokes. For example, Jethro once asked Gary how he liked his jacket. Gary said, "It's nice. Where'd you get it?" He answered, "I found it on my bedpost last night." Bada boom.

Jethro Burns and Al Petteway.   © *Oelze*

Fun facts: Chet Atkins and Jethro Burns were married to twin sisters. Whenever Jethro played the hall, all the mandolin players in town would come to listen. One night there was John Duffey, Akira, Doyle Lawson, Dick Smith, and Jimmy Goudreau on stage with him. They so admired his jazzy style.

"It was also in his contract to provide five cases of beer for Jethro every time he came to play. And he could drink beer," says Gary.

Robert Earl Keen (b. Jan. 11, 1956, Houston, TX)

Known for his storytelling Americana music style, the Texas singer-songwriter started as a fan of both Eric Clapton's band Cream and Willie Nelson. His signature tune is "The Road Goes on Forever." His songs have been covered by Joe Ely, Lyle Lovett (his former roommate, with whom he co-wrote one of their best-known songs, "This Old Porch"), The Highwaymen, Nanci Griffith, and the Dixie Chicks.

Nanci Griffith helped Keen get his first record deal, *No Kinda Dancer*, done back in 1983. Gary says, "And 18 records later he's still playing here." His two 2021 shows sold out despite the pandemic, and Keen had some time to tell how he got to the Birchmere.

"I was booking myself when I started. I listened to some Seldom Scene records, and found out that this was their home base. That's when I started calling Gary to get a spot. I must have called him 20 times. Finally, I got booked touring with Guy Clark and Townes. I ended up with Keith Case, who was their agent, too."

When asked how he got Keith Case to represent him, Keen replied, "It was the same deal. I started calling him, and then taking him out to lunch every couple of weeks, Finally I said, 'Look, your regular cut is 10-15% and I'll give you 30% if you'll represent me.' He didn't take that deal either, but I did wear him down in the next year and a half. I always thought if I'm not doing it for me, nobody else is going to do it.

"When I finally met Gary, I was surprised. I had this idea that he might be like an *Inside Llewyn Davis*-type disheveled promotor but he wasn't. I thought maybe I should have been a little more sophisticated in my earlier approach with him. He was very kind from the minute we met, and I feel like all my performances at the Birchmere went well."

Keen continues down memory lane: "The second club hosted a BMI Songwriter's Workshop, which was more like a panel seminar. I remember Bill Lloyd [singer-songwriter], Mark Wright [head of Universal music in Nashville] and me. So, we were talking about the music business. Many people came and one frumpy young woman in the audience just kept grilling the crap out of everybody with questions about the songwriting business.

"Mark started an answer that began with 'When I first started out playing in Bumfuck, Iowa...' and Bill whispered to me 'You know, *everybody* has played Bumfuck, Iowa." And this woman was just relentless with her questions. She's asking us, 'Why are you doing this? And what about that?' and I thought, 'Wow, this woman is pretty serious.'

"So, I went up to her afterwards and she introduced herself as Mary Chapin Carpenter. I thought, I've heard that name before. And the next year her career just exploded."

Rancho Grande

Robert Earl Keen toured with Fred Eaglesmith, a Canadian alternative country singer-songwriter known for his humorous monologues and storytelling. "He is one of the best conversationalists I know," says Keen. "When we would run out of encores on the shows, we'd end up singing "Rancho Grande" together which is a traditional Mexican song. We started doing that one night at the hall and the entire kitchen staff came out and started singing with us. They were so happy."

On Townes

"I had a really great relationship with Townes Van Zandt. I was a huge fan and used to go see him play in Houston and Austin. I toured with Guy and Townes around '89 for a couple years so I got to see him before and then during the real dark days. Like when he'd fall off stage, or he sold his guitar and bought a saxophone and would blow it on stage until he turned blue and collapsed.

"One night he played a club, the Cactus Inn in Corpus Christi where it sold out at 160 seats. And people came in and saw Townes onstage asleep. Everyone was quiet and just waited for him to wake up. And he did and started singing "Dollar Bill Blues," and I'd never seen anything like that before. Just bizarre.

"But he had a "come to Jesus" moment and started to only drink beer, and I could never tell if he got drunk on beer but I knew when he was hitting the vodka. The word on the street was how awful Townes was but I saw him do some great shows that were kind of mind blowing. Townes was out there, exuding, playing out to the crowd. He invited you into his mind. He was bringing you in. It was really like a different kind of transcendental feeling because his songs were so beautiful and colorful that you were sucked into that world. And you weren't even paying attention to the person who was playing the guitar, really. You're just in this world of beautiful colors or tragic stories. That was amazing for me.

"But Townes as a person could be caustic and liked to be cruel. It was weird to be taken down a notch by him. One time we were in Boston and were supposed to go to Northampton.

"We went to get a rental car and Townes hands the agent a library card. This is classic Townes. The agent said, 'Sir we can't accept this,' and Townes protested, 'No, it's a real library card.' He gave them this doleful look, so they'd take pity on

93

him. He got enjoyment out of making people uncomfortable in real life.

"In his final days, almost everyone distanced themselves from Townes except Guy Clark's wife, Susanna."

James Ridout Winchester, Jr. (b. May 17, 1944, Bossier, LA)

This southern songwriter moved to Canada to avoid serving in the army during the Vietnam War, returning in 1977 when President Carter granted amnesty to draft evaders. While in Canada, he began to write songs that often evoked his southern homeland, including his first, "The Brand New Tennessee Waltz." Waylon Jennings, Reba McIntyre, Lyle Lovett, and the Everly Brothers have recorded this song.

Jesse and Mickey in June 1989.   © *Oelze*

Robert Earle Keen remembers, "My first tour was opening for Jesse. He was kind of a different guy altogether. I'd say introverted, yet demonstrative on stage. He'd end his show with "Rhumba Man," and look like Woody from *Toy Story*. He was really thin and sometimes a little frightening, but a great player. And one of the best songwriters.

"The Birchmere has a "hearing a pin drop" kind of unity in the hall, but Jesse took it down to "half a pin drop" level." Robert Christgau's Record Guide notes: "Winchester's first LP was apolitical on the surface and not without its conservative tendencies, but its brooding lyricism and barely contained ferment reflected the force of will it took for him to flee this country."

Gary states, "We all liked Jesse. I always thought his albums, being mostly recorded in Canada, could have sounded better if he would have used US recording studios. His last studio record done in the US in 2009, *Love Filling Station*, produced beautifully by Jerry Douglas, was a big success and gave his concert draw a boost. With Jerry's assistance, especially his silky-smooth lap steel accompaniment, I thought he sounded as good on a record as he did live at the Birchmere."

Kristoffer Kristofferson (b. June 22, 1936, Brownsville, TX)

Kristofferson greets fans outside the hall in 2015.   © Oelze

"Simple yet profound," is how Willie Nelson once described songwriter Kristofferson's lyrics for an *A&E Biography* documentary. About his voice, Willie added with a smile, "It's a good thing he can write. He saved country music and brought it from the dark ages to today."

From Golden Gloves boxer to Rhodes Scholar, decorated army helicopter pilot to Nashville recording studio janitor,

Kristofferson's history reflects the individualism and experience that he brought to his songwriting. He once told TV interviewer Charlie Rose that the drugs, sex and rock and roll life was wonderful. "I agree with poet William Blake who said 'The road of excess leads to the palace of wisdom.'"

Since the mid-'80s, Kris has played the hall accompanied by his wife, Lisa. His last and final performance in 2019 included members of Merle Haggard's band, The Strangers. He added Haggard's "Sing Me Back Home" "Okie from Muskogee," "Fighting Side of Me," "Daddy Frank (The Guitar Man), and "I Think I'll Just Stay Here and Drink" to 24 of his own songs, including "Me and Bobby McGee," "Help Me Make It Through the Night," "For the Good Times," Casey's Last Ride," "Loving Her was Easy," and "Sunday Morning Coming Home."

There was no indication to the packed house that Kris was experiencing any cognitive decline. His family thought it was dementia. In 2014 his doctors correctly diagnosed his illness as Lyme Disease. He expressed support for this history project in 2020 but declined to be interviewed because of memory problems. He formally retired a few months later.

Former Birchmere soundman Tim Kidwell remarked, "Gary had a great comment that Kris's voice never has been that great. It's actually deteriorated over time, but as an artist and musician he sure could present his songs. And he was so nice. Oh, my God. His wife was in the booth during soundcheck. His soundcheck was half a song. He'd tell me 'I don't need anything. I want to stop right now. I'm perfectly happy.' His catering requirements were tortilla chips and Gatorade."

Kidwell also tells this story: "The mother of David Beebe, the Birchmere lighting director, was a great fan of Kristofferson. Dave brought his mom and dad to a show as a birthday gift for his mother. Kris's wife, Lisa, heard about this and went to the merchandise store and got five CDs, and took them to Kris to sign. After the show, she invited Dave and his parents backstage to meet Kris. It was wonderful, and it showed me how much Lisa cared about the fans and also about Kris."

After his mother died, Dave and his dad returned to visit with Kris at another show to thank the Kristofferson's for their kindness.

Dave Beebe with Norma, his Dad and Kris.
Photo by Lisa Kristofferson.

Last show in 2019.   *© S. Moore*

Mike Nesmith in 1993 and with staffer, Chris Adams in 2018.

© *Oelze*

Robert Michael Nesmith (b. Dec. 30, 1942, Houston, TX)

He will always be remembered as wool-capped Mike from the TV show and star-making teen phenomenon, *The Monkees*. But Michael Nesmith and his First National Band—recognized as an often-overlooked pioneer country rock band—bypassed all the well-known hit songs by his first famous band when FNB played the club in 1993. It was 20 years later when Nesmith resumed touring, and a 2013 show at the Birchmere was on his schedule. (Nesmith's fellow Monkee, Peter Tork—who along with Nesmith pushed the show's producers to allow them to play their own instruments after the first album—also played the hall in 2013 and told his own Monkee tales.)

Nesmith and his backing band delivered a low-key set that focused on his solo and FNB catalogs and included his most well-known tune, "Different Drummer," made famous by Linda Ronstadt's first band, The Stone Poneys. However, Nesmith's version was slower and mournful.

In his *Washington Post* review, Dave McKenna paraphrased Nesmith's introduction to "Different Drum": "1950s sidewalk cafe. . . the whole scene bustles like a painting from Renoir . . . There is a distance between them . . . She wants to be a mother and he wants to be a lover . . . There is a sadness."

The only Monkees song on the setlist was the first Nesmith composition the group recorded, "Papa John's Blues," a catchy, Tex-Mex flavored tune. Fun fact: James Burton played the chicken-picking lead on the original Monkees recording. Burton was guitarist for Ricky Nelson, Emmylou, and Elvis.

Only on the song "Grand Ennui," with Marty Stuart's bassist Chris Scruggs playing rocking solos—even soloing with his teeth like Hendrix, who once opened for The Monkees in 1967—did the audience start moving. Nesmith asked if the senior parental dancing at their seats might embarrass "the children." Mike took a look around the chairs and answered his own question, "The children aren't here!"

John Robert Hiatt (b. Aug. 20, 1952, Indianapolis, IN)

With a career that expands over 30 years, John Hiatt songs have become part of the American songbook. Indeed, the Americana Music Association bestowed on him a lifetime achievement award. Starting as a Nashville songwriter at age 18, he evolved into a performer and a multi-genre singer-songwriter equally fluent in blues, rock, and country styles his material interpreted by artists ranging from traditional to alternative rock. Since 2004 he has played the Birchmere over 34 times, and holds the record for 10 sold-out shows.

Hiatt's songs have been covered by Birchmere alums like Buddy Guy, the Everly Brothers, Rosanne Cash, Aaron Neville, Freddie Fender, New Grass Revival, Nitty Gritty Dirt Band, Cliff Eberhardt, Suzy Bogguss, Robben Ford, Albert Lee, The Desert Rose Band, Rodney Crowell, Nick Lowe, and Odetta. "A Thing Called Love" by Bonnie Raitt is another well-known cover of a Hiatt song. When Kyle Osborne interviewed Hiatt in the Birchmere dressing room in 2012, he was touring to support his CD, *Mystic Pinball.*

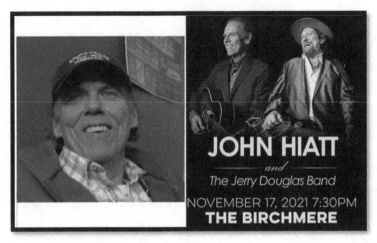

Hiatt's 2021 show poster with Jerry Douglas.

Hiatt said "I make a new record when I got the songs. There's a heightened sense of excitement over the work for me the older I get. This [music] is what I do. I'm running out of time, so, I might as well step it up."

He was playing consecutive nights at the Birchmere ~~mirror~~ and it's clear that he has a comfortable relationship with his audience, conversing with them from the stage throughout the show. And hours after the show, John was still in the parking lot, signing autographs for a few diehard fans.

Osborne asked him, "Why are they so comfortable with you?"

Hiatt responded, "I really appreciate them, and the fact that they come out. They offer us [musicians] the opportunity to do what we love."

Hiatt played the hall through all stages of his career. He told Osborne: "Yes. It's always fun to play here. It's set up to where you feel like you're out in the audience already. The thing we're always trying to do is build the bridge, you know, between the audience and us and meet with music and there's something physical about this room. You feel like you're already halfway there as long as you can give them something good."

Chapter 7 – What'd I Say

Blues and soul music is satisfying, sorrowful, erotic, and can make you have to dance. It can have a joyful sense of humor yet is born from, and gives a powerful voice to, people who have historically felt themselves at the margins of society. The Birchmere has presented thousands of R&B musicians over the years. Here are a few.

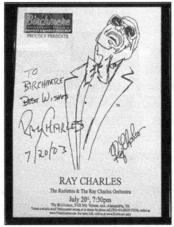

His last autograph at a music venue.

Ray Charles Robinson (b. Sept. 23, 1930, Albany, GA)

Gary Oelze considers the most remarkable Birchmere event to be the 2003 concert by Ray Charles. Blind since the age of seven, Charles combined his blues, classical piano, country and western, and jazz influences, the cornerstone of what has become known as soul music. His performance was the beloved artist's last concert. Charles had played his 10,000th concert at the L.A.'s Greek Theater a few days prior and his tour was canceled soon after this Birchmere show. *The Washington Post* reviewed it.

The Ageless Genius of Ray Charles
by Joe Heim, July 23, 2003.

Performers at the Birchmere will often receive a rousing ovation at the end of a concert. But when Ray Charles visited the club Sunday night, the sellout crowd stood, clapped and roared for several minutes before he had played a single note.

In the hour that followed, the legendary singer, pianist and arranger showed once again why he has earned that sort of acclaim—and love.

With backing from the superb 17-piece Ray Charles Orchestra and the five Raelettes—his wonderful and amusingly coy backup singers—Charles explored his familiar repertoire and yet made it all sound new, vibrant and, at moments, magical.

Charles doesn't just sing a song; he tells you a story. He growls and yelps and moans, cries out in despair and smiles his wicked smile. And so, his songs take on life as each word, each raspy phrase brims with passion and urgency. "Georgia on My Mind," for example: Charles revived it, drew out every melancholy note, and the song's lingering, soulful sadness filled the air. He restored feeling to other hits as well, including "I Can't Stop Loving You" and the still hilarious "Hit the Road Jack." (Charles grumbled asides like "I don't think you know who you're talking to" as the Raelettes responded with the insistent chorus).

At 72 years old, Charles is such an icon of American music that his remarkable artistry—his myriad contributions as one of the great innovators of soul—is often overlooked. But if he's become better known over the years for pitching Diet Pepsi or singing "America the Beautiful" to huge crowds on the Fourth of July, this intimate show was a brilliant reminder of the breadth of the man's musical vision and creativity.

His management cited "acute hip discomfort" as the reason for the tour cancellation. Ray issued a statement: "It breaks my heart to withdraw from these shows. All my life, I've been touring and performing. It's what I do. But the doctors insist I stay put and mend for a while, so I'll heed their advice."

Ray Charles' majestic presence was an involved production. Birchmere's now director of sound production, and then stage monitor engineer, Bud Gardner, remembers getting ready for the show:

"The band came on a bus with the gear and all that. But Ray showed up in a black limo later on with his tour manager. I was still fresh working at the Birchmere.

"Ray didn't come to the soundcheck. We had to add six feet to the side of the stage using 2x4 plywood to accommodate the band. It was about seven o'clock when Ray pulled up in the limo. We made a human wall so people in the parking lot couldn't see him. We all welcomed him, and he grumbled a pleasant hello.

"The two dressing rooms were already crowded and the women needed to have their own bathroom and privacy. Charles asked Tim Kidwell, then front sound engineer, if there was a place where the crew hangs out. Tim said, 'we have a tech room.' Ray agreed that that would work for him if he had a chair.

"Mr. Charles it's just a tech room," Tim told him.

He answered, "Son, I'm blind."

Gardner continues: "Ray was rushed into my tech room with a guy on each of his arms. I just basically sat in the back of the small room and stared at him as he sat with his two assistants. Ray didn't eat. We all sat there in silence."

Bud concludes, "At showtime, they walked him out and onto the stage. And he went on. Ray had his own sound guys, so one of them sat at my console and ran the stage monitor sound. It was a long show, and Ray sure didn't phone it in.

Riley B. King (b. Sept. 16, 1925, Berclair, MS)

B.B. King's 2011 New Year's Day concert began with fans lining up in front of the stage to take pictures of glistening red Lucille, one of the most famous electric guitars on the planet. When the 85-year-old Rock and Roll Hall of Fame blues master took the stage, he didn't have to introduce her.

Dave McKenna described the show in his *Washington Post* review: At one point in his two-hour show, he plucked a single note on Lucille and wiggled his finger while the note was solely and soulfully sustained. As the tone filled the room, he cradled his head down in his other hand. He smiled, demonstrating that he could get more emotion from a single note than other guitarists could attempt with a hundred.

"King cautioned the audience, 'Don't ever get to be my age,'" after briefly forgetting a lyric. Minor flubs did not matter much to the blues guitar master. He could always rely on Lucille to compensate with her fluttering vibrato, octave slides, and trademark mix of major and minor riffs. Listening to King play now makes it impossible to mistake his influence on generations of blues and rock guitarists."

He was first known as the "Beale Street Blues Boy," then shortened to "Blues Boy," and finally to B.B. King.　　　　　© *Oelze*

King's relaxed, two-hour show included "Everybody Wants to Know Why I Sing the Blues," "Rock Me Baby," "Key to the Highway," and Wille Nelson's "Night Life." King once quipped, "I fell in love with that man [Nelson], and I ain't gay, *yet*"... He even added a sing-along version of the country classic, "You Are My Sunshine," especially appropriate for the Birchmere's regular patrons in the sold-out audience. His finale was his signature blues song, "The Thrill is Gone."

King stayed in his tour bus before the highly anticipated show, emerging that day only for the soundcheck. Around 7 pm, general manager John Brinegar was summoned from his office to come to the green room. "It was time for the boss to get paid in cash," John explained. "An assistant in the green room escorted me to where Mr. King was relaxing in his tour bus, listening to jazz on his laptop, and eating cheese and cantaloupe. Lucille was beside him, resting against a seat."

Brinegar recalled the encounter with a smile, "He was jovial and friendly. He had a big family, and many were attending the show. I had taken care of them with tickets, and he was aware and thankful I had handled that. He said, 'John, sit down and share some food with me,' and we began talking about music and other guitarists. He was familiar with the work of everyone I mentioned, including a young player from the U.K. named Davey Knowles."

John had counted B.B.'s pay twice before he did it in his presence. It was a very old-school method of paying an act in cash, reminiscent of the days when players were routinely stiffed by shifty club owners. John felt like he was in the presence of the Godfather, and King acted like he did this every day." Actually, he did it nearly every day. He was logging about 300 live shows a year from the 1980s until he died in 2015.

At the end of his New Year's Day show, King stayed seated in his center stage chair, meeting fans and signing autographs. Several brought guitars for his signature. He was heard to roar, "No Fenders. I only sign Gibson guitars!"

In addition to the Birchmere, other famous Washington venues for the bluesman include the Howard Theatre in his early days, Constitution Hall, Wolf Trap, the National Mall, and the White House.

Delores LaVern Baker (b. Nov. 11, 1929, Chicago, IL)

In 1991, LaVern Baker became the second solo female R&B artist to be inducted in the Rock and Roll Hall of Fame, after Aretha Franklin in 1987. Baker's 1950's hit singles include "Tweedle Dee," "Still," "Bop Ting-a-Ling," "I Shed a Tear," and her number one song on *Atlantic Records,* "Jim Dandy," was certified gold in 1956. During her Rock and Roll Hall of Fame ceremony, songstress Chaka Khan proclaimed that Baker was "one of the first women to capture the essence of rock & roll."

Khan has played often at the hall, and a 2019 concert at the Warner Theatre produced by the Birchmere. Chaka was inducted in the Rock Hall in 2021.

© *Oelze*

LaVern played one of her last shows at the hall in 1996. Gary remembers, "We had to lift her onstage in her wheelchair because diabetes had claimed her legs but she was still a powerful entertainer." *Washington Post* writer Geoffrey Himes did a feature article on her career and reviewed the Birchmere show: "...She threw herself into numbers such as the slow blues "Do Right, Baby," a reading of the riot act to wayward men, which Baker punctuated with sharp shouts and a wagging finger...On her hit 'Saved," she cried, 'I used to smoke and drink and dance the 'hootchie-koo,' as if testifying in her old Chicago church. Then she demonstrated the dance by swinging her elbows and swiveling her hips in her wheelchair."

She billed herself as "Little Miss Sharecropper" when she began her career at the age of 17. Another of her hits was "See See Rider," as she spelled it. Bonnie Raitt, told Steve Jones of *USA Today* that Baker's hit song "'Jim Dandy" was one of the greatest records I heard as a kid."

Jamesetta Hawkins (b. Jan 25, 1938, Los Angeles, CA)

A member of both the Rock and Roll and Rhythm and Blues Halls of Fame, Etta James was only 15 years old when her song, "The Wallflower," also known as "Roll With Me Henry," became a cross-over number one hit recording on Billboard. James could do it all. R&B, jazz, gospel, and rock. She played a show with and befriended a 19-year-old Elvis Presley in Memphis when he recorded at Sun Studios, and she opened for the Rolling Stones on their 1978 tour. She first performed at the Birchmere in 2001. In his *Washington Post* review titled "Pure Emotion at the Birchmere," Mike Joyce wrote: "From the start it was clear that James wasn't going to resort to routine interpretations or untested songs. Opening with "I'd Rather Go Blind," James revisited this classic tale of a woman betrayed with a mixture of empathy and resignation, as if all the lessons she's learned about the treacherous nature of relationships were weighing on her mind. Then she changed the mood all together with "At Last," her signature song, in which her voice and spirit seemed lifted by the very notion of an enduring romance. While she didn't dramatically belt out the ballad as she once did, she used her voice cagily, ratcheting it up and down and measured tones until the song reached an exultant climax."

She brought her eight-piece band back to the hall on May 15, 2009. Gary recalls, "Her band started the show with a long set. Etta arrived in a wheelchair and took a seat center stage. She played a short 40-minute set to a full crowd. No encore."

Malcolm John Rebennack Jr. (b. Nov. 20, 1941, New Orleans, LA)

Appearing six times from 1986 until 2010 was Rock 'n Roll Hall of Famer Mac Rebennack, known to his fans simply as Dr. John. His music was born in R&B and jazz and evolved into a genre-bending swampy funk blues style. His voodoo "doctor" persona was inspired by his New Orleans roots and live shows, a wild mixture of Mardi Gras and musicianship. Although he only had one hit record, "Right Place, Wrong Time," the Doctor was incredibly prolific, winning six Grammy Awards and generating an impressive discography. His unmistakable music also found its way onto numerous film and TV soundtracks.

His career was almost predestined when his family introduced him to the jazz of Louis Armstrong and King Oliver. His grandfather sang him minstrel songs, and his aunts played piano. By 13, he was performing with Professor Longhair, and would graduate to a chair in L.A.'s famed Wrecking Crew, working as a session musician. Over the years, he appeared on thousands of recordings by other artists.

Rebennack first found professional notoriety as "Dr. John, The Night Tripper." Dr. John appears in Martin Scorsese's documentary film of the Band's farewell concert, *The Last Waltz*. The gumbo-fed doctor's turn, "Such a Night," is a highlight of that celebrated film. In later years, he was honored for his charity fundraisers for Hurricane Katrina relief.

Despite the Birchmere's "Quiet" rules, Dr. John's spirited two hour set in 2000 provoked much spontaneous dancing. When he bid goodbye with his trademark silver cane in hand, music writer Dave McKenna observed, "It may have been the wrong place, but it was surely the right time for such abandon."

Dr. John in 2010.   © *Oelze*

Dr. John confided to reporter Kyle Osborne backstage: "I don't think much about where I'm playing, because that can make me crazy, and I'm already crazy enough. I'm just glad I'm breathing." From his last show at the club, Dr. John flew to play as the opening act for the Neville Brothers, and headliner Buddy Guy—both Birchmere alums—at the 17,500-seat Hollywood Bowl.

I Ain't Mentioning No Names

Gary once tapped Jon Carroll to open for Dr. John at one of his '90s club appearances. Both would do solo sets. Jon, the pianist in Mary Chapin Carpenter's band and former Starland Vocal Band member, loves to tell this story:

"I was a bit nervous because I hadn't played too many solo shows in those days. Mac and I were alone, just the two of us, in that boxcar dressing room waiting for the call to go on, while Mac sat in a big chair, and we were sharing stories about pick-up gigs and how we never knew what to expect.

Jon Carrol at the house piano.   © *Oelze*

"Mac nodded, knowingly chuckled, and in that low jazzy voice of his said [Jon does an impression of Mac]: 'I know what you mean, man. I was sittin' in wid deez cats last week at Mikell's club [NY] and—I ain't mentionin' no names—but dis one cat was playing deez fills dat wuz so sideways dat, I swear, I could not find the one! I mean, I ain't mentionin' no names, but I'm tellin' ya, I could NOT find da downbeat after some o' deez crazy-ass fills! And I'm from New Orleans!! I tell you wut, I'd never hoid nuttin' like dis dude's fills, man.' "Then he kinda trailed off' 'But I ain't mentionin' no names.'"

They shared a twenty second pregnant pause before Mac erupted, blurting out: "It was Jack DeJohnette!"

"Right then, a knock came on the door," Jon continues, "and I scooted out and on for my set. But I couldn't stop wondering about it on the drive home that night. What was going through his head during that long silence, obviously an internal debate: Could it have been 'Who's this guy (Jon) that this'll never get back to Jack DeJohnette?' or maybe just, 'Ya know what? *'Fuck* Jack DeJohnette!'"

For the record, Jack DeJohnette is one of the most accomplished and influential jazz-fusion drummers of the 20th century. He's played with Herbie Hancock, Miles Davis, Chick Corea, Pat Matheny, and nearly every other jazz genius.

George "Buddy" Guy (b. July 30, 1936, Lettsworth, LA)

Buddy Guy began his professional blues career in the late 1950s as a session guitarist at Chess Records. Guy added his talent to the recordings of Muddy Waters and many other Chess artists. It is easy to pick up Buddy's distinctive lead guitar on Koko Taylor's 1965 hit, "Wang Dang Doodle."

However, the label didn't foresee his potential as a solo artist. They didn't want to let him record the way he played live. When Chess eventually freed him to begin his solo career, he slowly started to get the attention and success he deserved.

Guy became well known early in the Washington, DC area. He opened for Led Zeppelin at the 1969 Laurel Pop Festival, played Georgetown's The Emergency the next year with musical partner Junior Wells, a blues master vocalist and harpist.

The Junior Wells-Buddy Guy band also played Washington's first blues festival, held at Howard University in 1970. From humble beginnings at The Emergency, Buddy would also find himself being honored with a 2012 Kennedy Center Honors award just a few blocks away from where The Emergency once was. Also being honored that night was Led Zeppelin.

After seven albums, his 1991 breakthrough record, *Damn Right, I Have the Blues,* earned a Grammy award and kicked off both critical and commercial success.

B.B. King and Eric Clapton jointly inducted Buddy into the Rock and Roll Hall of Fame in 2010. Clapton, one of Guy's most devoted disciples, cites him as "without doubt the best guitar player alive. He combined the Delta Muddy Waters style and urban blues—the phrasings of T-Bone Walker and B.B. King— into his unique, sophisticated style."

Guy first came to the hall in 1987, returning to play 16 shows over the next 31 years. In 2004, Guy, dressed in overalls and sitting on a stool, played a rare acoustic guitar show that featured country licks and Delta blues songs by Muddy Waters, Willie Dixon, and even a version of Ray Charles' "What'd I Say." "I used to do this before I knew what electric light was," joked Guy.

The audience at his last appearance in 2018 was impressed by his energy at the age of 82. Washington writer Mark Engleson reported in *Parklife DC* that Buddy "showed the audience all sorts of tricks, playing his Fender Strat over his head, behind his back, one-handed, and even using the friction from pressing his body and his polka-dotted shirt against his guitar. I'd heard before the show that Buddy has a habit of parading around the audience while playing his guitar. Buddy lived up to his reputation. The crowd rose to its feet as he strode through the crowd like the Pied Piper. I was just a few feet from this legendary, iconic artist."

Some patrons recall shows where he strolled throughout the club making his rounds among the tables, through the kitchen, and outside to the parking lot.

Engleson: "Plugged-in and back on stage, Guy gave demonstrations of guitar styles he learned from legendary guitarists he called "the masters," like the boogie style of John

Lee "Boom Boom" Hooker. He set his guitar on its back and played Clapton's "Sunshine of Your Love" riff, playing with a drumstick. After these stunts, Buddy's language could get charmingly salty when he offered an 'I just want to f**k with you,' accompanied by a warm smile."

Buddy in the kitchen with waitress, Teresa O'Brien.   © *Oelze*

Guy was known to say from the stage, "I never play from a setlist because I want to play for *you*," pointing to the audience. Yet his fans always knew that his most famous songs would be played, often opening with "Damn Right, I've Got the Blues" and always including "Feels Like Rain," a blues song written by hall favorite, John Hiatt.

Daryl Davis (b. March 26, 1958, Chicago, IL)

Expert blues and R&B pianist and historian, Daryl Davis talked about his story, coming to the DC area in 1971 and his

friendship with Buddy Guy.

"I'm a close friend of Buddy. He played a lot with Big Mama Thornton, [who recorded "Hound Dog" three years before Elvis Presley]. The team of Buddy on guitar with Junior Wells on vocals and harp was legendary. On one of Jerry Lee Lewis' last albums, Buddy recorded a duet with Jerry Lee, the old song "Hadacol Boogie.'"

Daryl, Buddy, and opening act, Christone "Kingfish" Ingram
© *D. Davis*

"I was a late bloomer in music, taking lessons in the early '70s from John Malachi, the renowned pianist in Billy Eckstine's orchestra. I then majored in jazz at Howard University. I saw the Seldom Scene and the Country Gentlemen at the Birchmere in the '80s, but here's the thing: Country, bluegrass, the blues–it's the same three chords. Sometimes they're in different orders, but it's basically the I to the IV to the V, with sometimes and II and a VI thrown in.

"The Birchmere and other clubs are where I could see what the musicians were doing. I even started playing in a country-bluegrass band early on around town. Musically, we're all related. It is society that separates us. I consider the Birchmere to be a leader and very progressive in uniting communities in the DC area."

Davis is also well known for working to improve race relations, by engaging with members of the Ku Klux Klan to convince them to leave and denounce their group. His 1997 book *Klan-destine Relationships* (New Horizon) was made into a documentary film, *Accidental Courtesy.*

114

He graduated from Howard University in 1980 to become a leader himself on blues and rock n' roll piano. For 32 years, Daryl was the preferred piano accompanist for Chuck Berry whenever Chuck toured the East Coast.

"In the beginning, I went to meet everyone who were my idols like Chuck Berry. I saw Muddy Waters and his back-up band, who became The Legendary Blues Band as they were known after they left Muddy. I was there when the Legendary Blues band first played the Birchmere. The band called me up on stage to play with them. This is where I met Muddy's pianist Pinetop Perkins. When Pinetop played in town, he'd stay at my house. We became fast friends."

Joe Willie "Pinetop" Perkins (b. July 7, 1913, Belzoni, MS)

Jump blues hopped its way into the Birchmere with "Pinetop" Perkins. Another dazzling pianist whose bite and bounce of The Legendary Blues Band came from Perkins' emblematic boogie-woogie style. Pinetop was in his 70s when he decided to leave that band and pursue a solo career.

"Pinetop showed me how to really play the piano, along with Chuck Berry's pianist, Johnnie Johnson," says Davis. With a Lifetime Grammy Award in 2011 at age 97, Perkins is the oldest performer to win a Grammy. He died of cardiac arrest one month later. Pinetop can also be seen in action alongside Muddy Waters, backed-up by The Band, in *The Last Waltz.*

Clarence "Gatemouth" Brown (b. April 18, 1924, Vinton, LA)

"Gatemouth" Brown, who created music from his Texas and Louisiana roots. Known for his flowing, deep vocals, Brown's music instructor once said he had a "voice like a gate," and the name stuck.

Brown, who began his career in 1945 playing drums in San Antonio, Texas, displayed a wide range of blues, zydeco, jazz, big band, and country swing tunes, blending these styles into a brew all his own. Guitarists Frank Zappa and Roy Buchanan, a Blues Hall of Fame member, both credited Brown as a significant influence on their guitar playing.

Brown played the Birchmere first in 1985 and again in 2000. with his band Gate's Express. Songs in his 90-minute sets included "Caledonia," "Take the A Train," "One O'Clock Jump and a country music. medley of "I Can't Stop Loving You," and "Release Me."

He returned to the hall in 1997 to promote his album, *Gate Swings*, which Geoffrey Hines favorably reviewed. Hines wrote "Clarence "Gatemouth" Brown has never put out a bad album. His tough-minded approach to the blues, country, Cajun and jazz ensures a minimum of nonsense and a maximum of variety, while his virtuosity on the guitar and fiddle ensures the highest standards."

"No info on who the little girl is," says Gary.   © Oelze

Izear Luster Turner Jr. (b. Nov. 5, 1931, Clarksville, MS)

Dave McKenna described Ike Turner's 2002 Birchmere show in the *Washington Post*: "The Turner who showed up at the Birchmere on Monday is a testament to bad living. Wearing a flashy black-and-green ensemble unzipped to reveal his pecs, he wowed a small but reverent crowd with a mainly retrospective 90-minute set that showcased his seminal role in the history of rock and soul music."

The high point was "Rocket 88," the 1951 Sun Record single he co-wrote and played on. It was released and credited to Jackie Brentson and his Delta Cats, who were actually Ike Turner and his Kings of Rhythm.

From the Birchmere stage, Ike claimed this to be the first rock n' roll song. A versatile musician, Turner switched from his Stratocaster to pound the piano, as he smiled to pianist Ernest Lane who, like his hit songs with female partner Audrey Madison and an eight-piece backup band. No mention of Ike's ex-wife, Tina Turner.

Ike's proclamation that his "Rocket 88" is the first rock n' roll song began a debate among Daryl Davis and Gary Oelze while researching this book.

Based on a 1947 song called "Cadillac Boogie," "Rocket 88" was a homage to the Oldsmobile car of the same name. *Time* magazine reviewed the song as "brash and sexy with rhythm and attitude and electric guitar and reimagined black music into something new."

Daryl Davis chimed in on "88's" claim to fame: "Some people say "That's All Right, Mama" by Elvis was the first rock n' roll song. Then there's "Rock Around the Clock," by Bill Haley. And "Rocket 88" recorded by Jackie Brexton. I say no to all of them.

I believe it was "Maybelline" by Chuck Berry. He was playing this music in 1952 before he even started recording. But how do you define "rock and roll?" First it has to have that backbeat in it. Before "Maybelline" everything 'swung.' Especially Bill Haley, because he was a Country & Western swing band when he started. He cut a country version of "Rocket 88." It's actually a "boogie-woogie," song. It doesn't have that heavy II to the IV back-beat. "Maybelline" does. And "That's All Right (Mama)" isn't rock 'n roll, it's a blues song."

Gary says: "My view is that the Bill Haley's 1954 "Rock Around the Clock" should be considered the first because of the cultural impact it had in the opening credits of the movie, *Blackboard Jungle*. We were used to listening to small radio speakers in our cars, but when that song blared out on huge sound systems in movie theatres, then that was the birth of rock and roll."

© *Oelze*

John Dawson Winter III (b. Feb. 23, 1944, Beaumont, TX)

"Rock and Roll, Hoochie Koo" is a popular Johnny Winter song even though Rick Derringer, in Winter's band during the song's 1970 release, wrote it. Those at the 1969 Woodstock festival say Johnny Winter's set was a highlight of that famed concert. So, it's a shame that his manager wouldn't let it be in the film, but it can be found on YouTube.

Raucous, torrid, and loud were apt adjectives for Winter's gigs, usually supported by a power trio of backup musicians. Audiences loved his shows, but at least one reviewer, Mike Joyce, noted early on that "Winter failed to take advantage of the intimate setting by playing acoustic slide guitar or otherwise substantially altering the pace of his 1990 show."

At his dozen Birchmere shows between 1990 and 2013, Winter would sometimes welcome fans into his tour bus. The Seldom Scene's Dudley Connell remembers seeing a Winters show. "He was great," says Dudley, "but a little loud for the club."

Albert King   © *Oelze*

Albert Nelson (King) (b. April 25, 1923, Indianola, MS)

Rolling Stone magazine once ranked Albert King as number 13 of the 100 greatest guitarists of all time. King played the hall three times beginning in 1990. The gifted blues man's career took off with his first hit record, "Don't Throw Your Love on Me So Strong," featuring Ike Turner on the piano. King was posthumously inducted into the Rock and Roll Hall of Fame in 2011.

Birchmere staff remember the left-handed guitar master, a big man at 6'4," using his first set as a soundcheck while simultaneously instructing his bandmates on what to play, and sometimes even how to play. "The Sky is Crying," "Kansas City," and Killing Floor" were standout songs he performed stage in 1990, fortified with burning riffs on his cool-looking Gibson Flying V guitar.

Another Albert appearing at the Birchmere was fellow bluesman **Albert Collins**, also known as "The Iceman." Collins, was known for his unusual tunings and using a capo on his electric guitar If you had happened to get Collins' autograph after his set, you might have noticed the "Big Bad Voodoo Daddy" added below his signature. Collins' other alias was adopted by the blues group **Big Bad Voodoo Daddy**, who have played the Birchmere several times.

Robert Cray (b. Aug. 1, 1953, Columbus, GA)

He's won five Grammys and played with the likes of Eric Clapton, John Lee Hooker, Chuck Berry, and Stevie Ray Vaughan. He is the bass player you see backing Otis Day and the Knights in the 1978 film *Animal House*. His own band, the Robert Cray Band, has played the Birchmere almost annually since 2006.

"The sound is great," says Cray. "I hear everything I want to hear, and we have a really good time playing the Birchmere. That's the most important thing. If you can't corral your sound in a room, it makes it really difficult to have any fun. And we always have fun there. That's why we always come back.

"Hearing is a funny thing," Cray said. "It's understanding and interpreting it, making sense of the various vibrations swirling around our heads," says Cray. "That's how two people can listen to the same thing and come away with opposite impressions. The sounds may be the same, but the comprehension isn't.

"What struck me the first time playing the hall was how quaint and intimate everything was, and now it's kind of like going home. We pull up to the side of the building and know which dressing room is ours. We look forward to ordering the catfish and red beans. Nobody in the band goes out anywhere else to eat. It's always fun. And then when we get on the stage walking up the ramp to the stage, everybody can see you. It's like being in somebody's living room and playing."

Chapter 8 – Pete, Tom, Janis, Joan & Arlo

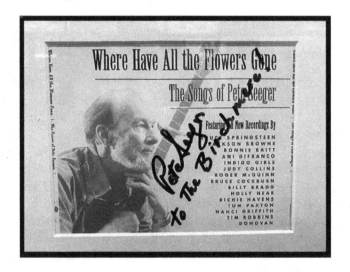

"The best way to get to know people is to go and listen to their music."

Woody Guthrie

It was bluegrass music that initially brought people into the Birchmere. It was folk music that steadfastly followed, especially after The Cellar Door closed its doors in 1981. "We inherited many of their folk acts when they shut down," Gary explains."

One folk show highlight was a 2006 Tribute to Woody Guthrie, one of America's most significant folk artists. His "This Land is Your Land" was a protest song that addressed the suffering of the Great Depression and became a lasting American standard, even sung at President Obama's 2009 inaugural.

Actually, Guthrie wrote the words only. The melody came from the Carter Family's "When the World's on Fire," which they adapted from a Baptist gospel hymn, "Oh, My Loving Brother."

At the time, Woody said he recorded it because "I was tired of hearing Kate Smith sing 'God Bless America.' God blessed America for me," which was the original title before he changed it.

Peter Seeger (b. May 3, 1919, New York City, NY)

The Guthrie tribute headliner was Pete Seeger, marking his only appearance at the Birchmere. Seeger began as a Guthrie disciple and sang with Guthrie, Lee Hays, and Millard Lampell in the Almanac Singers from 1940-1943. One of their first gigs was at the old Turner's Arena in Washington, DC about six miles from today's Birchmere. Their music was powerfully political, anti-fascist, and pro-union. "Where Have All the Flowers Gone?" and "Turn!, Turn! Turn!" are both beautiful examples of Seeger's songwriting although Pete contributed the melody only to the latter. The words are from the Bible.

Folksinger and fellow activist Billy Bragg wrote upon Seeger's death in 2014: "Pete believed that music could make a difference. Not change the world, he never claimed that—he once said that if music could change the world, he'd only be making music—but he believed that while music didn't have agency, it did have the power to make a difference." Billy Bragg has played the Birchmere seven times.

The 2006 tribute show began as a benefit for a regional project called Culture Works. The organizer was guitarist and singer Joe Uehlein, an Ohio native who moved to the Washington area in 1975. "It was ground zero for the bluegrass scene at the Birchmere, and I was a fanatic," says Joe.

His first bluegrass band, Groundwork, and his later group, The U-Liners, had played the hall since the early '80s.

Joe says, "I pitched Pete Seeger to headline a Woody Guthrie tribute show for the benefit to Michael Jaworek, who wasn't immediately sold on this idea. He was aware of Pete's physical condition and vocal abilities at 87, and he was right. Pete was slowing down."

"After Jaworek gave me an October date, I enlisted Cathy Fink and Marcy Marxer, Woody's granddaughter Sarah Lee Guthrie, Johnny Irion, Baldemar Velasquez and my band, The U-Liners.

When Pete, with his wife Toshi, arrived for the show he had some disturbing news. He told Joe that his memory was failing and he couldn't remember song verses, but he'd be fine on the choruses.

"Not even on "This Land is Your Land?" Joe asked.

Pete replied, "On *all* the verses."

However, later in the day, Pete suggested playing "The Sinking of the Reuben James," and he wrote the lyrics from memory on a sheet of paper in the dressing room. "When he actually sang it, he didn't look at the paper, and did it perfectly." Joe says.

***

J. Freedom du Lac reviewed the Guthrie tribute in the *Washington Post*: "While his voice has seen better days, Seeger remains an expert storyteller who can summon dates, anecdotes and songs with remarkable ease...the second act, which included a brief onstage interview with Seeger and was highlighted by a wonderful medley of some of Guthrie's whimsical children's songs. He has something of an encyclopedic mind when it comes to music. No wonder, then, that he received multiple standing ovations, the first simply for showing up."

Preceding the second set's music, Joe interviewed Pete on stage. We include the highlights of this interview, because it happened at the Birchmere:

Beginnings of the Almanac Singers

Pete: The transport workers had a strike and they asked us to sing in Madison Square Garden for 20,000 people. Woody was on the West Coast writing songs for the Bonneville Power

Administration. Sure enough, Woody hitchhiked East and knocked on the door on June 23rd. It was one day after Hitler invaded the Soviet Union. And the first words out of Woody's mouth was "Well, I guess we won't be singing any more peace songs." I said, what do you mean?" He says, "Well, didn't you read? Churchill says 'all aid to the gallant Soviet allies.' I ask, "Is this the same man who said in 1920 to strangle the Bolshevik infant in its cradle?"

Sarah Lee Guthrie, Seeger, Johnny Irion, and Baldemar Velasquez.
© J. Uehline

Woody says, "Yep. Churchill's flip-flopped. We got to flip-flop too." And he was right, but we still sang union songs across the country.

Millard Lampell and Lee had written "The Ballad of Harry Bridges." I think I just helped by finding a tune for their verses. Woody learned it. And when we got to San Francisco, we sang it at a meeting of the longshoremen. I remember we walked through the aisle and some of the longshoreman said 'What's a bunch of hillbilly singers doing here? We got work to do.' But Harry says, 'I think you might like to hear these guys.' We sang the "Ballad of Harry Bridges" and got a standing ovation. We had to sing it twice on the way down the aisle going out. They were slapping Woody on the back so hard that he almost fell over.

Talking Union

Joe: I always thought the talking blues songs were pretty cool. Tell us about Woody's "Talking Union" song.

Pete: Woody taught me the talking blues, but he did not write "Talking Union." That was Lee Hays, a son of a Methodist preacher in Arkansas. If I was asked about the geniuses I've known in my life, Woody would be one, but Lee Hays would be the other. Yeah. Lee wrote that.

Cathy Fink, Pete, and Marcy Marxer.   © *J. Uehline*

"Union Maid"

Pete: The wife of an organizer once said, "You have all these union songs about brothers this and brothers that. How about a song for the women? And the next morning in the union office, Woody was tap, tap, tapping on the typewriter. I just watched him. I don't think I helped him at all, although later he claimed I helped him. But all I did was sing it with him. It's an old German tune, you know? And it was a pop song in 1907 named "Red Wing."

Career Advice

Joe: Later in your years you did a lot of work with the peace movement, the environmental movement. It is really hard to imagine a soundtrack for America through the 40s, 50s, without Woody and you, and then through the 90s without you. What advice would you give to people today? What do you think it's going to take to make a difference?

Pete and Joe in the dressing room.   © *J. Uehline*

Pete: Try and stay away from commercial work. I was saved most of my life by my lefty reputation, but now with this Springsteen record, I've blown my cover.

Joe: Well, what do you think about that, Pete, with a huge rock star doing this? [referring to Bruce Springsteen's released 2006 album, *We Shall Overcome: The Seeger Sessions,* his first—and so far only—album of entirely non-Springsteen material.

Pete: Well, he is a fantastic singer and he's a very, very honest guy. I don't always agree with him. He put a new tune to "How Can I Keep from Singing?" I think the old tune was better. However, I don't get in big arguments like that. Let the audience decide. Most people have changed my tunes. Peter, Paul, and Mary changed my original tune for "If I Had a

Hammer" and frankly, I think they improved it. I really should pay them some royalties because until they rewrote it, the song didn't take off. Probably the same thing is true of "Turn! Turn! Turn!" Roger McGuinn rewrote the melody slightly but in important ways. And then it really took off.

Roger McGuinn in 1979.   © *Oelze*

On Changes

Pete: However, there are times not to change things. There was a melody written 403 years ago, in the year 1603 by an Irish harper, Rory O'Callaghan. The reason he wrote the melody was that his cousins had all been slaughtered when the English captured Castle Derry. It was known during his lifetime as "O'Callaghan's Lament." After he died, harpists and other musicians played this beautiful melody. And if somebody tried to put words to it, it was discouraged. Wordless, it said everything you needed: "Don't forget. Don't forget. Don't forget."

After the English took over the country, a London woman put out a book of Irish traditional airs, and she gave it a new title, "Londonderry Air." An English lawyer put the words of, "Oh, Danny Boy" to it and now it's all over.

Everyone on stage for the finale: Pete Seeger, Cathy Fink & Marcy Marxer, Sarah Lee Guthrie & Johnny Irion, Baldemar Velasquez and Joe Uehlein & The U-Liners. © *J. Uehline*

Thomas Richard Paxton (b. Oct. 31, 1937, Chicago, IL).

By the time an unknown Bob Dylan hitchhiked to Greenwich Village in 1961 Tom Paxton was already playing his original songs in Village coffee houses.

He is well-known today for "The Last Thing on My Mind" and "Bottle of Wine." Who remembers the Ken L. Ration TV commercial, "My Dog's Bigger Than Your Dog." That's Tom Paxton's song, too.

He was the perfect emcee for the Birchmere's first tribute to Woody Guthrie in 2000. Pete Seeger had played a few Paxton tunes at the 1963 Weaver's reunion concert, and Paxton had played at Guthrie's' 1987 farewell concert, both held at Carnegie Hall. Woody had died the previous year from Huntington's disease at age 56.

The first Guthrie tribute included Cathy Fink and Marcy Marxer. Other musicians were Wilco and Billy Bragg, who had joined forces for the 1998 album *Mermaid Avenue* two years previously. The *Mermaid Avenue* project was made possible by Guthrie's daughter, Nora, who gave Bragg and Wilco access to hundreds of unfinished lyrics that her father never put to music, and the musicians did the rest. The resulting album is the best-selling Woody Guthrie album of all time.

Tom's first promo picture on the Birchmere wall.

From the Alexandria home where he's lived for 20 years, Tom Paxton discussed his long history with the Birchmere:

"When the Cellar Door closed in 1981, I arrived at the Birchmere. It was very dark, and I was apprehensive. Gary and Pudge welcomed me. When I took the stage, I got a big welcome, and I thought, 'Well, this is a good place to play for 40 years.'"

Folksinger Dave Van Ronk had played a week before. Van Ronk often said, "Dylan is usually cited as the founder of the new song movement, but the person who started the whole thing was Tom Paxton. He tested his songs in the crucible of live performance."

When asked if Tom thinks this assertion is true, he answered, "I think Dave made too much of that. But I was writing my own songs before coming to New York in 1960, and I was very serious about it."

During his stint in the US army, Paxton would drive from Fort Dix, New Jersey to hang and learn at the Bitter End club. The Army folksinger character in the Coen Brothers film, *Inside Llewyn Davis* is clearly inspired by Paxton, even singing "Last Thing on My Mind" in the film. Paxton says, "I was lucky when I came out of the Army. I went to an audition to replace an original member of the Chad Mitchell Trio. They picked me to see how it worked, but it didn't. They didn't think my voice blended well enough. But during that week I was with them, I sang them the only good song I had, "The Marvelous Toy." That got me the attention of Milt Okun, who signed me as his first client at his new Cherry Hill Music Publishing company.

The Chad Mitchell Trio recorded "The Marvelous Toy" without Tom, and it began to climb the *Billboard* chart in the fall of 1963. There were expectations that it might become a Christmas favorite that year, but the assassination of President Kennedy derailed it.

The song would become newly significant when Peter, Paul and Mary included it on their 1969 children's album, *Peter, Paul, and Mommy.*

***

Paxton says, "My greatest experience at the Birchmere is when I did an album, *Live for the Record*, in 1996. I had a bunch of friends to help me. John Gorka, David Buskin on piano, a bunch of guys from Nashville. And Lucy Kaplansky. She's a fantastic singer. Her intonation is as good as anyone I've ever heard.

"Roy Husky, Jr. played upright bass. And Billy Wolf, then the Birchmere sound engineer, did all the mixing on that album for me. He is a genius. Apparently, that was a hell of a job. There were many fluffs that he had to deal with.

"But it was a wild night. There was a big snowstorm, and John and Lucy were late. We only had time for one run-through of the songs, but they nailed them. I didn't think anyone would get there in the snow, but it was full. It was an exciting night."

Paxton often played at the second hall. Asked about the two locations, Tom said, "I was concerned when I learned they were going to move. The second place had such a funky feel about it. I wasn't sure if we weren't going to lose that. But Gary put me in a car and showed me around the new place. I said, 'Oh, wow. This is certainly different. It's much bigger, and I wonder if it is going to work.' And when I played there, I said 'All right.

This place is sensational.' For my money, it's one of the top five acoustic concert halls that I play in the country.

"I knew and loved Guy Clark. I got to know him and Patti Griffin well. We played a show in Austin when Patti's *Other Voices in the Room* album came out. When we were saying goodbye, Guy told me, 'You know, you are a sweet cat. I thought that was very high praise.' Gary adds, "Guy Clark once told me, 'Like a good guitar, Paxton just gets better with age.'"

Paxton: "I didn't know Townes Van Zandt very well, but whenever I hear him on tape now, I think 'What a talent that was.' My wife and I went to the Kerrville Festival. in 1997 when they had their Hall of Fame black-tie "do" in Austin, where everybody gets all gussied up. We got off the plane, and I saw Townes. He looked like hell. We talked a bit. He told me he wasn't going to the affair. When I caught up with my wife at the baggage area, I told her, 'I saw Townes. If he lives another two weeks, it will be amazing to me.' And he didn't. He died shortly after that night."

Dick Cerri and Gary   © Oelze

World Folk Music Association

It was a 1983 conversation between Paxton and Dick Cerri, the popular DC-area radio show host of *Music Americana*, that launched the World Folk Music Association (WFMA). They wrote their rationale at that time agreeing "that there was a strong need to keep the people who loved folk music 'in tune' with the folk scene." Cerri ran the regular WFMA showcase nights at the Birchmere from the mid-'80s, introducing new folk musicians and providing them with a career start. Tommy Makem, of the Clancy Brothers, headlined a Dick Cerri World Folk Music Association celebration show on Jan 13, 2001. Makem performed "The Rambles of Spring," "Wild Mountain Thyme," "Wee Willie," "Four Green Fields," and (as a group finale) "Take Me Home Country Roads."

WFMA benefit shows began at the beginning and continued for 25 years. The last one was held in 2010 and presented "The Women of Folk Music," featuring Lisa Taylor, Hot Soup!, Doris Justis, The Nields, Grace Griffith, Lynn Hollyfield, SONia disappear fear, Priscilla Herdman, Cindy Mangsen, Anne Hills, Catie Curtis, Maura Kennedy, and Carolyn Hester. All of these artists benefited from the decades of support that Cerri provided.

"John Denver Remembered" WFMA Tribute.

Then-newcomer Nanci Griffith with Carolyn Hester in 1982. Gary recalls, "This was their first national tour together. They started in California and played gigs across the country. By the time they ended their tour at the Birchmere, they weren't speaking to each other. I don't know why."   © Oelze

Carolyn Hester also appeared for the first time the same month that Paxton did. A figure in the 60s folk scene, she was known for her traditional folk music and giving a young harmonica player named Bob Dylan his first recording gig on her third record. It would be on this project that her producer John Hammond discovered Dylan and signed him to *Columbia.*

Hester also turned down an opportunity to become a trio with folk singers Peter Yarrow and Paul Stookey. Mary Travers joined them instead, but it could have been Peter, Paul, and Carolyn, had she accepted.

Gary chimes in, "Peter, Paul and Mary played the Birchmere but only separately, never together."

Tom's 80th Birthday Bash performers. Back row (l to r) Robin Bullock, Don Henry, Tom Paxton. Dave Buskin, Tom Rush (front) Marcy Marxer, Cathy Fink, and Debi Smith.   © Oelze

In the Fall of 2017, The Birchmere threw an 80th birthday party for Paxton. The performers on stage were Tom's band, The Don Juans, admirers Cathy Fink and Marcy Marxer, Debi Smith, David Buskin, and "Celtic guitar god" Robin Bullock.

Writer Ron Ray wrote a terrific review of the evening in *No Depression: The Journal of Roots Music*, with the headline "A Legend's Grace at 80, Tom Paxton's "Birthday Bash" a triumph at Virginia's Birchmere.

In November 2010, Tom Paxton and Janis Ian performed together with both artists singing together on stage. Ian posted on her website: "It's really a once-in-a-lifetime thing, for the audience *and* for us. Heck, how often do you get to see two performers who've known each other 45-plus years and can still carry a tune?"

Janis Eddy Fink (b. April 7, 1951, New York City, NY)

Janis Ian recalls her first New York gig at The Village Gate club in Greenwich Village, opening for Tom Paxton. She was 13 years old. "I finished my song and the crowd gave me a standing ovation. But I'd been told to do just one song, so I began walking off stage. Tom grabbed me from behind and yelled 'Get back out there, kid!"

The two-time Grammy winner, and composer of two essential folk staples, "Society's Child" and "At Seventeen," Ian was also the musical guest on *Saturday Night Live's* TV premiere show singing "At Seventeen."

Ian reflects on her Birchmere experiences: "There were clubs like The Main Club in Bryn Mawr, Pennsylvania and the Birchmere where you would want to hit town a couple of nights early and actually go see your friends performing. Clubs with attention to details like having a washer and dryer. What a luxury.

"The Birchmere was one of the first clubs in the United States that I'm aware of that had these. When I did TV shows for the BBC in England, I could drop my clothes off, and they'd do them for me.

Current washer and drier in dressing room.

"Also, not insisting that you eat off a performer menu, which is usually all of the greasy stuff they're trying to get rid of. There's a couple of infamous clubs, one in the Northeast that I no longer play, that basically feeds you pasta. The owner expects you to do two shows and work for four or five hours on bad pasta.

"Gary's Birchmere is one of the few clubs I never worry about food. We are always there early enough before the show. And we've never had an issue.

"My favorite story about the second hall involves my wife, Pat. It was 1989, and she had never been on tour with me. She didn't know about touring, so I said, 'Well, why don't you come to the show I'm doing at the Birchmere?' We got on a plane, and they bumped us to first class. Pat said, 'Wow, this is really a rough life.'

"When I did my soundcheck. Pat came up on stage. She'd never been on a stage, and she says 'It smells like beer.' And I said, 'Yeah, it's a club.' And she says, 'There are stains in the carpet.' And I said, 'Yeah, it's a club.' And so, it was very funny watching it through her eyes.

"But then I went on and did the show. Me and my little band finished and we went downstairs, and I asked her, 'What did you think?'

"And she said that it 'was amazing when the lights went down and the stage lights came up, all of a sudden it was magic.' And I said, 'Yeah, that's what it's supposed to be.

Because when a club, no matter the kind of condition it's in, if they take the time with lighting and sound and make the audience comfortable, we're allowed as performers to create magic."

Comments on the Organization

"Gary's running a big organization," Ian continues. "I try not to bother or involve him in things where he's not needed. The staff are incredibly patient. That's the first word that would come to mind, incredibly patient. Because, for instance, my audience wants absolute quiet. They get annoyed when they're served. But they want the wait staff to magically know when they want a refill and then bring it to them in absolute silence. And they don't drink a lot, so the tips are bad. And yet the wait staff are always really wonderful to them. They work really hard at it. I always try at the end of my shows to remember to say to people, 'Look, tip the people who are waiting on you because they're losing money tonight. So please be nice to them.'

"The Birchmere has always been well-run. And it's very easy to find somebody running a club and hiring their friends and not knowing how to be a boss and not knowing how to hire people who know how to be a boss. And then it all goes to shit. It's like Gordon Ramsay's *Kitchen Nightmares* TV show. I could do a "club nightmares" show, which I played where they forgot to order the lights. We had to scramble around buying flashlights and gaffer tape to hang them up so that I would have a little light on stage. I mean, many clubs are owned by people who go into this because they think it'll be cool to hang out with their friends, do drugs, and drink.

"You want clubs like the Birchmere to survive. You want places that like the arts to endure. You want those clubs open. If all of us turn around and stop going to those clubs and only play the larger venues, then what clubs are going to have enough financially to take a chance on new acts? The circle has to keep going. Once you break that circle and stop being part of the circle, there's a big gaping hole. I don't want to be the cause of a big gaping hole, particularly not at this point in my career."

Janis shared this about Pete Seeger: "I've known Pete Seeger and performed with him on and off my entire life."

"Your *entire* life?" we asked.

"Yes, when I was three years old. I sat on his knee and sang with him," she confirmed.

Joan Chandos Baez (b. Jan. 9, 1941, Staten Island, NY)

© *Oelze*

Joan Baez played shows in 2008 and 2010. She signed one of her wall posters "Loved my stay." Calling his 2008 *Washington Post* review "Diamonds, No Rust," Buzz McClain reported, "She made the bitterest sentiments sound positively sweet as she and her acoustic band performed songs about war, politics, social injustice and childhood sexual abuse in a generous two-hour-plus set. The protest songs were to be expected—delivered with typical Baez sincerity and melodic charm—but the delightful surprises were the up-tempo lighter moments, including songs penned by Steve Earle ("Christmas in Washington") and Merle Haggard ("Sing Me Back Home"). Call it "honky-folk."

Arlo Davey Guthrie (b. July 10, 1947, Coney Island, NY.)

Arlo is famous for his 18-minute debut, *Alice's Restaurant Massacree,* a satirical anti-Vietnam war talking blues, and for his hit recording Steve Goodman's train tune, "City of New Orleans." Of course, Arlo is also the son of Woody Guthrie. And he toured with Pete Seeger for 40 years. He says he loved every one of those shows with Pete that they "never rehearsed."

Arlo first played the hall in 1995, returning a dozen times, including in 2020 when he spoke about his appreciation for the place.

"The Birchmere is special for many reasons," Guthrie began. "First off, it's the audience. Regular folks know where to go to feel comfortable and they won't get ripped off. It is amazing to me that so many others have tried to do the same thing as the Birchmere but don't quite pull it off. The others might last a few years, but they can't do it in the long haul.

"The staff is like a family. That's also how I feel about my band. On this 2020 tour I had the short team, but some musicians have been with me going back to 1975. Some have left to have kids, and the kids went through school. They retired from their other jobs and asked me, 'Can we come back?' And I said, 'Yeah. Sure.' And it was like we didn't miss any time at all.

"Also, the sound is different wherever you go, of course. But the Birchmere has kept up with the technology. So, you are not dealing with antique stuff. The sound guys here know what they're doing. This makes it easy for us. We come in, and we set up. We know what we're in for," Arlo said.

Gary reminded Arlo about the night he played and the audience was light, so Arlo wanted to return some of the money. Guthrie replied, "I don't remember that. I don't remember much after 30 years, but I think the nicest thing when I come to the Birchmere is that I get to see old friends. Tom Paxton came last time to say, 'Hi.' Now Tom doesn't need to hear me. Do you know what I'm saying? He wants to catch up with an old buddy. And I get that. And it is fun."

In 2014, Arlo and Tom Paxton played a concert for Theodore Bikel's 90th birthday, a week after his wife Midge passed away. Paxton remembers, "Arlo and I were both staying at a hotel in Beverly Hills that had a funky rooftop restaurant. I went up for breakfast and saw Arlo sitting there, alone. So, I joined him and we sat and talked for about an hour because he had lost his wife about a year before that."

Arlo's final Birchmere show in 2020.   © *S. Moore*

From the club's dressing room Arlo reflected on lessons he learned from his father: "One of the things I learned from the guy is that you have to make trade-offs for who you want to be. And for sometimes who you *have* to be. Those trade-offs aren't always fun. I would not be who I am today had I not been in the proximity of somebody who had that kind of struggle with himself.

"You have to go long out of your way to get to a wilderness where you can ask questions in a place where you don't have voices talking at you and trying to influence you.

"That's where my dad went. He went to those places and not just in geography, he went to them in his mind, and it is hard. And if you see an artist do that these days it'll be fairly rare, but when they do, it becomes important."

Woody Guthrie was willing to defy boundaries and take risks to become comfortable with who he really was. Arlo's father spent his life trying to champion people's importance and both individual and collective human rights.

Gary and Arlo in the dressing room. © *S. Moore*

The dressing room conversation drifted to stories that Arlo tells in his act. One of Arlo's monologues involves his first big paycheck from the success of "Alice's Restaurant." He bought a Ferrari convertible. His mother, Marjorie, disapproved.

"Arlo, we are folk musicians. We don't drive expensive sports cars," she told him.

"But, Ma. I bought it from Pete Seeger," Arlo responds as the audience laughs.

When asked if he really bought a Ferrari from Pete Seeger, Arlo, who is open about his Libertarian political beliefs, confessed, "No. It was an MG, and I got it from Pete's son, Danny."

When Bob Dylan hitchhiked from Minnesota to find Woody, Arlo answered the door to inform Bob that his dad was in the hospital. When asked what Arlo remembers of that brief encounter, he said, "It was 1961, and I was 13. I can't tell you what Dylan looked like, but he was wearing old work boots, which I thought were cool. Nobody who came to our house back then wore work boots."

Arlo was also 13 when his father persuaded him to perform in public. Arlo shared that he has never authorized a biography because he doesn't think he's that important. He did once work with a writer to complete a memoir that he only shared with his kids and grandkids.

He also added that reasonable accommodations and food on the road were important. He said, "We are not touring to save for retirement. This is what we do."

Unfortunately, this would turn out to be Arlo's last tour and one of his final shows because health problems stopped his long ride. He formally retired from performing the following October, citing medical issues.

On his website, Arlo concluded, "A folksinger's shelf life may be a lot longer than a dancer or an athlete. But at some point, unless you're incredibly fortunate or just plain whacko (either one or both), it's time to hang up the "Gone Fishing" sign. Going from town to town, doing stage shows, and remaining on the road is no longer an option."

The one and only Arlo.   © *Oelze*

Chapter 9 – More Good Folk

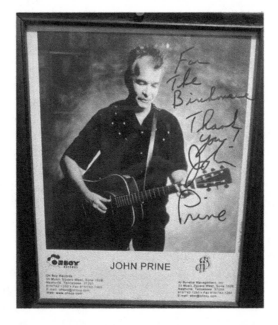

JOHN PRINE

One otherwise ordinary afternoon, Gary returned from early morning fishing to learn that Elvis Presley had died. He'd been a loyal fan since he'd seen Elvis perform near his Kentucky hometown in 1956. His wife Linda said "People are going to Memphis for the funeral. I want to go." When Gary heard this, he said, "Well, let's load up the car."

The Oelzes arrived at Memphis Forest Hills Cemetery after a 16-hour drive. Mourners watched police motorcycles with flashing lights preceding a white Cadillac that carried Presley's father, Vernon, followed by the hearse bearing Elvis' casket. A third white Cadillac followed with Presley's divorced wife, Priscilla, and their nine-year-old daughter, Lisa.

Public grief and hoopla best describe the atmosphere in the cemetery where vendors sold food and drink, tee shirts, and newspapers packed with sensational stories about the King.

One pertinent quote from a fan summed up the turnout and supporters' affection: "There have been thirty-nine presidents but only one Elvis."

Abundant flowers were handed out to the hundreds lined up to visit the gravesite. Undeterred by the long line, Gary and Linda waited their turn to pay respects by placing their flowers on the grave.

Then, with no room at the Memphis Inns, the Oelzes drove back to Nashville to find a place for the night. "We stopped at the Pickin' Parlor, a legendary music club where Elvis' first guitarist, Scotty Moore, and other prominent Nashville cats hung out.

"We sat us at a table with a guy sitting by himself, and we chatted about Elvis over drinks, listening to the music," recalls Gary. "We discovered that he went to the funeral, too.

"It was typical at the Pickin' Parlor for surprise guests to take the stage. The bluegrass band leader stood up to introduced his 'talented friend, who just happened to be 'one of the world's greatest songwriters.' The guy at our table stands up and grabs a guitar and starts to sing. It was John Prine.

"I knew his music, but he didn't look like the Prine I had seen on his album covers. We ended up talking with him outside. He was driving a 1950 Ford with a stack of records in the back. On top of the pile was the Mike Auldridge solo album, so we talked about Mike. That's how I met Prine."

***

Gary cites a possible reason Prine didn't appear often at the Birchmere: "John thought the audience was too close to the stage. He had many die-hard fans, and of course they were the first in line so they could get the close seats. I think he felt freaky that some of these people were at every show he played, so he didn't feel comfortable with the Birchmere audiences up so close."

On a similar note, singer-songwriter Shawn Colvin says that she loves the intimacy of the people being close up to the stage but she avoids looking at them. "I kind of fake it," she says. "I love the fact that they're so close but looking at them can distract me."

Writer Buzz McClain wrote about Prine's 1999 Birchmere debut in the *Washington Post,* leading with "John Prine took a little time out of his sold-out performance at The Birchmere to pay tribute to the late singer-songwriter Roger Miller, who "could write a goofy song, then turn around and break your heart." Prine too possesses that same rare gift for contrasting ludicrous scenarios with poignant vignettes, sometimes within the same song."

John Prine has the sad distinction of being the first Birchmere artist to die of COVID-19 complications during the 2020 pandemic. He passed on April 7, 2020, at 73 at Vanderbilt University Medical Center in Nashville.

Christine Lavin (b. Jan. 2, 1952, New York).

Singer-songwriter Christine Lavin's music deftly blends comedy with emotional expressions of romance. In addition to her solo albums, she was a founding member of the folk group the Four Bitchin Babes in 1990.

"Dick Cerri gave me airplay on his *Music Americana* radio show, and it was at his World Folk Music Association [WFMA] presentations where I eventually earned my first paycheck with a comma," she said in 2020 in the dressing room. She was there for a performance of her ensemble album, *On A Winter's Night,* a group effort that included Cheryl Wheeler, Patty Larkin, John Gorka, and Clift Eberhart on this particular tour. The *Winter's Night* tour is a seasonal favorite.

On Lavin, guitarist Clift Eberhart said, "Christine got me my first record deal, and started my career. She's unselfish. She's an entrepreneur and she's helped artists her whole life."

House promoter, Michael Jaworek, walked in the dressing room and Lavin greeted him with a "Hey, sir," and then commented "Here's another "up" aspect of the Birchmere."

She continued: "Just by playing us on the radio, it made all the difference in the world. Dick Cerri was helping us bring the audience in. I had never played for a large audience back in New York.

Lavin doing her first gig at the Birchmere in the '80s.   © Oelze

"I became really good friends with Linda and Gary in those early days. I remember coming to see Lucy Blue Tremblay [Canadian folksinger] and driving nine hours from upstate New York to see David Wilcox. Great show.

"The original Bitchin' Babes were Sally Fingerett, Patty Larkin, Megon McDonough, and me. We named our first album *Buy Me, Bring Me, Take Me, Don't Mess My Hair: Life According to Four Bitchin Babes*. It was a live recording, and Billy Wolf just taped that off the board at the Birchmere."

Lavin's 2010 biography, *Cold Pizza for Breakfast: A Mem-wha?*, is rich in details about her decades in the music business, and recounts the unlikely formation of the Bitchin' Babes. At the beginning of the book, Janis Ian states, "Lavin is the unsung heroine of the latter-day folk movement. Her tireless support of talented songwriters has brought out the best in many, given chances to more than a few, and put her head and shoulders above most people claiming to be "star makers." Her autobiography, like her life, is a work of art."

Cheryl, Gary, and Christine in 2020.   © *S. Moore*

Cheryl Wheeler (b. July 10, 1951, Timonium, MD)

Cheryl is an acclaimed singer-songwriter with an impressive catalog, covered by a Who's Who of artists, and affectionately known for her humor.

Country singer Kathy Mattea talked about meeting Wheeler: "I recorded a song of hers called "Further and Further Away." I've been on stage with Cheryl and she always invites me to sing on that song. She is brilliant. She can be subtle. She can hit you over the head. She can be playful. She can be clever and she can make you cry unexpectedly. It's like going through the back door of your mind to something you didn't even know was there. I think Cheryl is a national treasure."

Also speaking from the Birchmere dressing room in 2020, Wheeler talked about her beginnings: "It was Jonathan Edwards ["Sunshine (Go Away Today)"] that brought me to the Birchmere. He produced a couple of my records. I played bass once in his band It would have worked better if I knew how to play bass. Fortunately, Jonathan liked simple bass parts. They always made me feel so welcomed here at the Birchmere. And that is not always the case at other places. Other clubs kind of welcome you, but the Birchmere is better at it."

Wheeler recounts this funny moment: "There was this custom in my family. You were supposed to take $25 and buy the most ridiculous piece of shit you could find and present it at family gatherings. And then take it home. Someone brought a replica of Muhammed Ali's hand."

"Cassius Clay's hand?" asks Lavin.

"Yes. So, we went for years sneaking this hand back and forth among each other in the family. Once around Christmas when I was at the Birchmere, a staffer came and said someone from the audience had given me a gift. I opened it and it was the hand. My family was here and did it as a joke.

"Today, the hand is glued and screwed under one of the shelves in my library. When my nieces and nephews visit it is the first thing they check out, to make sure it's still there."

© *Jana Leon*

Patty Larkin (b. June 19, 1951, Des Moines, Iowa)

Patty Larkin is an accomplished singer-songwriter, also known for her innovative guitar playing. She studied jazz guitar at Berklee School of Music and is a founding member of the Four Bitchin Babes.

She recalls, "I felt the first time I walked in that the Birchmere was the best place I could play. I was blown away by the photos on the walls of the second club. I was thinking about that today. I had never seen pictures like those early ones with Roseanne Cash. All the people who had played here.

I thought 'Are you kidding me?' There was something about this place being rooted in folk and country that I had never seen in other places I'd been.

"I was sad when they moved from the second Birchmere where I started. I loved the sound and feel, but as I pulled in for the 2020 show, I thought 'really smart move.' Facility, accessibility. Gary has always been kind, with a reputation of presenting very high-quality music. People might come here not even knowing what music they might be hearing. but they trust that Gary and Michael are booking great people."

Debi Smith and The Smith Sisters.   © *Oelze*

Debora Smith Jaworek (b. Jan. 30, 1953, Philadelphia, PA)

"I go back to the first Birchmere. There was a woman named Lynn Eddie who ran an open mic night. I did a set there. I'm Irish and I learned to play the bodhran drum in an Irish group called the Hags. That was Ivy Harper, Terry O'Neill, Wendy Morrison, Linda Davis and myself. Mary Chapin Carpenter also sang lead in that group, but not when I was in it. DC was the crossroads then for Celtic, bluegrass, traditional country and folk, and the Birchmere was the manifestation of that music.

"After the Hags, the Smith Sisters—Debi and my sister, Megan on electric bass—started happening, the Birchmere was very much a part of our launch. Our first LP came out, *Bluebird*, produced by Merle Watson.

"At that same time, we toured Russia with Doc and Merle and got much publicity from the *Washington Post*. Richard Harrington and Geoffrey Himes would write about us.

"I don't know how we did this, but we talked Gary into not having a cover charge. People were lined up around the block and the club was so full that some couldn't get in. This is when I started developing a deeper relationship with Gary. Also, Mary Chapin was there before she became Mary Chapin Carpenter. Bill Danoff and Jon Carroll from the Starland Vocal Band were there. It was terrifying but fun. It was a huge moment for the Smith Sisters.

"We did shows from the early '80s until around 1993. We then did a live CD called *A Canary's Song* that included Al Petteway."

The *Washington Post's* Mike Joyce wrote: "Except for some typically terrific guitar work from Al Petteway, the Smith Sisters go it alone on their new album...Debi's acoustic guitar melodies are gently underpinned by Megan's electric bass lines and often beautifully augmented by the ever-tasteful Petteway. All in all, it's the kind of intimate retrospective that will delight the duo's longtime fans and no doubt attract some new ones as well."

***

"Gary Oelze is a very big-hearted person," says Debi. "He has been so kind to our family, not only to my husband, Michael Jaworek, who has a wonderful job at the Birchmere as their promoter, where he loves to get up every day and go to work.

"Gary has always been very sweet and gracious to my parents (Viv and Dave, now 95 and 96) and us when we come to the shows. He has had my group and I perform at the club for many years; it is my favorite place to play. But the greatest

150

gift he has given us has been for our son, Lee Jaworek. Lee has mild autism and is a fine artist/painter. He calls his art "Artism." Gary has generously let us use a room in the building for an art studio for Lee. It gives Lee someplace to go to paint; he even takes some lessons there. It has been a huge blessing for us."

The Jaworek family: Michel, Lee, and Debi. © D. Smith

Julie Gold (b. Feb. 3, 1956, Haverton, PA)

Julie Gold opened for the Smith Sisters for *A Canary's Song* live recording. At that time, she was already known for writing "From a Distance."

Debi Smith says, "Julie was so funny that night of the live CD show. She made us very relaxed to perform." Gold remembers that night: "The Smith Sisters were beautiful and charming, and they had more hair between them than I've had in my entire lifetime. I never saw so much hair. And then, of course, Megan Smith plays the bass. So that was magnificent. You don't really see too many female bass players. And Debi played that Irish drum that looks like a pizza delivery.

"This was early in my 'touring' career, if you'd want to call it a tour. I never really toured, but I remember feeling like, 'Wow, every piano is different, but this Birchmere piano is really louder than the act on stage.

"When Patty Larkin left the original Bitchin' Babes group in 1992, I was the reluctant babe just because I'm not a natural harmonizer and these women know how to do it. I sit at the piano and play my own songs and that's what I do. The scariest thing to me is 'Let's jam.' I play what I've practiced and what I've taken time to learn or have written."

Gold remembers: "Playing with the 'Babes was a lot of fun, Gary paid us in cash. We'd go back to the hotel, and we'd get candy and throw it all on the bed and literally jump in it."

Debi Smith replaced Julie Gold in the group. "From the Hags to the Sisters to solo and then the Bitchin Babes," says Debi "I call that a promotion." Their third Babes album *Fax It, Charge It, Don't Ask Me What's for Dinner* was released in 1995.

"I still perform at the Birchmere regularly as part of the Bitchin' Babes," Debi says. "When I joined, it was founder Christine Lavin, Sally Fingerett, Megon McDonough and myself. Currently the members are Christine, Sally, Deirdre Flint and me. Revolving members have included Cheryl Wheeler, Marcy Marxer, Mary Travers, Suzy Roche, Janis Ian, and even a "man-babe," John Gorka."

Marching in a Common Band

It was Christine Lavin who introduced Julie Gold's song "From a Distance" to Nanci Griffith, who first recorded it for her 1987 album, *Lone Star State of Mind*. Bette Midler made it world-renowned, earning the Grammy award for 'Song of the Year" in 1991.

When asked what it feels like to have written an internationally beloved song that is so much a part of people's psyches, Julie Gold responded, "It is surreal. This is my answer, and it's not meant to sound trite if I just rattle it off: "I fished in a humble pond and God granted me a whale. I was the messenger and now I'm the steward. I take that very, very, seriously. And I am so incredibly grateful beyond words that this miracle happened to me."

The Kennedys

As the alternative folk group, The Kennedys, Pete and Maura Kennedy have played the Birchmere often. Pete's memoir, *Tone, Twang, and Taste* (Highpoint Life) incorporates many Birchmere adventures.

Nanci Griffith with Maura and Pete Kennedy.   © *Oelze*

Pete begins this discussion: "I just happened to live in the Barcroft apartments across Four Mile Run drive from the first Birchmere. I was old enough to play at the Red Fox Inn, and when the Seldom Scene switched to the Birchmere I began to walk across the street and go there. My dad really liked Jethro Burns so he'd come in and see him."

Maura adds: "His dad's name is also Pete Kennedy, so my husband would announce him from the stage, 'Ladies and gentlemen, the original Pete Kennedy.' His dad would stand up and wave to the crowd."

Maura Kennedy was born and raised in Syracuse, NY, lived in Austin briefly and moved to DC. "I was not expecting the Washington area to be such a great music scene but it was. And the Birchmere, of course, was the heart and soul of that."

Other Kennedys' Birchmere memories include playing Tom Paxton's 70th birthday, joining in the Hank William's tribute series, and doing the last show by the songwriting team Lowen and Navarro in 2009. Eric Lowen was very sick with ALS and the Birchmere invited all his friends for this poignant show. He died from ALS at the age of 60 in 2012. Over the course of their career and a dozen albums. Lowen & Navarro's catalog includes "We Belong," which became a hit by Pat Benatar.

Eric Lowen, Pete Kennedy, Dan Navaro, and John Jennings in 2009. Lowen and Navaro's last performance at the hall. © Oelze

On another occasion, Bruce Hornsby was scheduled to play a private event. "It was a Democratic fund-raiser and Gary called us with the news that Bruce had broken his left hand. Gary asked us to fill in for Bruce's left hand," Maura recalls.

Crosby, Stills & Nash

Gary: "I like to tell people that Crosby, Stills, and Nash played the Birchmere in 2015. While that is true, I need to add that they played separately."

David Crosby's first show in 2015 is remembered by staff for how sour he was for most of the day. However, in the middle of his set he surprisingly apologized to everyone for how he had acted during the day, and then added "This might be the best club I've ever played."

Stephen Stills headlined six times, and appeared twice with Judy Collins. Graham Nash played five times, including a very strong 2020 show just before the hall temporarily closed down from the COVID pandemic.

David Crosby in 2017; Stephen Stills in 2015. © *Oelze*

Graham Nash in 2020. © *S. Moore*

A selective list of other illustrious folk artists that graced the second Birchmere hall includes: Al Stewart w/Luka Bloom, Ann Hill, Aztec Two Step, Barenaked Ladies, Baskin and Batteau, The Chad Mitchell Trio, Chris Smither, Cindy Lee Berryhill, Dave Matthews Band, Eric Anderson, Bill Danoff and Friends, Gamble Rogers, George Turman, Glenn Yarborough, Holly Cole, Holly Near w/John Pacino, Indigo Girls, James Lee Stanley, John Fahey, John Sebastian, John Wesley Harding, Kate Bennett, Kate Wolf w/Mike Auldridge, The Kingston Trio,

Kristin Hersh, Laura Nyro w/Bill Holland, Livingston Taylor, Loudon Wainwright III w/Kennedy Rose Lucie, Lucinda Williams, Magpie, Maria Muldaur, Mary McCaslin w/Jim Ringer, Michael Tomlinson w/Karen Goldberg, Mike Cross, Mimi Farina, New St. George, Washington Revels Mummers, Nicolette Larson, Phil and Gaye Johnson, and Richie Havens, Bruce Cockburn, Robin Williamson, Schooner Fare, Speidel, Goodrich, Goggin & Lille, The Brothers Four, The Chenille Sisters, The Hard Travelers, The Roches, Tom & Steve Chapin Band, Utah Phillips, Tom Rush, and Judy Collins.

Judy Collins.   © *Oelze*

The Birchmere also has a long tradition of presenting community events and fund-raisers.

Chapter 10 – Mary Chapin Carpenter & Company

"Mary Chapin Carpenter was very shy when I first met her. She was playing at open mics around town and opening for my headliners. She once came to a Rosanne Cash show. She asked me if I would give a tape she had made of her songs to Rosanne. I said 'No,' but asked her to wait while I went to the green room to arrange for Rosanne to meet her and accept the tape in person. Of course, Roseanne agreed. But when I went back to get Mary Chapin, she had left the building leaving her tape on the soundboard."

Gary Oelze

© Oelze

Mary Chapin Carpenter (b. Feb. 21, 1958, Princeton, NJ).

Mary Chapin Carpenter grew up listening to the Beatles, the Mamas and the Papas, and folk music favorite Judy

Collins, and was playing songs like "Leaving on a Jet Plane" while in high school. Carpenter moved to the DC area when she was 15. She returned to the city after graduating from Brown University. Despite an early shyness onstage, she began hosting an open mic night at Gallagher's Pub in the upscale Cleveland Park section of Washington, DC. After five years playing cover songs at local clubs, she began writing her own, very personal, songs. She has since won five Grammy Awards and is the only artist to have won four consecutive Grammy awards, 1992-1995, for Best Female Country Vocal Performance. She was inducted into the Nashville Songwriters Hall of Fame in 2012. Carpenter's five Grammy Awards were for Best Country Female Performance for "Down at the Twist and Shout" (1991), "I Feel Lucky" (1992), "Passionate Kisses" (1993), and "Shut Up and Kiss Me" (1994) and for Best Country Album, "Stones in the Road" (1994).

In one of her first interviews in 1986 by Stephen Moore for the *Journal* newspaper, she discussed her budding career. "I think you are influenced by everything that you hear. It has to shape you in some way.

"I've always enjoyed listening to people who convey an idea in a line—simply and acutely—and I enjoy literal songs. Songs that tell stories."

Carpenter also discussed her long collaboration with John Jennings:

"John and I have been together for about four years. We met through a mutual friend, Bill Danoff. Bill put a little group together to go out and play gigs. We had a good time and played for about a year. It was Bill, John Jennings, Danny Pendleton and me.

"About a year ago [1985], John Jennings and I started a demo tape in John's basement. We looked at it like an artist demo. The idea was to send it out to people with the hopes that someone would say 'Hey, I like that voice; do you know who is this person?' But the more we worked on it, the more John would say 'Why don't we use your own songs?' I was resistant however because my songs are personal and I thought people would want to hear songs that they knew. John was very encouraging and stubborn, too! So, I went along with the idea.

The more we kept working on it, the more we liked what we were doing.

"After six months it became a full-length tape, no longer a demo, and we transferred it over to Bias Studio in Springfield Virginia. And then we decided to try to make a record for release locally. The independent record scene is thriving and healthy. We thought it was possible to get our records released around town.

"When we finished, I got hooked up with Tom Carrico [a local agent for Studio One Artists which included durable rockers The Slickee Boys]. Tom was the one who said, 'Well, we've got nothing to lose if we shop it around a little.' So, I said 'Sure, why not?'

"For nine months we got some positive feedback on the tapes we sent out and eventually got two offers from two independent record labels that I think very highly of. [*Rounder* records and *Homecoming*, a label founded by John Stewart, formerly with the Kingston Trio]. We were literally three days away from signing up with one of the independent labels [*Rounder*] and at that point I was the happiest girl in the world. And then CBS called.

"Actually, we had sent tapes to CBS earlier in the year but they had evidently gotten lost or forgotten about. CBS had been talking to Gary Oelze, the owner of the Birchmere and manager of the Seldom Scene, a few days prior, asking Gary what was happening on the local music scene in Washington. Gary mentioned us, and CBS called and requested our tape. They understood we were about to sign with the independent label and said 'Well, send us your tape and we will listen to it right away and won't hold you up. We did and they called us up the next day with the offer. I cried. I just couldn't believe it. I still feel that it is beyond my wildest dreams."

When asked if CBS made her go to Nashville and rerecord her homegrown album, Chapin answered: "No. I was just talking to David Bromberg. He's a friend, and he said it is really unusual that a major label didn't make us rerecord a tape we sent them. I take it as a personal compliment to John Jennings and his production of the album. The only song they rejected from the album altogether was "Granola Baby." We thought the song injected a bit of needed levity to the album, but the song sort of drives me up the wall, so I'm glad it won't make the album."

***

John Jennings with Mary Chapin. Lyle Lovett says, "John always had a smile on his face. He was as so articulate in his playing. His personal joy always came through his music. The way he played sounded like the way he spoke to me. Jennings brought all of his positive energy that he had in life to his music." © *Oelze*

Gary Oelze recalls: "In the beginning, John Jennings would come in with Pete Kennedy in different configurations of bands that I would use as opening acts. I became friends with Jennings and met Chapin through him. We all called her Chapin back then. I admired her talents as well as John's. She had a voice like an angel, but she was very shy on stage. Often, she would look down when she sang and wouldn't look up at the audience. I think she opened or joined in on about 30 shows, and, then she would sing something she wrote. And I remember thinking that I would rather publish her than record her.

"I knew she and John were working on that album together when I travelled to Nashville to negotiate the potential sale of the Seldom Scene's 15th Anniversary concert at the Kennedy Center in 1986 to CBS. I was talking with Larry Hamby, then vice president of signing new acts at CBS Records-Nashville."

Oelze mentioned Carpenter and got Carrico to send Hamby a tape. The CBS executive was so taken with the demonstration tape that he quickly signed her to a contract.

Larry Hamby

"Larry would drop by the Birchmere when he was in DC to catch the O'Kanes and others. Larry asked me what was going on in DC musically and I mentioned Chapin's name. I told him I was hiring her off and on while she was working on her songs. I told him that she had sent him a tape, and he replied, "Do you know how many tapes I get, Gary? Thousands.""

"Larry finally got the tape, and took it to Roy Wunsch [president of Sony Records, Nashville division] This led to Carpenter being signed to Columbia. Larry sent me a thank you letter writing 'I think of you often as I see Chapin's career blossom. You must be so proud.'"

Although Columbia didn't rerecord the resulting debut album, *Hometown Girl*, they did advance money needed to get the album to market. It sold 60,000 copies but did not recoup its costs. "Some labels might have dropped her then, but I think everyone saw the promise of what could come," Carrico says.

"They kept her on because they knew how good she would be." Her follow-up 1989 album, *State of the Heart*, was a blockbuster success generating four top ten singles.

In 2020, Mary Chapin talked about her former musical partner, the late John Jennings: "John knew what a special place the Birchmere is. He played with me many times and on his own there. He just revered it as the amazing place it is, like the same way I do. For those of us who have known the club—whether we think of the old or new Birchmere—it's so important that they always put the music first. Obviously, there are some very special clubs around the world that take the same approach, but the Birchmere is unique."

The Greven Guitar Story

Carpenter shared this story about acquiring her number one guitar: "One day I told Gary about this amazing guitar I had played in the Guitar Shop on Connecticut Avenue in Northwest DC. I had been there [with John Jennings and guitarist Al Petteway] getting my Martin guitar repaired. Gary told me I should go back and buy it.

"'I don't have money,' I told him.

"So what?" he answered, matter-of-factly.

A surprise guitar.   © Oelze

"I said, 'So what, yourself.' I was living hand to mouth in a slummy Takoma Park, Maryland apartment and I didn't have the money. Soon after that, he hired me to open for someone at the club. I did that and was leaving to go home. I stopped to see him to get paid, and he said, 'Hold on a sec. I want to show you something.'"

Gary led her back to the old dressing room that had a couple of closets, opened a door and pulled out a guitar case. He opened the case and there was the guitar. The same Greven guitar from the shop. Mary Chapin was stunned.

Gary told her, "The only way you're going to be able to figure out if you really love and need to have this guitar is to have a chance to play it for a little while. So, I've arranged for you to take it home. Steve Spellman, the head of the shop said it's okay."

And then Gary pulls out a wad of bills. Mary Chapin was expecting $40 for her gig. "He gave me like 200 bucks. I told him it's too much, and he says maybe it can be a down payment on that guitar. He blew my mind."

Mary Chapin took the guitar home and put it on a stand in her room for the first day, and just looked at it.

"I couldn't quite believe it was in my possession. Wow. And when I finally played it, then I could not let it go. Gary was proven right about that. I had never been to a bank to get a loan but I asked my Dad to co-sign for me and then I paid it off. If Gary Oelze hadn't done this incredibly kind thing, there is no doubt I never would have acquired that guitar, it's my number one and I've written so many songs on it."

For the record(s), her number one, go-to guitar is this 1983 Greven maple J model. She has owned and played it for almost 35 years. It amplifies well but is extraordinary live, acoustically. Just like Mary Chapin Carpenter's performances.

In January 1987, less than four years after appearing as a "friend" of Bill Danoff, Chapin headlined the Birchmere for the first time with her band that featured John Jennings, Robbie Magruder on drums, and Jon Carroll on piano. She has returned to the hall several times over the years. Her main DC area venue became Wolf Trap.

Gary says, "All I did was tell CBS to sign her. For my part in her story the only thing I asked for was Mary Chapin to come back and play the Birchmere. I'd pay her anything. She did everything else to earn her multiple successes, including her five Grammy awards."

Lyle's Awkward Birchmere Story

Lyle Lovett tells this story: "I was booked in the Kennedy Center in 1984 as part of a Kerrville Festival road show gig. Two runners picked me up in a van at the airport and took me to the gig.

"I was booked to play the Birchmere in 1986 and Gary called me.

"Hey, do you mind if we have a local girl open for you?" he asked.

"Whatever you want," I told Gary.

"The reason I'm asking is that she has a five-piece band and Larry Hamby from CBS is coming. It's kind of a showcase for her to maybe get a record deal," he said.

Mary Chapin and Lyle Lovett.   © *Oelze*

"I felt really on the spot. If I say no, it could affect this person's chance on getting a record deal. But I'm just playing solo. Having a band open for me is kind of weird. As I was hesitating and trying to process all of this, Gary says, 'But they've agreed to learn some of your songs and play with you.' Oh no, I thought. This has just gone from bad to worse.

"So, I asked Gary 'Do I have to do this?'

"'No,' he said, 'But they're going to prepare some of your songs and you can go over them together at the soundcheck.'

"I said, 'Okay, fine.' I had met Larry Hamby. I knew he was the real deal.

"And then I met the local girl and her band. It included the runners who picked me up at the airport for the Kennedy Center show, Mary Chapin and John Jennings. 'Hey, I know you," I said.

Lyle sat with Larry Hanby in the audience during their opening. "He was captivated and then we played the five songs we had prepared. They were right on. And Larry offered her the record contract after that performance. Everything worked out great."

MARY CHAPIN CARPENTER
& SHAWN COLVIN
TOGETHER ON STAGE!
FRI/SAT/SUN. NOV. 8,9,10 | THE BIRCHMERE

Shawna Lee Colvin (b. Jan. 10, 1956. Vermillion, SD)

Shawn Colvin won Grammy awards for both Best Record and Song of the Year in 1988 with "Sunny Came Home." Colvin taught herself guitar. Her first break was singing backup for Suzanne Vega, another great singer-songwriter who has played the Birchmere seven times.

In 2021 Shawn talked about her experiences, "I was playing there when Mary Chapin Carpenter had just been signed, and she introduced herself. She was very sweet and low-key, almost shy, and we went out in the back alley and became fast friends.

"My next memory is playing in a trio with Mary Chapin Carpenter and Cheryl Wheeler. That was so much fun. I felt like I had arrived, playing with those two."

Colvin continued building her career, moving to New York City to become a member of the Buddy Miller band. Larry Campbell was also in this band. She reminisced, "Buddy is just a monster singer and guitar player, and that turned a corner for me in my life, being in his band. He's incredible and yet has no ego. He produced a record for me about ten years ago, and I thought, 'How is he going to produce a record? He's too nice.' But he did it. No problem. He'd just say, He'd just say, 'Let's try that again.'

"I had met Cheryl in New York where a posse of us folk musicians and songwriters knew each other. I'm such a fan of so many of Cheryl's songs. When we played that trio, Cheryl did a song called "Estate Sale." We had previously referenced Bruce Springsteen, so when she finished "Estate Sale," I said, 'Oh, Born to Rummage.' This got a big laugh, and I thought at that moment, 'I can do this. I can go toe-to-toe with the witty Cheryl Wheeler and Mary Chapin. I am an equal.' Mary Chapin and I have done duo shows together there since then."

Gary Oelze admitted, "Sometimes Shawn would take the train down for her shows, and Officer Mark Uzell would pick her up and take her back to Union Station. On occasion, I think there was a police siren going on to make sure she got there in time for the late train, but don't quote me on that."

Gary and Officer Uzell escort Shawn Colvin after a show. © *Oelze*

Colvin extolled the club, "Once you start playing the Birchmere, Gary and everyone there treats you so wonderfully and like family. You feel really treasured. Gary championed me, and the audience is always so stellar and welcoming. They love being there. It's a club that has magic and this respectful spirit. You know, we're going to take care of you. Like there's just a warmth there. They bothered to get to know you. It's a spectacular place. Very rare. It's one of my favorite places to play in the world."

Colvin explained her way of playing at clubs like the Birchmere, "Sometimes I do the merch table on my tours; sometimes I don't. I'm also one of those musicians who doesn't really look at the audience, making eye contact and looking at them. It's intimidating for me. I don't want to see anybody flipping through their phone or something. I just don't want to catch somebody not paying attention. It'll make me feel insecure. So, I keep my eyes in the kind of straight ahead to the back of the room. It's an audience you trust. If you've got something new, it's okay to try it out on these folks because they're going to be with you a hundred percent."

Janis Ian, Cheryl Wheeler, and Lucy Kaplansky.   © *L. Kaplansky*

Folk singer Lucy Kaplansky is close friends with Shawn Colvin, and shared some of her memories: "I've been singing with Shawn since we met at Gerdes Folk City in the '80s," says Lucy. "We've sung on each other's albums and are good friends." Colvin agrees heartily, "Lucy is an amazing singer. We can harmonize with each other and just go off the beaten path and do whatever comes into our heads. Tom Paxton is right; Her intonation is stellar."

"My first show at the Birchmere was with the Kennedys," recalls Kaplansky. "One very memorable show for me was on September 14, 2001. The 9/11 attacks had just happened. I had a gig at the Birchmere, which is a few miles away from the Pentagon, and I had no idea how I'd do a show. What on earth would a show be like after that?

"Bob Feldman, the man who ran my label, Red House Records, told me: 'People want to feel something together, so just go do it.' He was right. I didn't know if anybody would come, but it was really full. People really wanted to be there." Kaplansky started her show with the familiar 19th century American folk and gospel song "The Wayfaring Stranger," a song brilliantly covered by Johnny Cash among many others. "The evening was very moving for me," said Kaplansky, recalling the intimate moment.

While Kaplansky attracted recording offers after performing with Shawn Colvin, she decided instead to finish her clinical psychology doctorate and open a practice in New York. Her love for performing resurfaced in the 1990s and Colvin produced her 1994 album *The Tide*, the first of several released by Red House Records.

Garrison Keillor brought his traveling storytelling and musical showcase in 1990. He last played the hall in October 2021.
© Oelze

Red House Records began in St. Paul, Minnesota when Bob Feldman first heard Iowa folk singer Greg Brown, another longtime Birchmere performer. The idea behind Red House was to have an independent record label for creative artists "to record without pressure to score the next hit single.

Both Feldman and Brown were recurring performers on the popular "A Prairie Home Companion" radio show.

Red House grew its artist roster to include Birchmere alums, John Gorka, Bill Kirchen, The Wailin' Jennys, Loudon Wainwright III, Norman Blake, Jorma Kaukonen, Cliff Eberhardt, Larry Campbell and Teresa Williams, and the husband/wife duo, Robin and Linda Williams. All of these talented Red House artists formed a direct conduit from the independent label to the music hall.

171

© D. Williams

Dorothy Snowden "Dar" Williams (b. April 19, 1967, Mount Kisko, NY)

At the beginning of this Birchmere history project, we discovered that singer-songwriter Dar Williams had written an absorbing book, *What I Found in a Thousand Towns*. Emily Saliers of the Indigo Girls (who played the hall 5 times from 2010-2018) wrote in her review: "A thoughtful and passionately explored journey of how American towns can revitalize and come to life through their art, food, history, mom and pop business, and community bridge-building. Dar Williams gives us hope and vision for the possibilities of human connection." Many of Dar's early songs explore the alienation of suburban life as small towns disappeared across America."

Dar recalled her Birchmere beginnings: "In 1994, I was at the Folk Alliance [a non-profit organization that produces an annual conference that is the world's largest gathering of the folk music industry and community]. I had just done a show with my ex-boyfriend, who I still had feelings for. I remember Michael Jaworek reading the whole situation and talking with me on the club's stairs. He was saying, yes, your ex-boyfriend is a really outstanding talented performer, but what about me?

He asked would I like to come to play the Birchmere. It was the first major club that took me on.

"I knew the importance of this opportunity because there's a constellation of venues across the country that are the best listening rooms for several reasons. First, there is the audience and what they bring to a show. They have a sense of humor, and they're good listeners, they come to experience things and their feelings and to be enlightened. They come for a lot of different kinds of happiness, and often not the easy happiness.

"Number two, for the artists, it's the respect and integrity with which they're presented by the presenters. And for everybody, it's the excellent sound system and the feel of the room."

Williams offered her list of exceptional clubs in the same league of the Birchmere Music Hall:

- Club Passim [Harvard Square, Cambridge, MA]
- Freight & Salvage [traditional music, Berkley, CA]
- Old Time School of Music [Chicago, IL]
- Swallow Hill Music [Denver, CO]
- Symphony Space [New York, NY]
- The Bottom Line [New York, NY – closed in 2004]
- The Great American Music Hall [San Francisco, CA]
- The Iron Horse Music Hall [San Francisco, CA]
- The Troubadour [Los Angeles, CA]

"And then there is the Birchmere. I think Gary was at every one of my sound checks. He was always stage left in the doorway out between the lobby and the kitchen in the hallway. He would float in, and he'd float out. Sometimes he was with the sound people. Sometimes he sat down and then left. But he was always back.

"I got the sense that he had that ability to understand, to experience his role without being hands-on, without being too interactive, but that he knew what his role is."

Musicians have rituals to prepare because you just don't know what will happen when you get out on that stage. But's that's part of the magic of live performances. You literally don't know what will happen, and that creates a certain tension.

'Gary knows that sort of arc of the performers' experience. He seems to understand that you've got to shepherd the whole environment. That you have an eye on everything, to hire the right people, to have the fitting room and the right sound and kind of publicity so that you have a great audience, and then you step away."

Dar Williams with soundman Bud Gardner in 1996.   © *Oelze*

Chapter 11 – Hometown Heroes

NILS LOFGREN

© *Jan M. Lundah*

Nils Hilmer Lofgren (b. June 21, 1951, Chicago, IL)

Nils Lofgren grew up in Bethesda, MD and studied the accordion, jazz, and classical music. At seventeen, Nils had a rock and roll epiphany while witnessing then-unknown Jimi Hendrix play the Ambassador Theater in Washington's Adam's Morgan neighborhood in 1967.

He took up rock guitar and piano, formed his first band, Grin, and landed a record contract. He played keyboards, acoustic guitar, and sang on Neil Young's *After the Gold Rush,* the first of several recording and touring associations with Young.

In 1984, Bruce Springsteen tapped him to join the E Street Band. Throughout a long and storied career, he earned renown for both his solo work and collaboration with a range of artists, and is a member of the Rock and Roll Hall of Fame.

Nils has not only played with Bruce, Ringo, and Neil Young, he's good friends with them. "I got to cut my teeth in the '60s and '70s, which was a heyday, and I celebrated 52 years on the road in 2020."

A few years ago, Nils called Gary Oelze with an offer he couldn't refuse. Nils explains: "My mom and dad loved music, and dancing was their hobby. We had a player piano, and my three brothers and parents listened to music together growing up. They always encouraged all four boys to participate. My father passed away and Mom eventually moved into a retirement community in Silver Spring, Maryland. We thought about giving the player piano to them, but when she passed at 91 in 2019, we called Gary and Michael Jaworek. We have a long history together, and they thought it a great idea to donate it to the Birchmere.

"Both parents came to so many shows and they'd bring a half a dozen of their friends. Although my mom was ill, she came before she died to see our show. The Birchmere would take great care of them.

The Lofgren family player piano.   © *S. Moore*

"Playing with my three brothers, Tom, Mike, and Mark, who would always join us there, was a great joy for me. The piano is near the bar. Gary isn't going to encourage people to drink and then navigate a player piano. That could get messy. But I hope they fire it up once in a while. It has a lot of old American standard and ragtime rolls. You hit a lever and it plays. We have many memories all singing together as a family. I'm glad it has a home at the Birchmere.

"My job is to do a good musical performance. I've done it in the worst places with half a PA system. With owners that are giving you dirty looks. With 14 people sitting on the floor and people getting into fights, and then the club trying to stiff you afterwards and not pay you. My attitude was 'Hey man, we had a deal. Offer me less money next time but please don't stiff me.' I have musicians playing with me. A couple of times it really got adversarial and scary.

"But it's the antithesis of that at the Birchmere. Through the decades it was Michael Jaworek who booked us and we'd work with him and the guys in the other departments to set up and handle things. Gary was always the happy owner who welcomed us and would tell us 'It's good to have you back.'

"Some clubs are stingy with letting family and friends in, but Gary was always accommodating if I asked him to sneak in another three or four couples. Sometimes he'd suggest he take care of my core family, and spread out some of my other friends because people stood in line to get tables, but that was fine with him, and he is always easy to work with."

Patron Nils

"I've seen many great shows," Nils say. "I always call and say, 'Hey, you know, I'm happy to buy a ticket. Can you get me a decent seat?' They always comp me, which is not necessary, but much appreciated. I've gone there plenty of times to hear great music. And Gary and the staff were always very friendly.

"When I was based in DC, I saw Danny Gatton, with friend Timm Biery on drums and John Previti on bass, doing their fusion trio work. I came to see Jerry Douglas and learned a little dobro on my own. Once I came with my brother Mark and his wife Kate to see Rickie Lee Jones. We had just walked in as her opening act, Martin Sexton, was finishing. We were floored by his beautiful singing and songs, and I actually followed him into the dressing room like I was stalking him. We've become friends over the years and I've sat in with him. He sang on my records. So, it's just been a good vibe all the way around and you know, God willing there will be more of it."

Early photo on the Birchmere wall. Tom and Nils Lofgren.   © *Oelze*

On the Road

"You know, you live in a hotel, you're in a strange town. Part of that is charming because you get out and walk the streets in a place you haven't been or are not familiar with. But there is something about playing to your own town. I moved from Chicago to DC when I was eight. And grew up in the DC/Maryland/Virginia area. There were so many great places to play in the early days and the Birchmere was one of them.

"And the Birchmere was more of a formal gig. People valued you a bit more in this setting where people listened. I always enjoyed not only playing there, but knowing I was home. It was a hometown crowd, and one of the rare occasions—maybe the only time in the year—I would drive myself to the soundcheck in my own car. And back to a house I was living in Maryland, spend a night in my own home for one night, and then back on the road.

"The backstage dressing rooms are really helpful. They have four rooms. You can be messy and spread out. There's a big communal room to eat in and visit with the players. It's nice to have extra spaces for band members and family which is an extra workload usually for women compared to most men.

178

Everyone can gather together and also have space for themselves.

"If you needed help, the good people working there would advise and help. If you didn't have a sound person, they had somebody there who was good. It is a great vibe. I'm looking forward to getting back there. God knows when that'll be, but it's really a big part of my history."

"Although I'm living in Arizona with my lovely wife Amy and son, Dylan. I'll always look forward to getting back to the Birchmere."

Jorma Ludwik Kaukonen Jr. (b. Dec. 23, 1940, Washington, DC)

John William "Jack" Casady (b. April 13, 1944, Washington, DC)

Jack and Jorma as Hot Tuna.   © *Oelze*

In 1960, two high school pals formed their first band, called The Triumphs, in their Northwest neighborhood of the Nation's Capital. By 1965, they were the lead guitar and bass players of Jefferson Airplane, psychedelic music pioneers and one of the first San Francisco-based groups to become *Billboard* hitmakers. Their blues-based Hot Tuna duo began as a side project in 1969, opening for their collective band, and a full-time endeavor when Casady and Kaukonen left the Airplane in 1972.

Both are longtime regulars at the Birchmere, and both enthusiastically contributed to this history project with a demonstrable passion for the club.

In fact, at age 80, Jorma returned to the Birchmere in January 2021 to play a solo show amidst the COVID pandemic. Jorma remembers: "I left DC after I graduated in 1959. I went to Antioch College for a year and then I went to college for a year in the Philippines because my dad was stationed there. And then I came back and I worked in DC for a summer. Actually. I was the night shift manager of the Sunoco station on Connecticut Avenue.

"DC's my hometown. It was and always will be. I've played a lot of places in DC, and would be hard pressed to remember all of them. There was Desperado's on M street in Georgetown. And I started playing the second Birchmere solo in the '80s which was like a house, and the one that's there now which I call Birchmere World.

"In a normal world, I'd be a great grandfather, but in this one, I've got a 23-year-old son that lives in Arlington, Virginia and my 14-year-old daughter is in high school in Ohio, where I live. My son and his buddies come to the Birchmere now because they know they're going to get a free catfish and beans and maybe a beer.

Or they could want to see dad and his buddies playing music. Who knows? But he's been coming to the Birchmere since he was a little kid. And now he's a grown man on his own. I mean, that's something right there.

"To come back to the Birchmere always reminds me of the early days when we were starting. It's like going home. I remember the city back then before there was a Capital Beltway. Northern Virginia and Southern Maryland were country back then. We'd swim at Dickerson's Quarry [a deep and dangerous private lake surrounded by steep rock in Montgomery County, MD].

"Now, we've played for so many years and know everyone. The last time Jack and I played we thought, 'Wow, these people aren't just resting on the laurels.' The sound just keeps getting better. When they have to invest in the sound system, they do. That's why I call it the Birchmere World. It's hilarious. It's got everything. It's got the statue of Pudge. It's got the store, and the stages.

Jorma's first signed photo on the wall.

"Some people say they miss the second one, but that's euphoric recall. I think if you back off and look at it objectively, the Birchmere we have today is a better venue.

"Here's the deal. I'm 80 years old, and I've been in this game a long time. And I feel blessed to be here. And not just to be able to play well—and I still think I can play well—but for the people who made the journey with us all over all these years. That's something to be thankful for, you know. It's been a long time since I played Wolf Trap.

"If somebody offered us a gig at Wolf Trap, I would say it's great to be playing there, but 'Wolf Trap-Smolf Trap.'" The Birchmere has always been there for us all these years. Guy Clark and Verlon Thompson had a song about all the places they'd played all over the world called "Everywhere...Yet." They mention the Birchmere in the first verse."

Jorma says he appreciates people who have attended his shows. "Check this out. My dad was in the service, so we traveled around a lot, but I graduated from Wilson High School in 1959. My high school girlfriend and I are still buddies after all these years. She comes with her elder son to see every gig I play there. Her name is Barbara Row. It's awesome. And if the Birchmere was some crummy bar, then she wouldn't come. The Birchmere is an inviting place to come. It always has been. But I'm all about the new venue. I think Birchmere World is the cat's ass."

When told we were going to interview his partner, Jack Casady, Jorma said, "People always think that Jack has a reputation for being mysterious. But he's a conversationalist MOFO, a real talker, with a memory that's unbelievable. And he was in DC longer than me. So, you're going to have a great time with Jack."

***

Jack had just returned from his first trip in his new RV when he shared his Birchmere memories. It was a 52-day journey from his LA home to and from Jorma's Fur Peace Ranch in Ohio for a series of quarantine internet shows by Hot Tuna.

He recalls: "When I think of the Birchmere it's a lot more than a checkered tablecloth, for sure. Jorma played as a solo there and then we came returning as the local DC hometown boys, so to speak, as Hot Tuna in the '80s. In the Airplane we had a reputation for playing where sometimes the fans and the level of noise made playing the acoustic music a little weird. But at the Birchmere we could really get into that acoustic, sonic world and not be disturbed by people partying.

"In the later years Gary did massive work on the sound systems where it's really top notch today. Jorma and I don't really need much sound reinforcement. We use pickups on guitars and bass, but I use a microphone on my acoustic . The hall sound is superb."

When asked why Jack and Jorma still think of DC as their home even though they've been gone since 1964, Jack responds, "When we came back as Hot Tuna, we came back to fans who have beautifully kept up with our careers, but music was handed down generationally when we were growing up. Particularly true in bluegrass and country music. And my advantage of being in Washington when I was 12 through 14 was going to the Library of Congress and sitting in those little booths where I could listen to the Alan Lomax field recordings of Appalachian music.

"And I collected and still have the records I bought at the Waxie Maxie's like Lost City Ramblers with Mike Seeger, or his sister Peggy, for example. [*At this point in the interview Jack clicks Facetime on his iPhone and walks down to his basement recording studio to show the boxes of these early records he stores there. He pulls out a few blues albums to illustrate his point.*] He continues "In those days I could go over to the Shamrock to hear Mac Wiseman, and then catch Ray Charles at the Howard Theater the next night, or see Louis Prima in the club circuit, and then head to the Dixie Pig bar over the DC line to play with Danny Gatton and a bunch of my pals."

William Knight Kirchen (b. June 29, 1948, Bridgeport, CT).

Although Bill Kirchen, aka the "Titan of the Telecaster" and skilled singer-songwriter, grew up in Ann Arbor, Michigan and didn't arrive to live in the DC area until 1986, local admirers and friends claim him as one of their favorite hometown performers, in the league of the "Telemaster" Danny Gatton. Bill was close friends with Gatton. His set during the two-night 1989 Gatton tribute at the Birchmere is considered a highlight of that event. "There's nobody in town who knows Bill who doesn't love him," says Gary.

His first instrument was the trombone in high school marching band. Drawbacks: No jamming and early morning practice around the football field. His next ax was his mother's banjo he found in the attic. When he saw Bo Didley play the old Avalon ballroom during a 1967 "summer of love" trip to California, Bill found his future. Kirchen found early success as guitarist with Commander Cody and His Lost Planet Airmen. Cody is **George Frayne IV** (born July 19, 1944 in Boise, ID). Frayne's boogie-woogie keyboard style was the foundation of the band.

That's Bill playing the staccato guitar riff on their hit, "Hot Rod Lincoln." These days Bill performs a medley of guitar leads when he performs "Hot Rod Lincoln" managing to nail the guitar riffs and tone of the Beatles, Hendrix, Zeppelin, Haggard, Stevie Ray and just about everyone who got close to rockabilly. It's fun and impressive.

Bill holding a second Birchmere chandelier. Jerry Jeff Walker's drummer Freddy Steady Krc has the other one. © *Louise Kirchen*

Kirchen started his Too Much Fun band that included John Previti on bass and Dave Elliott on drums when he came to DC. He has also enjoyed a decades-long musical association with Nick Lowe. He's recorded with many talented artists, including Link Wray, Gene Vincent, and Elvis Costello.

Bill continues: "My next show at the first Birchmere after Commander Cody was opening for Marty Stuart. And I loved seeing Alison Krauss play there. She is fantastic."

Bill adds, "In the beginning I never liked Jimmy Dale Gilmore's music. I've told him this. I'd heard his tapes and what, to me, was this high and wavering vibrato voice. I remember thinking this is too weird. I don't know what's going on there. But then I went to see him at the Birchmere. I sat there and saw him sing. I fell in love with him. It all made sense to be coming out of him, standing there, his demeanor and rapport with the audience. His funny way of approaching things. We became fast friends, and ended up doing a tour together. Thank you Birchmere."

Bill with wife, Louise from their web concerts.   © *B. Kirchen*

Too Much Fun won ten WAMA awards in 1996 including Musician and Songwriter of the Year. Kirchen became a contemporary of many other D.C. guitarists who played the club besides the late Gatton, a fraternity that includes Dave Chappell, Billy Hancock, Evan Johns, Tom Principato, Linwood Taylor, and Jimmy Thackery.

"I once asked Bill if Jimi Hendrix was as good a guitar player as he gets credit for, and Bill didn't answer," says Gary.

Cleveland "Cleve" Francis (b. April 22, 1945, Jennings, LA)

In 2020, Cleve Francis, a country music singer-songwriter and *cardiologist*, celebrated his 30th year as a Birchmere headliner.

Growing up poor in Louisiana "Cajun" country, Cleve taught himself guitar at the age of nine, inspired by the music of Sam Cooke, Hank Williams, Nat King Cole, James Brown, Mahalia Jackson, and Elvis Presley. While attending William & Mary University he developed a coffee house following, performing soulful folk music. After graduating in 1973 from the Medical

College of Virginia (now Virginia Commonwealth University Medical School)—the first African-American to do so—he became a board-certified cardiologist.

Dr. Cleve.   © *Oelze*

Along the way, he met DC musician "Big" John Hall, who played in the rhythm and blues group, The Heartbeats when he treated his brother for (ironically) a heart attack. Cleve gave Hall a tape of his music and this led to an offer to record in Nashville. His first song, "Lovelight" was aired on Country Music Television. This led to a three-year contract with Capitol Records. When the President of Capitol, Jimmy Bowen, asked Cleve what he did for a living and heard he was a doctor, he replied, "Well that's your problem."

In 2019 Music writer James Culum described in *Zebra Times* what happened next: "Francis would end up taking a three-year sabbatical and moving to Nashville. After the release of his first single, "Lovelight" the Singing Doctor was featured on *Good Morning America* with Bryant Gumbel and Katie Couric. He went on a radio tour around the country and then appeared on *CNN, CBS This Morning, The Today Show* and *Good Morning America*. Articles were written about him in *The New York Times, Washington Post, Chicago Tribune* and *Atlanta Constitution*—all stories about the cardiologist who spent his nights as a country western star. His contribution to country music has also been recognized at the National Museum of African American History and Culture with his photo, bio and selection from his album *Walkin'*.

© *C. Francis*

Around 1990, his friends suggested he audition for the Birchmere. However, Gary has never auditioned or even interviewed an applicant act. Cleve remembers approaching Gary and Michael Jaworek asking for a spot with Gary saying, "Well, maybe your patients will come and see you and fill some seats." Gary doesn't recall saying that, but agreed to give Cleve a chance. He started playing the hall twice a year with tickets starting at $8.50 in the beginning, and he and his players sold out the hall annually for thirty years. He's charted four country music songs, "Love Light," "How Can I Hold You," "Walkin'" and the aptly named "You Do My Heart Good." He appeared at the Grand Ole Opry in 1993.

Indeed, patients did support the good doctor, with one of his very ill patients once arriving by ambulance to attend his show.

Gary notes "Cleve is a one of a kind Birchmere performer. First, he's a black country artist, unusual in the field. Second he's a cardiologist—which would keep anyone busy—who nonetheless loves music so much that he added late night gigs to his busy days treating patients."

(l to r) Robbie Schaefer, Julie Murphy Wells, Michael Clem, Eddie Hartness. Honorary member, Jake Armerding, on fiddle. © EFO

Eddie From Ohio

"Too energetic to be labeled just "folk"', and not angry enough to be pegged "alternative," Eddie from Ohio continues to defy description with their unique blend of vocals and acoustic instrumentation," proclaims the band's website. February 3, 2021 marked their 30th anniversary. They've played the hall over 50 times and have been awarded Wammies for "Best Contemporary Folk Group" by the Washington Area Music Association six times since 1997.

Their considerable success is none too shabby for a Virginia-based band that got their start in 1991 playing covers in neighborhood bars. EFO was founded by three James Madison University graduates (Robbie Schaefer, Eddie Hartness and Michael Clem) who teamed up with Virginia Tech alumna Julie Murphy (now Murphy Wells). All four are native Virginians and many of their songs reflect their Old Dominion roots.

Performing Songwriter magazine described the unique sound of the band: "The manic strumming recalls Ani DiFranco or Dave Matthews, but there's also a deep undercurrent of high, lonesome mountain harmony that should appeal to fans of Alison Krauss and Union Station."

Founder Michael Clem (bass, harp, guitars, vocals) recalls the Birchmere influence on their music: "My first experience with the club goes to 1984. I was in high school and a friend took me to see the Seldom Scene. It was the first time I saw a dobro with Mike Auldridge in action, with everyone except Starling from the original lineup. I was just sold—hook, line, and sinker—when I heard them.

"And that summer we had a little bluegrass group and got the thrill of a lifetime when Dick Cerri had a cassette audition for his WAMU *Americana Showcase* and he picked our band. We taped a performance on the Birchmere stage.

"Fast forward to the 1990s when we formed Eddie from Ohio. Playing the Birchmere was the brass ring at the time that there was this love triangle between radio and the club, with WHFS especially important in playing new music in town and advertising groups' appearances. That's when I first saw Tuck and Patti, and Robben Ford. Many great experiences.

"We started EFO—the band's name came from a friend who coined the nickname as a tribute to the lead singer of the band Firehose, Ed "From Ohio" Crawford—and we worked the local clubs and people took note. We were trying to get a Birchmere gig, and David Buskin came in with a big band. He said, 'Sure, you can open for me, but you'll have to set up on the side of the stage.' We thought about that and thought 'We'll wait.' And it was Leo Kottke who said, 'Yes, you can put them out in front of me.' And that was our first show, opening for Leo."

"Running the sound for us was Billy Wolf whose mixes were like climbing in the sound hole of an acoustic guitar. We got permission to release a seat as a cassette we called the *Six-Pack*, with original songs. It was priced to sell at our shows. Billy took a shine to us and that was huge to us. He has since produced several albums by EFO."

Notably, Eddie From Ohio holds the Birchmere record of selling out consecutive three-night shows at the third location. Since 1999 they've sold out 35 times.

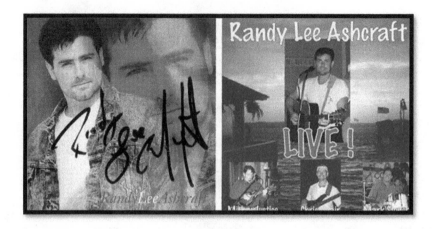

Randy Lee Ashcraft   (b. April 23,1962, Hamilton, OH)

Randy was a fledgling country singer-songwriter when he drove from his Salisbury, Maryland home to the Birchmere in the '90s to see his favorite performers, Guy Clark and Lyle Lovett.

"I love the Birchmere," Ashcraft says. "In 1997 I won the *Jimmy Dean True-Value Country Music Showdown* talent contest for performing original compositions "Fall in Love Tonight" and "Tame My Heart." I represented Maryland in this national competition. The final awards celebration was filmed in Orlando, Florida with singers Dean and Ray Stevens hosting. This award led to my winning another performance award at the *Independent Music World Series* held in Philadelphia, PA."

For these efforts, his growing fan club base flocked to the club for Ashcraft's two headlining sold-out Birchmere shows. "Gary came to the dressing room and welcomed me. And he let me record my second Birchmere appearance using their soundboard and release it as my first CD, *Randy Lee Ashcraft LIVE.*"

Another song, "Shore Thing," which promotes the beauty of Maryland's Eastern Shore, earned him a Maryland Governor's award in 1999. Today, Ashcraft and his band, The Salty Cowboys, are a successful Ocean City, MD country band.

Jane S. Barnett (b. Washington, DC)

Barnett is an Associate Professor teaching voice at Berklee College of Music, mentoring emerging singer-songwriters. © *J. Barnett*

With her own style of "Brooklyn-branded Americana music," singer and guitarist Janie Barnett grew up just south of Old Town Alexandria, close to the Birchmere clubs. Her first musical inspiration was seeing John Hartford perform at the Smithsonian Folklife Festival in the late 1960s. She was in middle school.)

She later worked the festivals and got to know Hartford well. "He was so formidable, gorgeous, talented and nice," Janie says. "I told him I was learning guitar and he said 'I bet you sing. You need to write songs. Don't get yourself boxed in.' He suggested everything I ended up doing in my career."

"The Washington area was such a rich environment for roots and folk music. The Birchmere was always presenting newcomers. Looking forward to new music was their booking policy as well as presenting the older performers. My grandfather was a musician, and my parents, a journalist and a government worker, were very supportive of my music."

Janie left home at 16 and moved to New England to begin her music career. "I'd return home to visit and I tried like hell to get booked at the Birchmere.

"Finally, around 1987, Gary offered me a gig. But it was a holiday weekend, and I wasn't sure if anyone would show up.

"So, I passed on the gig, which was a *big* mistake! I pounded on Gary and later Michael for a gig with no luck. I landed my first gig at the Birchmere in 2018, opening for three sell-out shows by the Bacon Brothers. And let me tell you, I cried after that first night with the Bacons. I'd never been happier playing on that stage."

Saffire – The Uppity Blues Women

Andrea Faye, Gaye Adegbalola, and Ann Rabson signed poster.

In 1987, Ann Rabson was teaching computer science at Germanna Community College in Locust Grove, Virginia, sixty-five miles south of the Birchmere. Saffire's inception began when she delivered an exam to the home of a sick student. Ann, a boogie-woogie pianist who also played guitar, discovered that her student, Earlene Lewis, played bass. They jammed and soon added another friend, Gaye Adegbalola, a singer-songwriter and guitarist. Andrea Faye replaced Lewis on bass in 1992, adding guitar, mandolin, and violin.

They began as feminist blues historians and developed into talented songwriters, recording seven albums for Chicago-based *Alligator* records including *Live and Uppity* in 1998, recorded at The Barns of Wolf Trap. Music writer Mike Joyce reviewed this album in the *Washington Post,* writing

"...Introducing the vengeful ballad "You'll Never Get Me Out of Your Mind," Rabson recalls how she composed it back "when I was getting rid of my second husband. I cannot think of any more joyous time. One thing I've got to say for that man, I got more songs out of that creep. "There's a lesson here for anyone breaking up with a songwriter: Don't expect to get the last word.

"The other members of the band—guitarist-harmonica player Gaye Adegbalola and bassist-mandolinist-fiddler Andra Faye—are in a mood to wash men right out of their lives, too, or at least some men. Adegbalola, who boasts a big, brassy voice, vents her wrath on "Bitch With a Bad Attitude," the title of which pretty much says it all, while Faye takes a more moderate approach with the classic blues lament "You Can Have My Husband (Don't You Mess With My Man)."

Gary says "They played the hall many times. They'd present great blues from the '20s and '30s by the greats like Bessie Smith, Big Mama Thornton, and Koko Taylor. Many of their audience weren't familiar with this music until Saffire fired up."

America's Dewey Bunnell and Gerry Beckley and Don in the middle.
© D. Chapman

193

Don Côqayohômuwôk Chapman (b. Feb. 15, 1954, Beverly, MA)

His North American native name "Côqayohômuwôk" means "spirit song" in his tribal Algonquin language. "I was named this by the Council of Elders because they knew me as a singer and musician. It's almost impossible to spell or pronounce, so it is kind of fun," Chapman jokes.

Don grew up in Alaska and heard Stephen Stills' guitar intro on "Suite: Judy Blue Eyes" on the first CSN album and was captivated by the musical style that came to be loosely known as Americana. As he explored the music, he became a fan of bands like America and Firefall. Then, moving to the Leesburg, Virginia area, I discovered that Larry Burnett, one of the original members of Firefall, lived nearby in Sterling, Virginia. It was about 2007. I met Burnett and played with him on some of the songs he had written for a solo CD. This led to Burnett and me opening for America and also the Association many times at the Birchmere. The America songs like "Horse with No Name" and "Sister Golden Hair" were big parts of my personal soundtrack. Their first album is iconic with the poster of the three Native Americans as they've got this huge reverence for Indian country. At the time, I was a senior policy advisor on Native American Affairs in the Obama administration.

So, I carried some gravitas when they found out about this. They began asking me questions. All of a sudden, I'm the cool kid in the Birchmere."

Chapter 12 – Twenty-Year Report

The Birchmere celebrated its 20th anniversary in 1986. The hoopla surrounding this milestone surprised some area residents with the realization of how special the place had become. Keith Case, the preeminent Nashville music promoter with clients like John Hartford, Tony Rice, New Grass Revival, Ralph Stanley, and many other Birchmere regulars told music writer Richard Harrington, "There's no other club in the country where my acts can have repeat performances to turn-away crowds as frequently as we can there. It's an absolute all-time favorite of every act that I represent."

One of Case's acts, Guy Clark, said, "As far as I'm concerned it's the best listening room in the United States. I've played them all over and that's the one that takes the most care that everybody's enjoying the audience and the performers as well."

People who may have resisted the place in the past because they thought it was a hillbilly haven got a different picture when they read the *Washington Post* anniversary account by Richard Harrington. "This is the only club like this on the northern continent," said Ian Tyson.

"I'm not a big bluegrass fan," Gary told Harrington at the time, "and I wasn't 'saving bluegrass' like a lot of these guys claim they're doing. I saw that it was a legitimate art form and nobody was treating it right."

The Birchmere had outlasted both the Cellar Door and the Red Fox Inn. On the latter, Gary commented then, "Everybody thinks Emmylou Harris, comes and sits in at the Birchmere like she did at the Red Fox. She doesn't but I let them think that."

Radio broadcaster Dick Cerri, said, "Gary Oelze takes running that club as if it's his home and people are his guests." By 1986, demand for bluegrass music was in decline. There was only a short supply of readily available bluegrass acts like Tony Rice and the Seldom Scene that could reliably fill the

Schooner Fare signed poster. Chuck Romanoff, Steve Romanoff, and Tom Rowe.

music hall. The Maine-based folk trio, Schooner Fare, was widely popular and cut a live album at the Birchmere around this anniversary. By then Gary was diversifying the acts, and nobody was objecting to this new direction.

John Duffey said, "I see it as survival, and I have no qualms about the change. The only traditional bluegrass that gets the crowds out is Bill Monroe, because they think it's the last time they'll ever see him again. After all, he's not exactly a spring chicken."

Meanwhile, despite a catastrophic fire in 1982, nearby Wolf Trap's Filene Center, was giving fierce competition to the Birchmere with an audience seating capacity of 7000 plus lawn seating.

A few previous Birchmere favorites like Buskin and Batteau and Nanci Griffith, had "graduated" to the spacious Wolf Trap park. Mary Chapin Carpenter would soon do the same, but return a few times.vHowever, many players like Emmylou Harris and Arlo alternated playing both venues.

***

Lee Michael Demsey is a longtime host of radio shows in the DC area. He has done bluegrass shows for WAMU (1982-2018) and can be heard on their HD channel, *BluegrassCountry.org*. He contributed his memories of the hall:

"My introduction to the Birchmere came in 1981, forty years ago. Where have the years gone?

"I met my future bride Leslie at WAMU-FM when she was a volunteer, and I was a rock jock who also engineered talk shows. As our first date in the summer of '81, she suggested we attend a Ricky Skagg's concert. He was making a transition from bluegrass to country with his third studio album, *Waitin' For the Sun to Shine*. He'd later return to bluegrass with exceptional success in both fields.

"Our date was at the second Birchmere. I'd heard of the club hanging out with WAMU's bluegrass hosts, mainly Katy Daley.

I thought it small yet perfect for most of the acts that played there. Clear sight-lines pretty much wherever you sat, a good sound system, and most importantly, a comfortably intimate experience with some of the best musicians that toured the planet. Bluegrass was the club's main focus in those days, but you could also find country, folk, blues, and Cajun acts. You didn't go to the Birchmere for the food in those days, but the reasonable cover price was well worth it every time.

"I saw some of the best shows ever in that mecca of music, from the Nashville Bluegrass Band to the New Grass Revival, the Tony Rice Unit to Mike Cross, Alison Krauss & Union Station to Peter Rowan and so many more. And there were those golden nights, mesmerized by Mary Chapin Carpenter (and her magical band), stretch her wings at the venue. I'll never forget my many Thursday nights watching The Seldom Scene—a very loose show, unrehearsed, without a playlist. John Duffey commanded the stage with humor (ahem!) and entertainment with his bandmates and their classic songs. Ah, those wonderful Birchmere nights in the 1980s.

"I recall waiting in line with fellow music lovers, anticipating the doors opening, making new acquaintances, and sharing our affections for the artists that would soon be taking to the stage. When you saw the people lined up down Mt. Vernon Avenue, heading back toward the parking lot, a half-hour before the doors opened, you knew the show would be an event.

(l to r) Katy Daley and Al Steiner, on-air hosts at WAMU and two
technical staff members, and Lee Michael Demsey.
© *Bluegrass Country Foundation*

"Some nights could be fairly sparse. Folk singer Eric Andersen booked a show at the last minute, filling a space between two other tour dates. He revisited the USA from his home in Norway. I don't think there were more than 10 people in the audience. Same for a show with Roy Book Binder. I was there to see the soon-to-be-legendary country artist, Vince Gill, who had bluegrass roots. He hadn't made it yet, but the dozen or so lucky people in his audience watched his entirely professional show, with his excellent vocals and instrumental dexterity.

"When the line extended around the corner on other nights, folks hoped and prayed they wouldn't get to the door to find they were at the cutoff point and had to go home, crestfallen.

"Many of us got to know the people who made the club tick, and who without them, there would have been no Birchmere. Among them were some food servers I knew, who had to quickly handle hungry, thirsty crowds.

Dave and Perrie Allen with daughter, Virginia Lee. She helped research this book and contributed photos. Very sadly she passed away in 2021 before publication. © *C.B. Smith*

"In the '80s I remember people like Perrie Spaulding, a waitress, who married Dave Allen, a fine songwriter appearing at the club many times. David Allen Stitch was a Texas songwriter."

Perrie Allen said, "Dave opened for Jerry Jeff Walker and I asked Dave out on a date. We got married three months later. We had our wedding party at the Birchmere. We moved to Nashville and Dave had a deal with two publishers. I pitched his songs to one of my favorites, the Nashville Bluegrass band, and they cut six of his songs. His song "Blue Train" won IBMA song of the year in 1992, but he died a few months before the award from cancer. Gary held a benefit concert for us.

"Lee Michael liked David's music and played him often on his radio show. One time on my birthday he asked me for my favorite Dave Allen songs he played his whole show around my requests."

Lee continues: "And there was Mary Beth Aungier, who went on to be Mary Chapin Carpenter's road manager, Terry Mayo, who would later marry Ron Rice, one of Tony Rice's musical brothers, sisters Neva and Sesi Warnock, and Teresa O'Brien, Connie Brandt Smith, and Peggy Tarbett (Mai), the wife of Pudge, who we'll get to in a moment.

"They were all "corralled" by the one-of-a-kind Linda Oelze, who was a mama lion to these dedicated workers. Gary Oelze was the owner/manager, but without his then-wife Linda, things wouldn't have run as well in those earlier years. Linda and the gals served as great "welcomers" to the performers, and many considered them their friends. And at the third incarnation, the current Birchmere, I always enjoyed chatting with a kindred musical spirit, Chris Adams from the waitstaff.

"The signs on the tables would remind you to be quiet. However, you still needed someone to be the "enforcer." Pudge was all-that-and-a-bag-of-chips. A burly guy, who often sported a scraggly beard, Pudge could scare the heck out of you.

"He'd snarl at you, and you'd do as he asked, or else. But Pudge (William Tarbett, though nobody really knew him by that name), was indeed a great guy once you got under the surface. These days there is no bouncer at the club, and it's left to the waitstaff and a security officer in the parking lot to keep order, but the golden days of Pudge are legendary at The Birchmere.

"Booking the acts for the Birchmere could be a tricky business. You had to choose acts that would draw people into the club but wouldn't cost so much that the club wouldn't make any money. It's a tightrope to walk.

"When Michael Jaworek came aboard in the job, things really took off. Michael has always had a great head for the business, and with his friendly disposition, he has been very well-liked. But don't let that fool you into thinking that he's a pushover. He can be a real tiger when it comes to wheeling and dealing with the bands and their agents. After all, his job is to bring in the right talent to The Birchmere, keeping up its reputation as one of the top nightclubs in the world, but not blowing the bank at the same time. His assistant in recent years, Ben Finkelstein, also does great work for the club.

"The Birchmere also had a record store which sold LPs in the earlier days and CDs, books and t-shirts as time went by. Bud Newman and later Neva Wernock ran the store well at the second Birchmere in the basement of the club.

"In more recent years, the job is handled by, among others, the very friendly and knowledgeable, Stuart Wodlinger.

"A nightclub is nothing without a great sound team. I never really got to know the guys who were the monitor techs, but the guy behind the board, who ran sound for the house, Billy Wolf, was as good as it could get. The musicians raved about his mix and so did the patrons. Billy left the club before they moved to the new location. He went on to be one of the most sought-after sound people in the business, from engineering albums to mixing and mastering them. If there is a hall of fame for this side of the music industry, Bill Wolf belongs.

"And now to the big kahuna, the boss man, the guy who could be seen running the soundboard near the kitchen in the early '80s, Gary Oelze.

"He could be a bit of a tough cookie at times, as one would have to be to turn a rather dumpy little venue into a music mecca. It takes more than grit and perseverance to get the job done. You could always tell when Gary had a hand in booking. When he was excited to have someone coming in, you'd know about it. He loved his country acts. He was so thrilled when people like Johnny Cash, Merle Haggard, and Waylon Jennings would come through. That was when Gary would really light up (not as in cigarettes, though he did a heck of a lot of that too). He relished making friends with his musical heroes. Gary's sly smile and country charm have made him a favorite with anyone who's had the pleasure of meeting him."

One year before the 20th anniversary would see one of the most remarkable performances in Birchmere history. Washington music critics would call it the entertainment event of 1985. Rodney Crowell, Rosanne Cash, and Guy Clark—with only their guitars—traded songs and stories for nearly four hours. The Birchmere afforded these performers the kind of living room intimacy in which they could reveal so much about themselves.

Rosanne Cash (b. May 24, 1955, Memphis, TN)

Johnny Cash's eldest daughter had her break-out hit album, *Seven-Year Ache* in 1981 and she is in the Nashville Songwriter's Hall of Fame. She continues to play the hall. Cash remembers well singing with Rodney and Guy:

"As far as I recall, it was not planned. Guy told me before he walked on stage that he might be going to call me up. But there was no planning, as far as I remember, Rodney may have a different memory. Guy was playing the Kerrville Folk festival and Rodney and I were there and he called me up to sing one song.

Rosanne Cash says "I love this picture with Guy standing there. He looks so protective and benevolent and that really touches me. He was very encouraging to me at that time." © Oelze

"I had been trying to impress Guy with my songwriting for a lot of years and the "Seven Year Ache" song turned his head around. When I first played it for him, he goes 'Who wrote that?' [laughs] Kind of competitively. So that's when I got Guy's respect. And you'd have to earn Guy's respect. I adored him. And I was proud to be called up.

"I remember being very nervous at the Birchmere that night because I was there with these two master song writers. All of my memories of the place are fond from the very first time I played there and every time I came back. I felt like I was welcomed back as part of a family, you know, 'here comes our sister back again.' And it's always been like that. I felt no judgment from the audience, no coldness. You know, like, 'OK, prove it to me.' It was always so warm. And I got to try things out there. I played some songs for the very first time at the Birchmere. I did this a couple of years ago; I think we called it *Blacklists River*. It was this show of songs from *Black Cadillac, The List,* and *The River and the Thread*. And I made it up for the Birchmere, and it was like a leap because we hadn't done it before. And the audience was so enthusiastic and so open to it, you know, to just trying this new thing. It was always so gratifying. I miss it. You know, I can't wait to come back.

"You never know about audiences. You just never know. It's always like rolling the dice every night to see what they're going to be like. But with the Birchmere, it's always like a homecoming, always welcoming. They're always enthusiastic. They give you a lot of slack to make mistakes. They're so present. It's one of the great venues in the country."

Gary, with Perrie Allen, later present a photo of the Cash, Crowell, and Clark show. © *Oelze*

Rodney Crowell (b. Aug. 7, 1950, Houston, Texas)

Crowell met Guy Clark in 1972 after moving to Nashville seeking a music career. Clark's songwriting was an inspiration for Rodney and a few years later Emmylou Harris recorded

203

Crowell's "Bluebird Wine" on her *Pieces of the Sky* album. (Crowell and Harris would become lifelong friends and professional collaborators and for a time, he played in her Hot Band.) Crowell recalls first meetings with Clark and the Birchmere: "I went down to meet Guy, who was playing at the Childe Harold and the Birchmere. I said, God, you know I could only relate this to Austin, Texas then. I hadn't been to San Francisco yet or Northern California where there was a similar vibe. For me, the second Birchmere just had it all the way.

"I think that we were just going to get up and do a couple of songs with Guy that night in '85, but as it turned out, we went up on stage, sat around and we just turned it into the living room.

"I'll admit that I prefer the original Birchmere for sentimental and emotional reasons. It was really shown to me that some places just have charisma and it had it. And I think, you know, you got to tip your hand to Gary Oelze, but you also have to tip your hat to that audience.

"But the current Birchmere is so user-friendly. You can get there early, do your laundry and walk down to RT's and eat dinner. I take long walks in the area. It just has a feeling of being at home and, you know, as long as they want me there. I would say the real gig would be that first time that Gary had Roseanne and Guy with me and I over there. But Emmylou and I had three nights standing there that was also really good fun."

Poets Award .

Rodney Crowell won a Country Music Association Poet's Awards in 2018. He joins an esteemed list of winners in this category who have also won this prestigious award. It includes Guy Clark, Billy Joe Shaver, Roger Miller, Buck Owens, and Kris Kristofferson. "I felt pretty cool about winning that. Yeah," says Crowell, "They should give that award to Mickey Newbury and Townes posthumously."

James Brady's birthday party at the hall. © Oelze

The club began accruing celebrity loyalists in the '80s. One was Ronald Reagan's presidential press secretary James Brady who often came with his wife, Sara to see the Seldom Scene.

In 1981, Brady was permanently disabled by gunshot wounds during an attempted Presidential assassination. He would arrive in a wheelchair to the shows.

One night, Sarah Brady called their favorite waitress, Linda, and asked her to hold a table, suggesting there would be a surprise when they came. When the Brady's arrived, Linda first noticed an empty wheelchair at door, and then in came Brady using two canes and walking to his table, hollering "Lovely Lin."

In the aftermath of her husband's shooting, Sarah Brady had organized the Brady Campaign to support the Prevent Gun Violence committee. She asked Gary to help her get the Seldom Scene to play a fund-raising gala benefitting the National Head Injury Foundation. That became the "Hoots, Boots, and Spurs" event at the Galleria Lafayette Center.

Gary: "John Starling came up to me afterwards and asked 'How in the hell did you get John Duffey to perform at an anti-gun event and *for free*?' and I told him, 'John Duffey respects me. He listens to me and trusts me.'"

The band at that time—or more specifically, Mike Auldridge and John Duffey—was having conflicts and dissension. They would eventually break up. On reflection, Gary thinks had he known about these quarrels, then he could have talked the guys into continuing.

Justice Thomas with Gary. © *Oelze*

In 1991 the newly appointed Supreme Court Associate Justice Clarence Thomas became a patron. Gary says: "He comes here with his wife, Virginia. He was friends with Johnny and June Cash. Clarence bought a bus like the country music stars use when they tour. He and Virginia get on the road and travel to campgrounds. He tells me some of the nicest and most interesting people in the world are at these campgrounds he enjoys visiting. What a gentleman he is."

Chapter 13 – Dirt Roads Paved in Gold

June Carter Cash and The Man in Black.   © Oelze

His mother wanted to name him John. His father preferred Ray. Simple initials were their compromise. The Air Force wouldn't permit the use of initials as a first name, so he became John R. Cash. He started using the name Johnny Cash when he became a member of Sun Records Million Dollar Quartet, with Elvis Presley, Carl Perkins, and Jerry Lee Lewis.

J. R. Cash (b. Feb. 26, 1932, Kingsland, AK)

After moving to Columbia Records, Cash topped the music charts in 1969 with his now-legendary *Johnny Cash at San Quentin* live album. His fame grew with his weekly TV music variety show *The Johnny Cash Show* (1969-1971) taped at Nashville's Ryman Auditorium.

By the time Cash played his only Birchmere show in June 1992, things weren't going particularly well for him. Columbia had abruptly dropped Cash from their label. Fans knew Johnny was a legend, but Columbia miscalculated that Cash was more history than hitmaker. He lost substantial money and prestige when investors for a planned "Country Cash" theatre in Branson, Missouri pulled out.

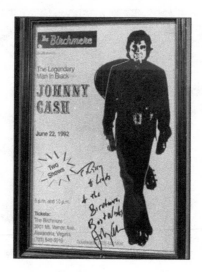

It would be four months after his Birchmere show when Cash appeared at Bob Dylan's 30th Anniversary show at Madison Square Garden. Record producer Rick Rubin, best known for heavy metal and rap music, took notice. Rubin convinced Cash to record his 81st album, *American Recordings,* with only Cash's voice and guitar covering his own compositions, along with songs by Kris Kristofferson, Tom Waits, Nick Lowe, and others. This album, released in 1994, revitalized Johnny as American icon, with *Rolling Stone* magazine proclaiming *American Recordings* "one of Cash's greatest albums because of his self-possessed, "biblically intense" take on traditional folk songs and Rubin's no-frills production. *American Recordings* is at once monumental and viscerally intimate, fiercely true to the legend of Johnny Cash and entirely contemporary."

Washington Post music critic, Richard Harrington delivered a mixed review of the Birchmere performance:

"Seeing Johnny Cash at the Birchmere Monday night was akin to having a president step off Mount Rushmore and onto the stage of the Alexandria club. Arriving on stage the legendary Man in Black was pure presence. Unfortunately, the show he put on lacked substance, a case of too little Cash and too much Carter Family."

The Carter sisters, Anita, Helen, and June with Johnny.   © *Oelze*

Harrington concluded his review with "Cash's voice, always somewhat suspect, was not in the best shape either, wandering in pitch and given to the occasional odd reverb. Too often he sounded like his face looked. On the positive side, the last time fans were able to sit this close to the Country Music Hall of Famer, they were probably inmates at Folsom."

Nevertheless, thrilled fans enjoyed Cash singing "Daddy Sang Bass," "Ring of Fire," "Folsom Prison Blues," "Get Rhythm," "Sunday Morning Coming Down," "Long Black Veil," "Ghost Riders In The Sky," and a 1970 ballad, "Big River." Duets with wife June Carter Cash included "Jackson" and "When I Look Beyond the River."

June, with her sisters Helen and Anita, delivered gospel tunes, with son John Carter Cash performing "Johnny B. Goode" and "Crossroads" in the 90-minute show. Gary remembers that Johnny was subdued that day and on stage.

"He appeared to be in pain and had a personal masseuse in his dressing room, working on his back. Yet, we all recall how genuinely nice he was to everyone."

Live on stage, and on poster behind the bar.   © Oelze

Merle Ronald Haggard (b. April 6, 1937, Oildale, CA)

One of the benefits of Johnny Cash coming to the Birchmere was his sharing a "good club" buzz with a few of his music pals, including Merle Haggard, the first of many country megastars that followed Cash.

In 1993, the Birchmere became an intimate California honky-tonk akin to the ones "The Hag" started in. Accompanied by his outstanding band, the Strangers, he played the room's warm acoustics like an instrument. When they came to "Today I Started Loving Her Again," he signaled to the band to lay back.

"He lowered his voice," Geoffrey Himes wrote the next day in *The Washington Post*, "till it found the borderline between a purr and a growl and captured the song's mix of anticipation and trepidation. When he sang, "Sing Me Back Home," he played a slow Telecaster guitar solo that was just as expressive as the vocal."

And while his '93 show was impressive; it was also short, clocking in at only 35 minutes. When he returned in 1995, he was a Country Music Hall of Fame inductee. To some, he appeared to be a little "sleep-deprived," but the show received good reviews from both audience and press. Standout solos from The Strangers included Don Markham on sax and Norm Hamlet on steel guitar. The show ended in an hour.

Haggard had angioplasty the next year and canceled his 1997 show due to "heart trouble," but his last show in 2011 went strongly with 21 songs. Clad in black suit and hat, Merle was in great voice, adding a playful fiddle solo on "Workin' in Tennessee." Others, like "The Bottle Let Me Down," "Old Man from the Mountain," "They're Tearing the Labor Camps Down," and "Swinging' Doors" were classic Americana. Adding the Cash cover, "Folsom Prison Blues" was an unexpected dose of fun.

Merle honored a shout-out for 'Mama Tried" from the loving crowd. The encore began with "Okie From Muskogee"—where he stopped the song after the first "we don't take our trips on LSD..." paused, and asked the audience, "Can we have a little more crowd response on that issue? A little more response, please." The crowd roared and started a call and response cheer following every verse, with Merle smiling.

"The Fighting Side of Me" ended his stirring show. He dedicated that last song to "all the armed forces that aren't going to get paid," a reference to the debt ceiling debate then seething on Capitol Hill.

Rubye Rose Blevins (Oct. 30, 1908, Beaudry, AK)

She was known professionally as Patsy Montana. She was the first woman country singer to have a million-selling single, "I Want to be a Cowboy's Sweetheart," in 1935.

When Montana died at age 87 in 1996, Cathy Fink and Marcy Marxer sent a follow-up to the short obituary that the *Washington Post* published. Below is an abridged version of their letter which the newspaper published.

Patsy Montana at the Birchmere. © *Oelze*

"On May 5 your paper ran a less-than-adequate, in fact embarrassingly brief, obituary of one of our national treasures, cowgirl singer Patsy Montana. Is this another slight on covering women in the arts? Would Gene Autry or Roy Rogers be remembered in a few brief paragraphs? Your paper found Patsy Montana significant enough to merit a major article and photo on March 30, 1983.

"Patsy had a lot of Washington fans who sold out venues such as the Wolf Trap Barns and the Birchmere to hear her golden yodel. They deserve what she deserves, a proper remembrance.

"In 1935, Patsy wrote and recorded the first million-selling single for a woman in country music, "I Wanna Be a Cowboy's Sweetheart." Not satisfied to sing the male western songs the record company executives chose for her; she took to writing many of her own songs from her own point of view— highly entertaining and definitely female. Today's female country artists owe a debt to Patsy for her nonchalant boldness some 60 years ago. Patsy's WLS co-stars, the Girls of the Golden West, used to sing, "Will There Be Any Yodelers in Heaven?" Heaven now has the best.

[Signed] Cathy Fink and Marcy Marxer

Patsy Montana and Cathy Fink. © *Montana Archives*

Ellen Muriel Deason (b. Aug, 30, 1919, Nashville, TN)

Kitty Wells, the "Queen of Country Music," made history when she became the first female country music singer to top the charts with her 1952 hit, "It Wasn't God Who Made Honky Tonk Angels." She is the only performer to be awarded the top female vocalist award for 14 consecutive years, and in 1991, became the third country music artist to be inducted into the Country Music Hall of Fame, after Roy Acuff and Hank Williams. Wells was 80 years old when she appeared at the Birchmere in 1999 with her husband, Johnnie Wright of the 1940's duo, "Johnnie and Jack [Anglin]." They had hit songs in the 1950's like "Oh Baby Mine," and "Goodnight, Sweetheart, Goodnight."

Their son, Bobby Wright, opened the show. Wright was also an actor who some patrons recognized as a cast member of the *McHale's Navy* TV show.

From Richard Harrington's review: "Wright, delivered a half-dozen classic country hits, including Hank Thompson's 1952 chart-topper "The Wild Side of Life," which blamed wild women for leading good men astray. That was pure prelude, of course, to the response: Her performance of "It Wasn't God Who Made Honky Tonk Angels." She didn't write it—a man named J.D. Miller did—but 47 years ago she sang it so convincingly that it became the first No. 1 country hit by a woman and, albeit

213

inadvertently, the first feminist song ever recorded in Nashville. Wells went on to become the biggest female country star of her generation, opening the doors that Loretta Lynn and Tammy Wynette stepped through in the '60s."

Kitty Wells and Jack Wright.   © *Oelze*

Waylon Arnold Jennings (b. June 15, 1937, Littlefield, TX)

Lash LaRue was a well-known western B-movie star of the '40s and '50s. He dressed in black and used a bullwhip instead of a gun. He was an inspiration for the Indiana Jones movie character. The first time Waylon Jennings played the hall, he told Gary how he and Johnny Cash once did a cowboy video. He told Gary, "Johnny and I were on this movie shoot, and somebody told them that some guy wanted to meet them. It turned out to be the authentic Lash LaRue. We invited him to our bus and enjoyed talking together."

LaRue ended up doing a duet with Cash and Jennings on their *Heroes* album. There's a picture of the three of them on the back of the album.

Jessi Colter and Waylon Jennings © *Oelze*

"I had an old Lash LaRue movie poster that I gave to Waylon when he and his wife, Jessi Colter, returned a second time," recalls Gary. "He thought the poster very cool. His second appearance in 1988 was solo with guitar and Jessi. He brought some backing tapes, which he activated with his foot as he played selected songs from his then autobiographical album, *A Man Named Hoss.*

Gary offers this anecdote: "At the beginning of the '88 show, there was some audience guy yelling questions and requests loudly. Waylon stopped the show and asked this guy to stand up. The fellow did.

"Are you from Texas? asked Waylon. The guy said, 'Yes.'

"Ok," said Waylon. "Now everybody knows you're here, so *sit down and shut up.*"

Waylon proceeded with an entertaining show featuring his well-known tunes like "Dreaming My Dreams with You" and "Luckenbach, Texas," colorful anecdotes, and duets with Jessi. He dedicated one song to his friend and actor, Robert Duvall, sitting at a close-by table. Duvall lives on his 360-acre farm in Fauquier County, VA, about 38 miles from the Birchmere. Waylon and Jessi were staying at Duvall's house. His driver told Gary that earlier that day Johnny Cash dropped by and the three of them went to a Haymarket, Virginia general store.

"The people there were amazed to see and talk with the three celebrities," the driver said.

Country Music Hall of Famer Jennings was one of the Outlaws with Cash, Nelson, and Kristofferson. His other claims to fame include playing bass in Buddy Holly's band. Holly also funded and produced Waylon's 1958 song "Jole Blon." The next year, Jennings generously forfeited his seat to Jiles Perry "The Big Bopper" Richardson on the plane that tragically crashed, ending the young lives of Richardson, Ritchie Valens, and Holly.

One of the stories Waylon recounted on stage was when he and Johnny Cash sawed several inches off all the furniture in a hotel room and then called for room service to see if they'd see any difference. When close friends Johnny Cash and Jennings played the Birchmere, they had both recently recovered from drug problems and were enjoying sobriety. This hotel escapade was obviously before rehabilitation.

Gary adds, "Waylon was a huge Mickey Newbury fan. Whenever he hosted the *Nashville Now* TV show, he'd invite Mickey to play guitar with him and sing songs."

Alvis Edgar Owens Jr. (b. Aug. 12, 1929, Sherman, TX).

Maverick honky-tonk singer Buck Owens returned to touring in 1989 after a long absence during and after his TV fame on *Hee-Haw*. He left his lucrative, long-running comedy show—which he said hurt his country music album sales—and after a ten-year hiatus got back to his basics with a successful European tour.

On stage in London, he proudly noted the Beatles' 28th anniversary of their 1964 cover of his 1963 hit, "Act Naturally." To mark the occasion, he even re-recorded the song with Ringo Starr at Abbey Roads studio. Gary: "When we found out that Buck was touring, we put in an offer, and his agent accepted it. We put the show on sale, and it sold out immediately.

"But then we unexpectedly get this call that he doesn't want to play the Birchmere. Damn. I called Rodney Crowell and then Vince Gill to find out why but they didn't know. Then Dwight Yoakum got involved. I think all three tried to convince him that the Birchmere was a great place. Dwight had recently

216

recorded some songs with his mentor, Buck, that brought Owens back on the charts. So, the agent called us back and said, 'OK. Leave it alone. Don't cancel the gig.'"

On the day Owens arrived, Gary went to his dressing room to welcome him. "I was surprised how tall he was because I guess I was used to seeing him on TV. He said hello, and then apologized: 'Gary, I'm sorry I canceled the show. I don't do these shows for money. I give all the money to the band. I just wanted to get out on the road to play a little music, but sometimes I get booked in any old honky-tonk. But I called my little friends Dwight and Rodney, and they told me the Birchmere is a great place to play. Michael Jaworek adds: "His agent, Stan Barnett, said reinstate the gig. I didn't understand. I'm sorry I canceled on you.'"

Sporting a leather jacket, red scarf, and black hat, Buck Owens, with his band the Buckaroos, did a great show that night. He sang his hits, including "Tiger by the Tail," "Crying Time Again," "Streets of Bakersfield," "Love's Gonna Live Here" and, of course, "Act Naturally." He surprised the crowd with a crazy honky-tonk rendition of "Wipe Out."

Gary noted that "Buck played his songs faithfully. No long instrumental turns, or medleys. He did not play his famous red, white, and blue Fender acoustic guitar but rather a more famous —among guitarists—Fender Telecaster. It belonged to his lead player, harmony singer, and best friend Don Rich, who died in a motorcycle crash in 1974. It was Rich who executed the brilliant licks on most of Owens Top Ten hit songs.

Buck's 24-song Birchmere set beautifully showcased his trade-marked twangy West Coast "Bakersfield" sound of country music: an inspiration to the styles of Merle Haggard and Dwight Yoakum. The *Washington Post's* Mike Joyce reported, "Whether sad, joyful or a tad corny, Owens sang each song in an unaffected, often stirring manner as if he just had to get something off his chest."

Owens at 1989 show. © Penny Parsons, and his wall photo.

Jackie Keith Whitley (b. July 1, 1955, Ashland, KY)

At age 33, Keith Whitley's career was soaring when "I'm No Stranger to the Rain" landed as the number one hit song on the country chart. One month later, the up-and-coming country singer was found deceased in his bed from alcohol poisoning, with a .47 alcohol blood level. Keith's fans were crushed.

Country Plus newspaper asked Gary Oelze to write a column in memoriam to his friend. Gary contributed this:

I feel Keith Whitley belonged to the DC area. Many of you probably don't know he lived up here in the early 70s, playing in a very progressive bluegrass band called Country Store with Jimmy Gaudreau, Carl Jackson, and later on, Jimmy Arnold. After his stint with that band, he re-joined Ralph Stanley's band, with whom he had been previously associated.

I first met Keith in 1978, while he was still with Stanley. He had come to see J.D. Crowe and The New South about joining the group. What impressed me at the time was his youthfulness, perennial smile, and great personality, which belied the amount of time he had already been in the music business. We were very lucky to have J.D. Crowe and the New South, with Keith, play the club for so many years. We knew

218

how talented he was a long time before the rest of the world. We became friends and he had many more friends here who he regularly stayed in touch with.

© *C. B. Smith*

Other memories

Today Gary looks back: "Some of my fondest memories of him were our all-night jam sessions. Keith had always wanted to sing country music, so on Saturday nights, after the New South had played and everyone had gone home, I would gather up Mike Auldridge on his steel guitar, Pete Kennedy on lead guitar, and numerous fiddle players Bobby Sloan, Gene Johnson, and Jeff Wisor with drummer Robbie Magruder and a host of other pickers. My brother, John, also brought in his drumkit. With Keith singing, they'd jam until Sunday daybreak.

"Ultimately, Keith left for Nashville to "seek fame and fortune." It took several years to get a contract, but he finally hooked up with RCA for a six-song mini-LP, *A Hard Act to Follow*. Although critically acclaimed by those in the know, too many critics in Nashville did not seem to be ready for the

219

traditional country, saying he was "too much like Lefty, Haggard, or Jones," things they were not saying a year or two later about George Strait, Randy Travis or Vicky Van Shelton.

When *Hard Act* came out in 1984, I called Keith and asked him to come up to the Birchmere for an album release show. I brought in his old New South bassist. Randy Hayes, Mike Auldridge, Pete Kennedy and Peter Bonta to back him up.

He finally started to get national recognition in 1986 with his *Miami To L.A.* release proving the old adage "that "it takes years to become an overnight success." He was back at the Birchmere that year with his own band and you could see in his face what he always wanted—to be a country music star."

© Oelze

Sesi Warnock, Keith, and Perrie Allen. © *C. B. Smith*

Chapter 14 – More Country Roads

© Cindy Dyer

Kathleen Alice Mattea (b. June 21, 1959, South Charleston, WV)

In 1984, Kathy Mattea recorded "Love at the Five and Dime," written and originally recorded by Nanci Griffith. Mattea looks back: "You know, when you have your first hit on a Nancy Griffith song, you take a crash course in Texas songwriting. You start to open up that can of worms and go looking through those catalogs. Steve Earle and I were coming up. We signed our first record deal on the same day. So, we knew each other and I used to sing demos for him. Steve and Nanci Griffith were my closest ties when I started.

"There were certain iconic rooms that you grew up hearing about like Nashville's Old Exit Inn. The Birchmere was one of them. One of my big memories is when I first played there in and Al Gore came to see me. He was my senator and when I began touring England his office helped me with visas. He loved the hall. Oh, my Lord. It's one thing that we have to do business together and I like you and you liked me and our offices worked great together. But it's a whole other thing for a guy to come out and bring a table full of ten people to your show and hang on every word.

"I was young back then and I was running a lot. I would jog in the afternoon. My manager was with us because our first time at the Birchmere was important. He asked me how my afternoon was, and I said, "Bob, I had the best run. I went to Arlington Cemetery and ran past a beautiful replica of the Iwo Jima statue."

"He said, 'Kathy. We are in DC. That *was* the statue.'"

***

Kathy says, "Great places stay great because the people who run them stay in touch with what made them get started in the first place, which is the same for us musicians. It's your responsibility to remember how lucky you are and how special this is from whatever point of view you come at. But that's the thing that always struck me. It's always like, 'Oh my God, you're back and you're supposed to be back, you know, you're our favorite.' And I just have this feeling that, every night, there's some version of that for everybody. And it's sincere."

Kathy continues: "The comfort and proximity of the people is what I feel like when I'm on stage there. It's not about the room. The room disappears and it's just you and the people. That's what I really like about it. It's not ornate. The room itself facilitates the connection between the artist and the audience. And everyone that comes there knows that it is the Birchmere. They are there, whether they know you or not, for a musical experience. That's a gift."

Just as Don Williams was the Birchmere's first national act, he was also the first national act that Mattea opened for, first opening gig ever. "Don also came into the studio when I wasn't there and secretly did the harmonies on "Live at the Five and

Dime" as a surprise for me. I later recorded Don's song "Come from the Heart."

As a presenter at the Country Music Awards in 1992, Kathy Mattea was the first major country star to speak out about AIDS, 30 years ago.

Kathy's first show at the Birchmere.   © Oelze

In 2018, Mattea released a new album, *Pretty Bird*, which was produced by Tim O'Brien, who together with Pete Wernick formed Hot Rize, one of the early bluegrass bands that played the Birchmere.

Nanci Caroline Griffith (b. July 6, 1953 Seguin, TX)

While a teenager, singer-songwriter Nanci Griffith began performing in Austin Texas where she was raised. In a 1989 *Austin City Limits* TV show she said "Loretta Lynn was the first singer I ever saw of the female gender who wrote her own dad-gum songs." (and played her own rhythm guitar).

Other Rooms, a 1993 album devoted entirely to songs written by Woody Guthrie, Bob Dylan, Townes Van Zandt, John Prine and others, featured guest appearances by Dylan and Prine, and earned Griffith a Grammy Award in 1994.

Pete Kennedy tells how he and Maura joined Griffith's Blue Moon Orchestra:

Nanci Griffith.   © *Oelze*

"I spent the summer of 1991 touring with Mary Chapin Carpenter, subbing for her producer and guitarist John Jennings, who was taking a break from the road to work on studio projects. The last gig of the year was a duo, just Mary Chapin and myself flying down to Texas for *Austin City Limits.* format for the show was round-robin, with Mary-Chapin, Nanci Griffith, Julie Gold and The Indigo Girls all sitting in a semicircle.

"I had never met Nanci, but I knew that her lead guitarist had just left the band. Since I was sitting between her and Mary Chapin, I just naturally played along with both of them during their spots. That sort of informal jamming is central to the Texas songwriting tradition. After the show, Nanci's manager asked me to join the Blue Moon Orchestra. Since I had just played my last scheduled show subbing for John Jennings with Mary Chapin, I felt lucky to get offered another gig, so I said yes!

"Iris Dement was touring with Nanci, opening the show and singing backup. When she left the band to pursue her solo career, I sent a cassette of Nanci's repertoire down to Maura in Austin. She made an astonishing 4-track tape where she overdubbed multiple vocal and instrumental parts in a deeply and perfectly rendered exploration of Nanci's work. I gave it to Nanci and the next day she said, "Who is this woman who knows everything about my music?" She hired Maura to take Iris's place, and that's how we both wound up as members of the Blue Moon Orchestra."

Maura Kennedy recalls this memory: "Nanci was always politically opinionated. Once at the Birchmere when George W. Bush was President she said something strong about "W." She didn't hold back. From the darkness in the audience, a loud voice shouted 'Oh come on back to Texas, Nanci. We aren't that bad.' It was the former Governor of Texas, Ann Richards."

© *Oelze*

Noble Ray Price (b. Jan. 12, 1926, Perryville, TX)

Elected to the Country Music Hall of Fame in 1996, Ray Price was an early and innovative musician and songwriter who shaped both the Nashville sound and Gary's childhood appreciation of music. Ray was among the first national acts to perform at the Birchmere. Gary tells his story:

"I was his fan my whole life. Ray was a friend and roommate of Hank Williams when they both came to Nashville. When Hank increasingly started missing gigs due to his alcoholism, Ray began using his band, the Drifting Cowboys. They became the Cherokee Cowboys when they backed Ray, and he took over the band when Williams died on New Year's Day, 1953.

Gary with Ray at his last show in 2012. © *Oelze*

Ray resented being compared to Hank and successfully found his own trademark baritone vocal style. In addition to Hank's former bandmates, later aspiring musicians to join his Cherokee band over the years included Willie Nelson, Johnny Paycheck, and Birchmere favorites Roger Miller and Buddy Emmons.

Gary first met Price at Waldorf, Maryland's Stardust Club in the mid-60's. During a backstage intermission chat made possible by noted promoter Jimmy Case, a bass player and early booker for Loretta Lynn. Ray asked Gary for a ride to his motel room so he could change his shirt. During the drive Gary asked him what happened to all his Nudie suits. Ukrainian-born Nudie Cohn, the "Rodeo Tailor," moved to Hollywood in 1947 to become the designer of distinctive signature cowboy outfits favored by country artists. Each suit was original and ornately embellished with colorful embroidered flowers and rhinestones.

"Ray was then immaculately dressed in what we called the 'Western tuxedo," says Gary. "Ray told me, 'All my old Nudie suits are on a rack at Nudie's store in Las Vegas for sale.'" Gary thought, "I didn't have 50 cents to my name back then, but if I did, I'd be in Las Vegas trying to buy one of Ray Price's Nudie suits.

Price eventually settled his style on impeccably tailored suits and would play the Birchmere six times, performing at his final show in 2012 at age 86. He passed a year later on December 16, 2013. Gary finds Price important for a myriad of impacts on country music.

"Price brought the fiddles coupled with the 'walking bass' sound to country music. The walking style of bass was more associated with jazz and blues when Ray put it right up front in his honky-tonk country music. Everybody else picked that up right away," Gary explains.

And the beat of his music increased to become known as the 'Ray Price Shuffle.' You can hear it on one of his first hit songs, "Crazy Arms," in 1956, which replaced Elvis Presley's "Heartbreak Hotel" as Number 1 on the country charts. Other honky-tonk singers like Faron Young, Buck Owens and George Jones were influenced by Ray Price. Between 1954 and 1974, he racked up total of 64 US country chart hits. "For the Good Times," his third million-seller, first introduced the songwriting chops of a Nashville janitor named Kris Kristofferson.

Gary continued: "Ray also told me that he got tired of 'all these New York producers making hits out of country music just because they have an orchestra.' So, Ray added strings and orchestral backings in the late '60s to his recordings, which did piss off some of the country fans, but he was successful. He used a 47-member orchestra to record his version of "Danny Boy." Johnny Carson became one of his biggest supporters."

Price would hire up to ten violinists from their local musicians' union in the shows he'd do on tour. Gary also noted that he'd have two separate bands out on tour at the same time. Ray would fly to the gigs while they'd be traveling from town to town by bus. "I don't know of any other performer who operated that way," Gary observes.

One poignant Birchmere show occurred on a Sunday night in 2000. The previous Friday, Ray had lost his best friend piano player of 34 years, Moses "Blondie" Calderone, the previous due to complications after open-heart surgery.

In the *Washington Post* review of that show, Buzz McClain noted: "Ray's encore could have been any one of dozens of hits. "I've Got A New Heartache," "Heartaches by the Numbers," and "I Can't Go Home Like This" went unsung but Price chose the Irish ballad "Danny Boy," and turned in a rendition—not maudlin, yet terribly mournful—that clearly was dedicated to Blondie. Sunday's show finished the tour."

Christopher Hillman (b. Dec. 4, 1944, Los Angeles, CA)

Chris Hillman is a Rock and Roll Hall of Famer, inducted in 1991 for his vocals, bass-playing, and songwriting in The Byrds.

A teenaged solid mandolin player, Chris Hillman formed his first bluegrass band, the Scottsville Squirrel Barkers, in 1961. An early gig was playing in Disneyland near the park ride, Space Mountain. One member of the group, Bernie Leadon, played with Chris in The Flying Burrito Brothers and later became the Eagles' final original member.

Hillman talked about his Birchmere memories: "What does an artist look for in a club? The answer is great sound and excellent sound personnel. The Birchmere has never, ever failed me. I began playing the second Birchmere in 1983 with my acoustic band [Al Perkins, Bernie Leadon, Bill Bryson, and John Jorgenson] and then many times with Desert Rose [Herb Pedersen and J. Jorgenson] and various other entities with Tony Rice and others throughout the years.

"I love Gary Oelze. He is one of the coolest guys. There are very few club owners like him. He is generous and cares about the artists. And promoter Michael Jaworek has always treated me so well, whenever I've played there."

"I can't say enough good things about Chris Hillman," states Gary. "He's been a gentleman throughout the years, playing beautifully with Herb Pedersen and John Jorgenson. I credit his Desert Rose Band with bringing back the straight-ahead country music that Chris helped reestablish in 1968 with Roger McGuinn and Gram Parsons on the *Sweetheart of The Rodeo* album."

First signed wall photo by Hillman, Bernie Leadon, Al Perkins, and Jerry Sheff.

Washington Post writer Joe Sasfy reviewed Hillman's 1985 return to the Birchmere: "Hillman has always seemed to be standing in someone's shadow singing harmonies. At the Birchmere last night, Hillman proved that his sweet tenor voice could almost carry a show all by its lonesome." With two critically acclaimed albums on the merch table, The Desert Rose band returned to the Birchmere in 1988, and has made a total of 12 appearances.

"Chris is a quiet person. He isn't flashy and wasn't the front man in previous bands, said Gary. "But his Desert Rose group was a hot-ass good band and he was clearly the leader. And Herb Pedersen is one of my heroes for the work and help he gave Rodney Dillard after brother Doug left The Dillards band to form Dillard and Clark with another former Byrd, Gene Clark. Rodney recruited Herb Pedersen to the band.

"Herb produced *Wheatstraw Suite* and *Copperfields,* two of the best bluegrass albums ever," says Gary.

Regarding John Duffey, Hillman said, "I listened to those first two Country Gentlemen *Folkway* albums. I was struck by their album covers in the record store. They were wearing ties, and it was so logical how they presented themselves as "gentlemen" bluegrass players. I thought these guys are *not* from Kentucky.

"I loved that band. John Duffey was a huge influence on my playing. His mandolin playing was smoking on "Little Bessie." And Tom Gray's basslines are so good on those songs. I was fortunate to play with Tom a few times."

Gary with Rodney Dillard.   © *Oelze*

Hillman said he met Duffey for the first time at the second Birchmere. "He came in and stood in the back with his arms folded. I was in awe. I thought, 'Oh my God. It's John Duffey.' So, I tried to play better.

"When I finished my show, I walked up to Duffey and told him what an inspiration he was to me as a musician. He replied, 'Oh yeah?'

Gary interjects: "I could have told Chris that would be Duffey's attitude because he hated talking about music with anybody."

Herb Pedersen knew John Duffey very well. When the Seldom Scene was looking for material to record for their fourth album, John Duffey wrote a note to Herb to ask if he had any songs to contribute. Herb long admired The Country Gentlemen and was inspired by Eddie Adcock to learn the banjo. Herb offered Duffey a group of songs written by him alone, and with his late wife, Nikki. It was the Seldom Scene's John Starling who received Herb's cassette demo tape. Starling picked his two favorites, "Wait a Minute" (H. Pedersen) and "Old Train" (H. Pedersen, N. Pedersen), and played them for Duffey. John liked both songs, and they appeared on the Scene's next album, *Old Train*. It is "Wait a Minute" that is The Seldom Scene's most famous song, and coincidentally, the song Herb chooses as his best composition.

Chris Hillman, Al Perkins, Bill Bryson, John Jorgenson in the kitchen, 1983. © *Oelze*

In 2015, the Desert Rose Band arrived to find the Birchmere dark from a power outage from a thunderstorm. "We were without power for three days," Gary remembers. "Desert Rose fans were especially disappointed, but imagine how I felt. I lost two sell-out shows. We also canceled Three Dog Night during this outage.

When asked in 2020 if the Birchmere has a power generator, Gary quipped, "We do now."

Chris is still an active musical force, partnering on various recordings and performing live. Hillman's autobiography, *Time Between: My Life as a Byrd, Burrito Brother, and Beyond* (BMG Books) was published in 2020.

Chris Hillman and Herb Pedersen of The Desert Rose Band. © *Oelze*

Chapter 15 – Rock and Roll Time

"LITTLE RICHARD"
THE INTERNATIONAL TREASURE

It was 100 degrees on a hot June Sunday in 2009. The Birchmere staff were waiting for Little Richard's tour bus to arrive. All of a sudden, they see the band come walking from the street, through the parking lot, rolling their bags and carrying their instruments. There were eleven of them. It turns out their inexperienced bus driver had a hard time pulling into the entrance, so Richard said, 'Let the band out' and he and the driver headed back to his hotel.

Richard Wayne Penniman (b. Dec. 5, 1932, Macon, GA)

Nicknamed "The Innovator, the Originator, and the Architect of Rock and Roll," Little Richard sold more than 30 million records and astounded audiences for decades with his flamboyant style and powerful voice. He was also among the very first members of the Rock and Roll Hall of Fame in 1986 with fellow inductees James Brown, Elvis Presley, Sam Cooke,

Fats Domino, Jerry Lee Lewis, Buddy Holly, Ray Charles, and the Everly Brothers.

Little Richard played two dates on June 2009, and the following year. Daryl Davis, a friend since his teen years, was there and remembers, "Richard had a large entourage that included his body guards, family, and friends, and others that did his bidding for him. Richard had been in a serious car accident in 1985. He crashed his sports car and suffered broken ribs and right leg, with head and facial injuries. He was very phobic of hospitals and would not go to get his leg operated on. He had to sit in a certain way so his leg wouldn't hurt. Over time his leg atrophied. He was in much pain. He needed a hip replacement but he wouldn't do it.

"He would ride around in a little motorized scooter, but he also had a wheelchair for tight spaces. He never let the public see him in the wheelchair."

***

Little Richard eventually arrived. John Brinegar escorted him in his wheelchair to the dressing room. At 76, he was in high spirits.

"John, honey, could you get me some tea?" he asked, "And could you bring some sugar, baby?" He unpacked a table full of cosmetic products and began his transformation into the fabulous Little Richard.

He was able to walk into the hall when he took the stage in rhinestones and satin. He announced to the crowd, "Hello, I'm the beautiful Little Richard," and launched into his slew of iconic recordings for 90 minutes. Between songs, he regaled the audience with funny stage patter and anecdotes—eating French fries in Las Vegas with Ann Margaret, for example. He'd frequently goose the delighted audience with a campy "Shut up."

Darryl Davis recalls, "He was able to climb up on top of the piano and dance a few steps. That was his routine." His set included "Good Golly, Miss Molly," "Lucille," "Keep A-Knockin" and "Tutti Frutti." His legendary falsetto "woooo's" and banging staccato piano riffs on the Birchmere grand piano filled the

234

hall, accompanied by an expansive band that featured a hot horn section and two drummers. He had the "big, fat, juicy" ladies (Richard's words) dancing in the aisles.

Richard's two covers that night were Fat's Domino's "Blueberry Hill," and a remarkable version of "Lovesick Blues," the song that propelled Hank Williams to fame."

And then there was more trouble involving the bus driver. "After the show, their tour bus backed over the front of Stephanie's mini-van, one of our servers," John remembers. "Her tire blew."

Little Richard returned four months later for another sold-out show. "He seemed a little frail that second time, "John says. "I saw him without his wig and noticed his thin gray hair. But his spirit and the 'Hi John, babies' were intact, and he seemed happy to be back at the Birchmere. He was still talking very loud. Little Richard always talked loud."

Isaac Donald Everly (b. Feb. 1, 1937, Brownie, KY)

Phillip Jason Everly (b. Jan. 19, 1939, Chicago, IL)

Pete and Maura Kennedy recall a memorable phone call from Gary in 1998. Pete begins: "He called to say "You have to come down and see this. The Everly Brothers are coming by to do three Birchmere shows." We showed up their first night and he put us front and center in the best seats. It took our breath away.

"Gary said that he "got wind that the Everly Brothers were going to Atlantic City to do shows. We put in a bid for three days and they took it. It was their last shows until a 2003 tour with Simon and Garfunkel who *opened* for the brothers on that one." Like the Beatles, Beach Boys, Graham Nash, and countless other musicians, Simon and Garfunkel were influenced by the Everly's' harmonies.

Previously, the Brothers had split up publicly on stage in 1973, with Don smashing a guitar as they exited.

Gary tells a story he heard about the Smothers Brothers meeting them for dinner to try and persuade the Everly's to get back together. "During the discussion, it was Tom and Dick that started fighting with each other. *They* almost broke up."

After 10 years of pursuing solo careers, Don reached out to Phil to reconcile, and they reunited in 1983 for sporadic projects.

Gary explained that they had a big band doing the Atlantic City show that included Albert Lee on guitar, Buddy Emmons on pedal steel, and Procol Harum's Gary Brooker on organ. The Birchmere shows helped them defray the cost of the band. Gary went to visit them backstage. "I thanked them for playing and welcomed them to come back," says Gary. "And then Phil replied, 'Sorry, we don't play clubs.' I was thinking, 'But this IS a club.' But I knew what he meant that they typically didn't book club tours."

In discussing the Everly Brothers, Gary talked with pride about being born in Owensboro, Kentucky, just one hour north of the Everly family's hometown, and meeting father, Ike Everly. "I loved the Everly Brothers. They had already gone to Nashville by the time I started playing guitar with my brother John playing bass. In 1957 we first played publicly with another Kentucky musician Floyd Stewart. I had a '56 sunburst Fender Stratocaster with a big Fender amp. Our first gig was a talent show where we didn't win but the judge of the show was Ike Everly. Ike was influential for his sons and also on introducing the fingerpicking style to a family friend, Merle Travis, also a Kentuckian."

Pete Kennedy adds "The brothers were fans of Bo Diddley, who played in an open G tuning. Don adopted this open tuning that blended well with Phil's regular acoustic guitar tuning."

Scotty, left, with Elvis on his signed poster.

Winfield Scott Moore III (Dec. 27, 1931, Gadsden, TN)

Writer Buzz McClain attended Scotty Moore's only appearance in 2002. Looking back on the show he reports: "What if Elvis Presley's guitar player was in the Stray Cats? That was Tuesday's cognitive dissonance—in a good way—at the Birchmere when pioneering rockabilly picker Scotty Moore joined Stray Cat bassist Lee Rocker for an evening of '50s classics played at a pleasantly blistering pace.

"After an opening 35-minute set of rockabilly guitar pyrotechnics by band members Tara Novick and Brophy Dale, with strong vocals and slap bass by Rocker, Moore, who was with Elvis from the beginning in 1954 to 1968, took the stage to a standing ovation. Age is just a number, and for Moore, who runs a Nashville print shop by day, that number is 70, and he wears it as well as he did his admirably fashionable suit.

"Alternately strumming and thumb-plucking a gorgeous brown Gibson electric guitar—given to him by the late Chet Atkins—Moore ran through the hits "Mystery Train," "That's All Right, Mama," "Blue Moon of Kentucky," "Heartbreak Hotel" and other tunes that are in the universe's musical DNA with eerie precision and calm. His unmistakable tone, all these years later, was ever-present in the mix, whether it was on the familiar solos or simply strumming rhythm.

"For his part, Rocker seemed singularly inspired, laughing as he spun or stood on his upright bass, and sometimes seemingly in awe to be sharing the stage with one of the trailblazers who invented what turned out to be his remarkable rock and roll career.

"The show closed with thunderous applause and another standing ovation, a well-deserved one. Elvis may have left the building, but thankfully, Scotty Moore is still in it."

Perkins onstage and with Rick Frank.   © *Rick Frank*

Carl Lee Perkins (b. April 9, 1932, Tiptonville, TN)

In an HBO tribute film that was never completed, Paul McCartney confessed to Carl Perkins that he and John Lennon used to play Carl's records at a slower speed and write down the lyrics. "See we couldn't understand your accent. But you were an enormous influence on all of the Beatles." They recorded his songs, "Everybody's Trying to Be My Baby," "Matchbox," and "Honey Don't."

Johnny Cash had a number one hit with Perkins' song "Daddy Sang Bass." Elvis Presley went cosmic with his "Blue Suede Shoes."

At Perkins' funeral in 1998, Ricky Skaggs, Wynonna Judd, Garth Brooks, Jerry Lee Lewis, and others paid tribute in word, song, and presence. Sitting quietly by meditating was George Harrison. At the end of the funeral, George, with acoustic guitar, said, "God bless Carl" and performed "Your True Love," the B-side of "Matchbox," issued in January 1957. "Matchbox" was the second record that John Lennon bought at age 16. His first record was Perkin's "Blue Suede Shoes." Paul McCartney claimed that there would be no Beatles without Carl Perkins."

(Courtesy to David McGee, the author of the Carl Perkins biography, *Go, Cat, Go!: The Life and Times of Carl Perkins, the King of Rockabilly* for the above research).

***

Gary Oelze first saw Carl Perkins in 1956: "It was in the Owensboro, Kentucky Coliseum. Johnny Cash was the opening act. Carl Perkins went on second, and the headliner was Johnny Horton. "The Battle of New Orleans," written by Jimmy Driftwood, was Horton's biggest hit song. Horton had a strong rockabilly delivery with many other hits songs, including "Sink the Bismarck" and the theme of the John Wayne film *North To Alaska.*

"When I visited Carl in the dressing room, I asked him, 'Carl. I read many history books on rock and roll. How comes Johnny Horton never gets the credit he seems to deserve?' That was my question.

"Perkins looked at me and replied, 'Gary. Johnny wore a hairpiece. Like I do. When he had his automobile accident, his head went through the windshield, cutting his head off. They found his head, but they never found his toupee.'

"I didn't know what the hell to say to that answer. That wasn't what I asked. But I sort of backed away and thanked him."

Later Gary talked to Rick Frank, a longtime Birchmere patron, and discovered that Rick and Carl chatted for about twenty minutes after Perkin's soundcheck. Carl discussed Sun Studio, singing with Johnny Cash, Jerry Lee Lewis, and Elvis (the Million Dollar quartet) with Carl signing Rick's copy of that album."

Frank says, "When I told Gary how friendly Perkins was, he asked how I got to talk with him. I said, 'You let me in to see his soundcheck.' 'Why did I do that?' Gary asked.

"I still chat with Gary about him letting me in whenever I come to the hall. Gary always asks the same thing, 'Why did I do that?' I don't have any idea, either, but I'm glad it happened."

Dick Dale, "The Father of Heavy Metal."   © *Oelze*

Richard Anthony Monsour (b. May 4, 1937. March 16, 2019)

Dick Dale was first known as "The King of the Surf Guitar" (also the name of his second album) and began developing his staccato guitar picking style to replicate the sound of the waves he surfed in Balboa, California. A senior in high school in 1954 when the California surfing movement was still wearing water wings, he is the pioneer surf guitarist.

His first five Capital records surf albums became national sellers beginning in 1961. Yet, his 1993 tour, which brought him to the Birchmere, was his first tour outside California.

The Beachboys' lead guitarist, Carl Wilson, said he took guitar lessons at age 14 to learn the Dick Dale guitar technique. This technique is almost impossible to learn without knowing one oddity in Dale's guitar method. He's left-handed, but when he began learning the guitar, he used a regular guitar and just flipped it over, so the low E string was on the bottom of the neck with the higher strings on top. With the low E string on the bottom, he used tremolo picking, creating the rumbling roar of waves through his powerful amp using high reverb.

He quit recording after his early albums because he thought his music could only correctly be heard live. Fortunately, he joined Stevie Ray Vaughn on a duet on the surf song "Pipeline" for the soundtrack of *Back to The Beach*, winning them a Grammy nomination in 1989. Dale's last Birchmere appearance was in 2013.

In Dales' 2019 obituary, Stephen Thomas Erlewine wrote in *Pitchfork* about the guitar master who was 81: "Dale's music evokes a specific time and place, one that is embedded in the popular subconscious. That's one of the reasons why Quentin Tarantino chose Dale's "Miserlou," a 1962 adaptation of a traditional Middle Eastern song, to soundtrack the opening credits of his 1994 masterwork film, *Pulp Fiction*. blends muscle and mind, connecting at a gut level while expanding sonic horizons."

(l to r) Bob Bogle, Nokie Edwards, Mel Taylor, and Don Wilson.

© *Oelze*

The Ventures

Appearing nine times between 1998 and 2019 were the famous instrumental group who had hit albums and singles in the 1960s. "Walk Don't Run," and "Hawaii Five-0," and other songs helped The Ventures sell 40 million records. The original group line-up first played the Birchmere in 1998 was **Nole Floyd "Nokie" Edwards** (May 9, 1935, Lahoma, OK) on lead guitar, **Robert Lenard Bogle** (Jan. 16, 1934, Wagoner, OK) on bass, **Mel Taylor** (Sept. 24, 1933, Brooklyn, NY) on drums, and **Don Wilson** on rhythm guitar.

The line-up that played in 2019, celebrating the group's 60th anniversary, included Bob Spalding (lead guitar), his son Ian Spalding (rhythm), Luke Griffin (bass), and Leon Taylor, the son of original drummer Mel Taylor on drums). Birchmere musicians influenced by the Ventures include Stephen Stills, Peter Frampton, Stanley Clarke, and Skunk Baxter.

In a *Washington Post* review of the Ventures at the Birchmere, writer J. Freedom du Lac added: "The Ventures' most significant contribution to pop music was probably their instructional album series, which launched a thousand bands and then some, from Takoma Park to Tokyo."

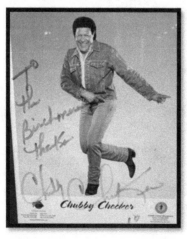

Billed as The Legendary Chubby Checker & the Wildcats.

Ernest Evans (b. Oct. 3, 1941, Spring Gully, SC)

Looking almost identical in his denim jacket to his signed wall poster, Chubby Checker was celebrating the 50th anniversary of the dance he helped popularize, The Twist, at his only show on June 6, 2010. He brought fans up on stage to do the dance as he has been doing since his career took off.

Mr. Checker also jumped around doing other dances, including "Pony Time," "The Fly," and the "The Hucklebuck," a dance with some sexy hip moves he had no problem thrusting.

"Back in the '60s, you couldn't do the Hucklebuck because it was nasty," he told the crowd. "But it's 2010— everything's nasty, so we're going to do it."

Southside Johnny.   © *Oelze*

John Lyon (b. Dec. 14, 1948, Neptune, NJ)

Known as Southside Johnny with his band, the Asbury Jukes, he's played the third Birchmere 32 times since 2005. Southside Johnny talked enthusiastically about his love for the Birchmere, the intimacy and great audiences, adding this memory:

"There are times when you're singing that you get so lost in your soul and feel the communion with the audience and the band that you forget who you are. Your ego falls away, your worries, all the quotidian crap, the day-to-day mundane stuff, and it's like a golden moment where you escape into this other consciousness. I had one of these experiences at the Birchmere early. It was a mind boggling experience. And I really had to climb down from where I was to get the next song started. The Birchmere lends itself to these experiences."

Former Rolling Stones bassist, Bill Wyman, brought his 11-piece Rhythm Kings band in August 2001.

William George Perks (born, October 24,1936, London, UK)

About the retired Rolling Stone's bass player Bill Wyman's 2001 sold-out show, writer Buzz McClain wrote, "Okay, it wasn't only rock-and-roll. There were moments of jump boogie and earthy blues as well. Nor was the evening entirely Stoneless; the Jagger/Richards composition "Melody" found its way into the set.

Former WHFS broadcaster Cerphe Colwell introduced the show and talked backstage with Wyman about "Melody." This song appeared on the Stones' *Black and Blue* album, and Bill told Cerphe that Billy Preston was very important to this song's creation. They also talked about fashion.

The rest of the show was vintage American rock featuring songs by J.J. Cale, Howlin' Wolf, and Dan Hicks and others.

Wyman's back-up musicians included guitarist Albert Lee, Georgie Fame (of the Blue Fames) and Gary Brooker.

(l to r) :Gary Brooker: lead vocals, keyboards; Geoff Whitehorn: guitar, vocals; Geoff Dunn: drums; Matt Pegg: bass, vocals; Josh Phillip: keys.
© *Bill Hanrahan*

And speaking of **Gary Brooker,** he brought a line-up of his progressive rock band, Procol Harum on May 6, 2003. They were supporting their *Wells on Fire* album. Crowd favorites, "Conquistador" and "A Salty Dog" from their first set, with their ten million-seller single, "A Whiter Shade of Pale" ending the show, were well-received.

The band schmoozed with about sixty fans afterward for pictures and autographs. Someone good-naturedly told them about wanting to hear "Whiskey Train" in their set. Drummer Mark Brzezicki began a drumbeat using his glass and their table with Brooker singing a few bars of the song for the smiling crowd.

David John Matthews (b. Jan. 9, 1967, Johannesburg, South Africa)

A few years ago, Gary Oelze received a CD from Dave Matthews. It was *Live Trax vol. 48: The Birchmere*. The liner notes of this six song CD reads: "This intimate acoustic performance from The Birchmere, in Alexandria, VA shows us a very young Dave Matthews and Tim Reynolds showcasing what are relatively new tunes for 1994. As the two settle in, Dave begins to share more info about the songs and this show becomes that much more intimate. Fans will know every song in this set, but we think it'll all sound fresh!"

Back in those days Gary wasn't very concerned with live shows ending up as albums without his involvement. "I thought it was good promotion," he says.

This board tape was made by then Birchmere sound engineer, Billy Wolf, during their show who explains, "I gave Matthews a mixed ADAT tape of the show. One of the tracks I mixed "Dancing Nancies" appeared on the Dave Matthews Band's first release *Under the Table and Dreaming*."

To date this record has been certified 6x platinum, which is six million copies sold.

246

The *San Francisco Chronicle* described **The Avett Brothers** as having the "heavy sadness of Townes Van Zandt, the light pop concision of Buddy Holly, the tuneful jangle of The Beatles, and the raw energy of the Ramones. The brothers played in 2008 and 2009.

Sir Raymond Douglas Davies, CBE (June 21, 1944, Muswell Hill, UK)

The Kinks' leader came to Mt. Vernon Avenue on February 28, 2010 with a 2-hour trip down Muswell Hillbilly Lane. Photographer Michael G. Stewart reported: "After one of the worst winters in metropolitan Washington, D.C.'s recorded history, the audience was badly in need of a sunny afternoon—and that's just what Ray Davies conjured up. From the opening note of "This is Where I Belong," the former Kinks' front man and songwriter invited the crowd to join him for two hours of what became an evening of "Singalong with Ray." Davies and his fellow guitarist, Bill Shanley, moved the crowd through spirited renditions of the Kinks' legendary songbook."

Ray Davies.   © *Michael G. Stewart*

A few other rockers who have played include: 10,000 Maniacs, 38 Special, Average White Band, Badfinger, Barenaked Ladies, Bill Payne, Chris Isaak, Craig Chaquico, Crash Test Dummies, Dave Edmonds, Dion DiMucci, Fabulous Thunderbirds, Felix Cavaliere & Gene Cornish, Foreigner, George Thorogood, Gram Parker, Justin Hayward, Little Feat, Nick Lowe, Marty Balin, Mother's Finest, NRBQ, Rick Danko, Ritchie Blackmore, Sir Douglas Quintet, Steve Hackett, The Commitments, The Pheromones, The Radiators, The Subdudes, and Todd Rundgren.

Chapter 16 – Bluegrass Redux

The Birchmere premiered as a bluegrass music club, and its history evolved into diverse entertainment. Yet, bluegrass continued to play a substantial role in the club's identity through the 1980s.

"One day I happened to be cruising the radio dial. I was about 13 when I heard the sound of a banjo. A five-string banjo. I thought, 'Boy that's a neat sound.' And I started listening to that station. It was Bill Monroe and His Blue Grass Boys that really turned me on—music that caught my ear. And Flatt & Scruggs, Hank Williams, and Carl Smith. The music I'm involved with now.

John Duffey, 1984

Bill Monroe   © *Oelze*

William Smith Monroe (b. Sept. 13, 1911, Rosine, KY)

Gary on Bill Monroe: "I was happy to meet the father of bluegrass. He was a very nice gentleman and a legend. When you think about how he first started in the '30s, traveling to play high schools, with a bass fiddle strapped on the top of a car, and keeping a band together during the depression, writing songs, and he's from Kentucky. He was a legend.

"I enjoyed his shows. He had a faithful audience. Always a good band. There was no cursing or shenanigans around Mr. Monroe. And no drinking. Some of his guys would come around the bar and sneak a beer. Monroe probably knew about that. John Duffey and Ricky Skaggs greatly admired Mr. Monroe.

"Personally, however, I would start the history of bluegrass with Lester Flatt and Earl Scruggs, when they joined Monroe's band. I don't want to get in trouble with the bluegrass theorists. Like I've said before, I wasn't a strong bluegrass fan, but I liked to watch Flatt and Scruggs. Lester had that accent, and Earl with that fabulous five-string banjo. His three-finger picking style became known as "Scruggs banjo picking" and they featured the resonator dobro guitar. They were so entertaining."

Earl Eugene Scruggs (b. Jan. 6, 1924, Cleveland County, NC)

At age 76, Scruggs brought his son, Gary, Marty Stuart on mandolin, Jerry Douglas on dobro, Brad Davis on guitar, Glen Duncan on fiddle, and Harry Stinson on drums to the Birchmere in 2000. He had endured 55 years on the road and sextuple-bypass surgery three years earlier. He explained to music writer Bill Friskics-Warren how his breakthrough banjo finger picking technique was born:

"I was raised with a banjo and a guitar and an autoharp," he remembers. "I came up at a time—we were poor in the country— we didn't have a radio, so everything I did was self-taught. When I was about 10 years old, I was just sitting there daydreaming with the banjo in my hand, and all of a sudden I was doing a three-finger roll, which metered out just fine. I played everything that I knew, and I played it so much until I learned little things to add to it myself."

Earl Scruggs in 2006. © *Oelze*

Gary continues, "That sound they brought to Bill Monroe when they joined his band was bluegrass for me. Earl played the Birchmere several times with his revue band from 2000) until 2006."

The Walk On

Gary will never forget the night Bill Monroe and his band showed up at the Birchmere by surprise. Gary explains, "We had tried to book them for a winter show, but Wolf Trap also had them booked for later in the summer. Wolf Trap felt that our booking would mean fewer ticket sales for their Monroe show, so they leaned on his agents to cancel our Birchmere offer. One night here comes Monroe, after they played Wolf Trap, to play a set for free on our stage."

Ron Thomason's band, Dry Branch Fire Squad, was playing that night. Thomason and the band were sitting in the dressing room chatting when Bill Monroe and his band suddenly walked in.

"It was the one big dressing room," Ron remembers. "They were really quiet, so we quieted down, too. I thought maybe that's what you do when Bill Monroe's around. About a month before, I had written an article—meant to be humorous—called

"Road Warriors, Donut Diet" for *Bluegrass Unlimited* magazine about what bluegrass people should wear on stage.

"Monroe and Ralph Stanley were irritated when bluegrass acts dressed like "hicks," and I understood that culture because I'm from it. Monroe and Stanley came from the old time when the musicians always wanted to wear their best suits. There were sacrifices in that because sometimes you barely made enough money to have a good-looking suit and hat. Even the Seldom Scene, when they first started, had clothes that matched.

"I had written there are going to be many ways to play bluegrass and many ways to dress. If you want to look like you're around the hay bales, then that's OK. We were sitting together in the tranquil dressing room. I heard Wayne Lewis, Bill's guitarist and singer for ten years, whisper to Monroe while pointing to me. He said, 'Bill, that boy wrote your story about how we dress and said nice things about you.'"

"Probably a whole minute passed in silence. Bill stood up and walked over to me, sitting in my chair. He looked down and asked me, "You believe that, don't you?' And that was it.

"He went back and sat down. I realized right there that this was the essence of Bill Monroe. It wasn't what you said or how you played; it was what you believed. I've never forgotten that. It was a signature moment."

Ronald S. Thomason (b. Sept. 5, 1944, Columbus, OH)

The Dry Branch Fire Squad drove from Ohio in their VW bus band van in 1979 for their first show. "And we couldn't find the Birchmere," Thomason remembers.

"We stopped and asked somebody on the street and he pointed up the hill and there were the buildings. But it looked like it was only a one-way street going up to it. We didn't want to be late, so we backed up the hill in our bus. We were pretty bad hillbillies."

Gary: "They told me they had a compass in their van but couldn't figure out if they were driving north or south."

"That's when I first met Gary Oelze," Ron continues. "I had heard about him, literally, from my friend John Duffey. John had described him to me as 'Gary's not exotic, but he is eclectic,' or something like that. But here Gary comes. He didn't introduce himself, but he showed us where to come and put our stuff. And we got to talking.

"I always had a bit of stage fright and it was way worse back then. The thing I'll never forget is that he kind of walked me through it. He probably won't remember this. We knew the Birchmere was a serious place, where we'd have to either shine or go home. And I met his girlfriend, Linda, and she sat with us and encouraged us, 'This is going to be easy for you all,'- she told us. Gary also said words that made us feel assured like, 'Don't get all bent out of shape. People are going to love you here.'

"This was in the days when many of the best bluegrass bands were sharply dressed up. The Dry Branch Fire Squad had brought two matching suits: blue and gray. I asked Gary which color should we wear. Gary replied, 'The audience is really not going to care.' But Duffey warned us, 'Boy, you're going to have to do your best, now!'

(L to R): Dry Branch Fire Squad: Dick Erwin, Ron Thomason, John Baker, and John Hisey.   © *Thomason*

"For this book interview, I've been trying to figure what my real opinion of the Birchmere is. The story of the Birchmere is what's happened there, and my early opinion was that John Duffey and Gary Oelze made each other famous. And that coupling early on was part of Gary's genius. He doesn't remember many of the people that he's helped along the way. And people he has helped in some cases haven't really appreciated it.

"At the second place we once brought Hazel Dickens. While we were unloading, Gary was talking with another band who wanted a spot. Gary didn't have one for them. Their argument was, 'You hired the Dry Branch Fire Squad, and we are a better band than they are.' Gary told them, 'When you get an audience wrapped all around the corner, waiting to get in, then you'll know you're as good as they are.' And it wasn't an ego thing for me. It was like, well, that's really nice to hear.

"The Dry Branch Fire Squad played their 35th anniversary show there in 2011. The only negative things I ever heard about the hall came from musicians that can't get booked there. I've played enough clubs in my life to know that the Birchmere stands alone."

Hazel Jane Dickens (b. June 1, 1925, Montcalm, WV)

Ron Thomason contributed this written remembrance of his friend, Hazel:

Hazel Dickens was the "real McCoy." Born to a "dirt poor" (her words) family in the "slums" (her word) of West Virginia and raised by a bilious coal-miner father who often assaulted his children and got away with it because he also passed himself off a (lay) minister. She learned to love and support her mother at an early age and to understand that women were simply better people than men when it came to the troubles that women endured at that time and in those places. At the height of her career as a singer/songwriter, many men and women from the old-time and bluegrass world often referred to her as "the world's greatest women." The moniker became so prevalent that one woman actually felt like she needed to explain to me that "she's just a woman."

Hazel Dickens and Ron at the first Birchmere,   © *Thomason*

Hazel was uncompromising regarding such things as morals, decency, politics, and courage. When Tough Tony Boyle ran the Coal Miners Union, he stole the miners' Black Lung funds from a Washington, D.C. bank. Joseph Yablonski tried to take the union back to the miners, and Boyle sent men from Kentucky to assassinate Yablonski and his family. The act caused the miners to fear Boyle, and that fear led to miners also fearing their own union.

Hazel took action that the miners would not; she gathered together musicians and took them with her to the coal mines and performed for the miners and their families while literally begging them to take up arms against Boyle. She was often beaten and derided. I was in one of those bands, and I was always scared that we might not get out alive. But Hazel kept it up until Boyle was finally arrested (and Yablonski's son became President of the UMW of A).

It could be said that she always spoke for the down-trodden in her music and her songs. Even though she had little herself. One night she came to the Birchmere "to see" the Dry Branch Fire Squad. She said she had heard of us and wanted to see

255

what the fuss was about. From that time on, she was my dear friend. And I have to say that being that was at times hard work simply because her standards in all things were very high.

In the early 90s, I was picked to give the keynote speech at IBMA. Hazel was there, and when she greeted me, she said, "You're a long way from Honaker, Virginia—nice suit." But the best was yet to come. My speech dealt full force with how I felt that the bluegrass community would never be a viable business until it sought and welcomed into its fold people of color, women, and folks of all types. It was a speech that was liked by many, but that was degraded and ignored by many as well. I told Hazel that I could never have given that speech if not for the friendship that started one evening at the Birchmere.

These are simply vignettes in a life well lived by an extraordinary woman whose name actually appears in songs written by others—a performer who sang in movies and starred in them too as well as wrote songs that were done by significant stars like Dolly Parton and The Seldom Scene, just to name a couple.

And it's relevant to the Birchmere itself: From the start, Gary Oelze provided a venue for every single race, creed, and color of performers without compunction. And that alone no doubt made "better people" of performers lucky enough to play the Birchmere were amazing. You didn't get a sense that there was any animosity between them at all. It was just a really warm night and great, great music.

Charles Otis Waller (b. Jan.19, 1935, Joinerville, TX)

The post-Duffey Country Gentlemen played early Birchmere gigs in the mid-70s. They continued until the passing of one of the finest bluegrass vocalists, Charlie Waller.

Twenty-two days before his death, Charlie Waller gave his final local D.C. performance with his Country Gentlemen at the Birchmere on July 26, 2004. *Washington Post* writer, Richard Harrington, reviewed Waller's show stating, "His smooth, powerful tenor was as unmistakable as ever, his enunciation natural and easy, with every syllable clear and beautiful. Waller's voice was strong, deep and distinctive, without the nasal quality of his predecessors. And beautiful. Some have suggested that had Waller chosen country music over bluegrass; he'd now be talked about in the same breath as George Jones."

Rick Allred, Kent Dowell, Charlie Waller, and Bill Yates.   © *Oelze*

The classic Country Gentlemen reunited at the Birchmere in 1989 for their 30th anniversary. Mike Joyce reviewed the show in the *Washington Post*: "Like most 30-year reunions, musical or otherwise, the Country Gentlemen's performance at the Birchmere Saturday night evoked a lot of memories and laughter. Especially laughter. But then, mandolinist John Duffey can crack up an audience any time he's within hailing distance of a microphone... If getting these songs into gear took some collective memory-jarring, once the band kicked off, say, "Stewball," "Sunrise," "The Spanish Two Step" or "Pallet on Your Floor," all the pieces quickly fell into place. Waller's whiskey-smooth voice, Adcock's jazz-inflected solos, Duffey's decisively crisp attack, Gray's solid underpinning and Aldridge's colorful embellishments."

Charlie's Country Gentlemen played the Birchmere from 1976 until his passing. "It is still a subject of wonder when bluegrass fans and pickers talk of Charlie," said Tom Gray.

"Although his body was failing in his later years, his voice always sounded great, up until the very end."

The "Classic" Country Gentlemen line-up—Waller, Duffey, Adcock and Gray—had parted company in 1969. The Birchmere produced a very successful reunion show, "The Grass of '80" featuring the original line-ups of the Country Gentlemen and Seldom Scene (which meant Dr. John Starling's triumphant return) at Lisner Auditorium. Gary decided he'd try and reunite another amazing early Birchmere bluegrass band, J.D. Crowe and the New South, for this show as well.

Gary runs it down: "The New South line-up was Tony (guitar, vocals), J.D. (banjo), Jerry Douglas (dobro), Ricky Skaggs (fiddle), and Bobby Sloan (bass fiddle). Their 1974 debut album was a top seller for Rounder Records. Both Rice and Skaggs left by the time J.D. and the group started playing the Birchmere. Regular shows with the New South helped the Birchmere immensely. The Lisner concert sold out, and the show was issued on Sugar Hill records as the 1982 double album *Bluegrass: The Greatest Show on Earth*. The "Almost New South" have a whole side of music including an impressive "Fireball." Gary is proud that the song, "Fireball" won a Grammy award. The show reviews called the reunion album "mind-boggling."

John McEuen (b. Dec. 19, 1945, Oakland, CA)

John McEuen was a founding member of the Nitty Gritty Dirt Band, whose 1972 *Will the Circle Be Unbroken* album, a collaboration with the likes of Doc Watson, Roy Acuff, Mother Maybelle Carter and other greats, introduced traditional country and bluegrass music to the Woodstock generation. He is also the man who gave banjo lessons to his high school pal, future comedian and budding musician Steve Martin; years later, he would produce and play on one of Martin's albums. The long list of artists with whom McEuen has performed or recorded reads like a Who's Who of contemporary music.

(Clockwise) John McEuen, Akira Otsuka, and Al Petteway. © *Oelze*

"John McEuen puts on one of the most entertaining one-man shows I have seen at the Birchmere. It was an honor to be asked to join him onstage with Akira," says Al Petteway.

In one of his first shows in 1982, McEuen on acoustic guitar, lit a smoke bomb on stage, did a cartwheel and charged into the audience playing a raucous guitar lead. It was McEuen having some fun.

Claude Russell Bridges (b, April 2, 1942, Lawton, OK)

Leon Russell unexpectedly lent his unique rock persona to the bluegrass genre when he first took the Birchmere stage in 1980. His opening act and backup band was the New Grass Revival. But for those who were familiar with his musical origins, his appearance that night was surprising but his ability to bridge genres wasn't.

Russell was a classically-trained pianist when he discovered rock and roll in 1959. As a former member of the legendary L.A. session musicians known as The Wrecking Crew, Russell played piano on hit recordings by Frank Sinatra, Barbara Streisand, The Beach Boys, George Harrison, the Ronettes, and hundreds more. That's Russell's gospel-tinged acoustic piano on Glen Campbell's "Gentle on my Mind" and Dylan's "Watching the River Flow."

(l-to-r) backstage. With Sam Bush in 1980, and on stage in 2009.

© Oelze

One of Russell's finest compositions, "A Song for You," has been recorded by 200 artists, with his "This Masquerade" covered by another 75 musicians with B.B. King playing Russell's "Hummingbird" on the Birchmere stage. "I was trying to write standards, not hits," Russell said when he was inducted in the Rock and Roll Hall of Fame by Sir Elton John in 2011.

Gary remembers this 1980 phone call from his doorman, Pudge: "He called me at home one afternoon and told me that New Grass Revival had checked in for their gig, and they brought Leon Russell with them. I said, 'Pudge, you don't even know who Leon Russell is. What's he look like?'"

"He's pretty weird looking with long white hair," Pudge replied.

"Sounds like Leon is here," Gary replied.

"Turns out Sam Bush had brought him. Leon liked the New Grass band and was considering taking them out on tour. He sat in the dressing room on the couch, very quiet, and didn't talk much. I recall he was wearing gloves; I suppose to keep his hands warm. I was surprised when he went on stage with them, just playing guitar. He never touched a keyboard. They sang old bluegrass songs. Leon's performance that night was a total surprise to the audience."

The Old Five and Dimer's bass player, Don Fuller, had a daughter named Ersten. Her mother, Wanda and Ersten would sneak in the side door to see acts. Wanda recalls, "Ersten was about four years old when Leon Russell came to play. At some point Leon and Ersten were talking in the dressing room, and he read a book to her."

Ersten remembers, "It was my *Hello Kitty* book, and he signed it."

Sam and Leon. © *Oelze*

Charles Samuel Bush (b. April 13, 1952, Bowling Green, KY)

Sam Bush is a virtuoso mandolinist (and fiddle player), one of the most accomplished alive, and a pioneer of progressive bluegrass. He was inducted into the International Bluegrass Music Association Hall of Fame as a member of New Grass Revival in 2020.

Sam Bush's friend and longtime bass player, Butch Robins played session work on Leon Russell's experimental shift from rock to country music on Leon's 1973 album, *Hank Wilson's Back.*

Russell mentioned to Robins that he was looking for a bluegrass band to tour with and Robins immediately suggested the New Grass Revival and asked Butch to get in touch with the band. Soon after, they were touring together for two years.

Russell would return to the club several times before he passed away in 2016. One atypical 1990 show billed as a one-man solo performance resulted in Russell accompanying himself on an electric keyboard, loudly demonstrating various kinds of synth sampling and electronic technology. Music writer Mike Joyce reported that "had there been a power failure at the Birchmere on Sunday night, some fans no doubt would have considered it a blessing."

In December 1982, the Birchmere held an all-star, two-night benefit to raise money for Sam's medical bills from cancer treatments. Important players who offered support to this benefit include Doc Watson, Del McCoury, Tony Rice, Jerry Douglas, Bela Fleck, Tony Rice, Vassar Clements, J.D. Crowe, Mike Auldridge, and his own Sam Bush Band.

Gary said, "Everyone who worked with Sam offered their support, and many offered Bush jobs playing for them over the years, but his dedication to bluegrass kept him devoted to his own music."

The Superpickers

Much of the work for bluegrass musicians in the '80s came in the sunshine of the ubiquitous festivals. "In the winter, the bluegrass players were practically unemployed," Gary explains, "So I put together these Superpickers shows, with Tony Rice, Jerry Douglas, Mark O'Connor, Vassar Clemens, Mark Schatz, Bela Fleck, and many others. Sam Bush was usually involved. It was Sam who suggested we get this young fiddle player named Alison Krauss. I had never heard of her. She was 14 years old when she first played our stage. Alison says it was when Tony Rice's *Cold on the Shoulder* album was released that she first saw him sing live. That album was hot in 1985."

Sam Bush, Tony Rice, and Bela Fleck. Bela came to the hall in his teens. He tried many innovative styles until he picked his band, Bela Fleck and the Flecktones combining bluegrass and jazz. He has also toured with Chick Corea and Branford Marsalis. © *Oelze*

Vassar Carlton Clements (b. April 28, 1928, Kinard, FL)

Clements, a bluegrass legend who began playing fiddle with Bill Monroe became known as the Father of Hillbilly Jazz, incorporating blues and swing into his music. He played the Birchmere often with the Bluegrass Album band and the Superpickers.

His last album, *Livin' with the Blues,* in 2004 was his only pure blues release, but he lent his swing and hot jazz riffs on recordings with Stéphane Grappelli, Jerry Garcia, Miles Davis band members, David Grisman and even Paul McCartney. He achieved over 200 collaborations with other artists throughout 50-years, and recorded with the Nitty Gritty Dirt Band on 1972's *Will the Circle Be Unbroken.* His wide-ranging projects included appearances in the films *Nashville* and *Welcome to L.A.*

Music writer, Richard Harrington noted a special gig in his *Washington Post* tribute to Vassar Clements upon his death in 2005: "Twenty years ago, Clements shared a truly memorable bill at the Birchmere with the Texas R&B guitarist and fiddler,

Vassar Clements   © *Oelze*

Clarence "Gatemouth" Brown. Both had an aversion to stylistic boundaries, so the night became an astounding and invigorating conversation about American music that embraced the bluegrass of Flatt and Scruggs's "Foggy Mountain Breakdown," the western swing of Bob Wills' "New San Antonio Rose," the galloping jazz of Duke Ellington's "Take the A Train" and more, with Clements and Brown effortlessly weaving in and out of each other's vivid inventions. And at night's end, the biggest smiles belonged to the musicians."

Alison Maria Krauss (b. July 23, 1971, Champagne, IL)

Gary: "The night Alison sang for the first time in 1985 at the Birchmere floored everybody. So, I hired her band, Union Station, and she did early Birchmere shows. A funny story is that she once called me from the road to report her band van had broken down. I told her to get it towed and try and get here as soon as she could. The tow truck arrived pulling the van. We went outside, and when the van door opened, Alison and the band popped out. She told me that the tow truck driver said it was illegal for them to ride back there, but if they kept hidden, it would be OK."

Alison signed with *Rounder* Records in 1986 at the age of 16 and released her debut album, *Too Late To Cry*, with Union

Station as her backup band. Her follow-up Union Station album, *Two Highways*, included a bluegrass version of The Allman Brothers' "Midnight Rider."

Alison Krauss at her 1985 Birchmere debut.   © *Oelze*

In 1988 she sat in with Tony Rice at the Birchmere. Tony was so impressed with Alison that he offered her a spot with him in his band. He told his biographer Tim Stafford, "I didn't know anything about Alison's singing but I liked the way she played the fiddle. She might have had two albums by then. At some point we were backstage, and Mark Schatz said 'play "Cry Darling Cry." I want you to hear Alison sing this'

"She went on stage and sang it into the fiddle mic and that was the only song she sang. There was a child-like quality to it. As good a voice as she had I didn't care about her singing. There was something unique about her fiddle playing and she fit right. There was no rehearsal or anything."

Gary concludes, "Alison was enormously flattered, but declined, telling Tony she had her "own thing going." By 1988, she was featured as a "Special Guest" when Tony played the hall, and by 1990 Alison Krauss, and Union Station was a Birchmere headliner. She returned in 1995 with three Grammy awards and membership in the Grand Ole Opry—the first bluegrass musician to be inducted in 30 years.

As of 2020, she has won 27 Grammy Awards from 42 nominations. She is the most awarded singer and female artist in Grammy history. In 2019, President Donald Trump awarded her the National Medal of Arts and in 2021, She was inducted into the International Bluegrass Hall of Fame.

Dudley Connell (b. Feb. 18, 1956, Scherr, WV),

Raised in Rockville, MD, Connell recalls, "My father played banjo, and my mother sang old-time ballads like *Bury Me Beneath The Willow, Remember Me* and mountain songs by the Bailes Brothers and Blue Sky Boys. He used to talk about all the music he saw, including bluegrass bands at Washington DC's Glen Echo Park. There was also a downtown bar called The Famous, where he saw Jimmy Dean and Scotty Stoneman.

"My life-changing experience with live bluegrass music was in 1974 at Ralph Stanley's Carter Stanley memorial festival in McClure, VA. I was still in high school. I think that's why I got into the traditional stuff so much. I went right from Jimi Hendrix to Carter Stanley in one fell swoop and because they both had that emotional edge that I like. One did it with a banjo, and one did it with an electric guitar."

Connell recalls his first experiences at the Birchmere: "Around 1974, I started listening to bluegrass on WAMU radio, and they had a 'Bluegrass Bulletin Board' segment where I soon learned about the Red Fox Inn and the Birchmere. So, my first time as an audience member at the original place was seeing J.D. Crowe and the New South with Keith Whitley and Jimmy Goudreau. I was utterly blown away. It was smaller than I had anticipated, and you were practically sitting on top of the artists. I was a fledgling musician, and I'd go see the best bluegrass bands pass through there and watch their hands.

"My band, The Johnson Mountain Boys, started developing in 1975, and eventually I approached Gary to give us a shot at playing there. He did and I think we drew 15 people. It was pretty bad but Gary kept plugging us in."

"Gary ran sound for us for years when we started there. So, we asked him if we could do a live recording, and he was cool that Peter Bonta produced it for us. *The Johnson Boys: Live at the Birchmere,* which was released in April 1983 on Rounder Records.

Eddie Stubbs, David McLaughlin, Larry Robbins, and Dudley Connell: The Johnson Mountain Boys. © *Oelze*

"Another early show I remember with the Johnson Mountain Boys was a WAMU fundraiser with the Country Gentlemen. That's where I first met Charlie Waller, Bill Yates, and Doyle Lawson. Again, playing one of the best clubs in the country and definitely the most excellent club in the DC area. This was like winning the brass ring.

"Most of the places that we played were like loud beer joints. Playing the Birchmere was like going to church. There's a certain edginess about that because people really listen, and most of them are pretty knowledgeable about the music. So, if you make a blatant mistake, then it's going to be heard. And that can be a little bit intimidating, but I personally always loved it."

The Johnson Mountain Boys, with Dudley on guitar and lead vocals, included Eddie Stubbs, vocals and fiddle—today the announcer at the Grand Ole Opry, Larry Robbins, bass, David McLaughlin, mandolin, and Richard Underwood on .

Their fourth album in 1984 was *Live at the Birchmere* on Rounder Records.

They played New Year's Eve shows with the Seldom Scene for many years. Their different traditional and newgrass styles complimented each other perfectly.

Joining the Seldom Scene

Dudley remembers: "John Duffey always kind of intimidated me a bit. I was a little afraid of him, but he was nice to me. I liked him, and he was respectful. I saw a notice in *Bluegrass Unlimited* magazine in the summer of 1995 that Mike Auldridge, T. Michael Coleman, and Mundy Klein were leaving the Scene to form their band, Chesapeake. The notice also hinted that the Seldom Scene might be no more which fortunately wasn't accurate. So, I called John about hearing he was dissolving the band. In his sort of sarcastic way, he told me, "We are really not dissolving the band. We're just looking for a new lead singer, guitar player, bass player, baritone singer, bass singer, and dobro player."

Dudley told John, "I'd love to get together with you and sing," and there was complete silence on the other end of the phone. "I thought, oh Jesus, I've stepped over the line. I've committed an error."

Fortunately, Connell sang parts to Duffey's satisfaction and the new Seldom Scene debuted New Year's Eve '95 at the Birchmere with Fred Travers on dobro, Ben Eldridge on banjo, Ronnie Simpkins on bass, John Duffey on mandolin, and Dudley on guitar. Mike Auldridge's band, Chesapeake, and John Starling played also. Dudley remembers being so thankful that he wore baggy pants because his legs were really shaking. "I was so nervous." He admits.

The Seldom Scene took the Birchmere stage with the audience giving them a standing ovation. Dudley looks back and says, "It was the reputation of the club and the band. The audience was applauding the fact that the Seldom Scene was not going to go away."

When the club celebrated 50 years in business in 2016, the *Washington Post* asked artists to explain what's special about Gary's music hall. Chris Eldridge, son of the Seldom

Scene's Ben Eldridge and Grammy-winning guitarist for the Punch Brothers and other solo and collaborative projects, said, "I basically grew up at the Birchmere. I have memories of just hanging out and eating pretzels while Dad was playing. I remember that atmosphere where music was a sacred, serious thing and people came to listen."

Carl Frederick Travers (b. Sept. 29, 1958, District Heights, MD)

One of the reasons the current Seldom Scene line-up continues to capture both the sound and feel of the classic group is due, in part, to Fred Travers' singing, gentle personality, and—most importantly—he learned dobro from Mike Auldridge. Fred grew up listening to country music and had played guitar and drums. But his encounters with Auldridge were a life—and instrument—changing influence. Travers says, "The Allman Brothers, especially the album, *Eat A Peach*, introduced me to Duane Allman's slide guitar.

Dudley Connell and Fred Travers in the dressing room before a 2021 show. Gary joked, "They look like hoboes."   © *S. Moore*

"The Seldom Scene was why my wife, Kyle, and I started going to bluegrass festivals because we followed them around. We were pretty much fanatics. The Scene was the band for me."

Fred described the momentous event that happened when he and Kyle got married: "I was trying to play dobro and her wedding present to me was a lesson with Mike Auldridge. I was just knocked out by it."

"I came to my lesson with three or four pages full of questions and we went through all of them. He was only supposed to be teaching me for an hour. We did enough playing for three hours. He made a tape for me. I practiced for seven months because he gave me so much information. He was the guy who showed me how to do what I do."

Norman L. Blake (b. March 10, 1938, Chattanooga, TN)

Norma Blake ranks among the best flat pickers in traditional American music. Blake was also an early favorite at the Birchmere beginning in 1977. He, with his wife Nancy and vintage 12-fret 1929 Gibson guitar, traveled in an old school bus for 25 years. They'd arrive around 8 am at the Birchmere, go into the green room, and play music together all day long with Nancy on mandolin and vocals. She also sometimes played "hillbilly" cello with her husband. Nancy was a trained classical cellist since childhood. Blake's credits are impressive:

Norman Blake in the dressing room. © Oelze

- Played radio shows in the '50s with the bluegrass band, Dixieland Drifters
- On leave while an Army radio operator in the Panama Canal in 1961, he played on the Lonesome Travelers' *Twelve Shades of Bluegrass*
- Played in *The Johnny Cash Show's* band from the Ryman Auditorium
- Recruited by Kristofferson on Kris's first tour
- Played on Joan Baez's hit song, "The Night They Drove Old Dixie Down."
- Played on Bob Dylan's album, *Nashville Skyline*
- Co-founded the Aeroplane band with John Hartford and Vassar Clements
- Played dobro on "Will the Circle be Unbroken" by Nitty Gritty Dirt Band
- Wrote "Church Street Blues," one of Tony Rice's best recordings
- Played on *Raising Sand* album by Robert Plant and Alison Krauss
- Played on *Oh Brother Where Art Thou?* soundtrack album

The first time Blake walked into the present Birchmere, Gary asked him what he thought. "It looks like it will hold a lot of hay," Blake replied.

One of Norman's best Birchmere shows was a 22-song, 2-hour set with pickin' pal Tony Rice in 1999. They pleased the crowd with Civil War and railroad songs and selections from their second duo album, *2: Norman Blake and Tony Rice* (Rounder records).

Hot Rize

Hot Rize with Pete Wernick on banjo, Tim O'Brien on fiddle and Nick Forster's electric bass, along with their comedic alter-ego, "Red Knuckles and the Trailblazers," were Birchmere bluegrass favorites. In fact, both bands were comprised of the same people but they evolved into two different bands with different personas and instrumentations that played the same gig.

Hot Rize signed poster and Peter Wernick with Stephen Moore.
© *G. T. Keplinger*

However, Gary recalls that one of their first shows in 1978 didn't draw well: "The band was disappointed but as they left, I told them 'We'll see you next time.' The band thought 'Yeah, sure.' However, their small audience loved them, and I felt like each member in the audience was going to tell a friend how great they were, and the next show would draw better."

Known as Dr. Banjo, Wernick is much admired for his contributions to bluegrass music in addition to Hot Rize. He is a teacher, author, and served a long term as President of the International Bluegrass Music Association.

Pete recalls, "It was the very beginning of our band, and nobody knew Hot Rize was going to be anything important, including us. And so being accepted by Gary who booked all these well-known acts like the Seldom Scene made us feel like, wow, okay, we passed the test. We were from Colorado, and one of the best signs back then that you're on your way was that Gary Oelze likes you. Gary for us was a prince, you know, we just thought, what better ally could we have?

"A friend also introduced us to the Scene's Ben Eldridge then. Ben explained to us that John Duffey was a really sweet guy and wasn't as scary as he might have appeared on stage. That was sort of interesting to know."

When Hot Rize played the hall in 2017, they earned their 39-year run status.

Ralph Edmund Stanley (b. Feb. 25, 1927, McClure, VA).

"The Lord gave me a gift," is how 87-year-old Dr. Ralph Stanley summed up his success in the dressing room before a 2014 Birchmere show. One of his first Birchmere gigs was in 1984, promoting a new gospel bluegrass album, *Child of the King.*

In a *Washington Post* review of this album, Richard Harrington said, "There are many songs about death (and dying mothers, in particular), but dying is always seen as a bridge between this life and a better one. Meantime, Ralph Stanley's music makes the stay on this side that much better."

Stanley got his start in 1946 singing and playing the banjo in the Clinch Mountain Boys with his elder guitar-playing brother Carter. Their mother had eleven brothers and sisters, and all of them could play the banjo.

Dr. Ralph Stanley   © *Oelze*

The 2000 movie, *Oh Brother Where Art Thou,* brought Ralph a Grammy for his work on the soundtrack, and provided the fame and fortune he never achieved with brother Carter, although both are in the International Bluegrass Music Hall of Fame.

"That movie was a lot bigger than I thought it would be," Ralph told Kyle Osborne in 2014. "It definitely put me on the map." He also admitted he liked playing the Birchmere, adding, "Many years ago, I used to play here every Saturday night." That's a wild exaggeration, but his yearly shows may have seemed like a second Virginia home to Dr. Stanley.

Gary remembers: "Curly Ray Klein would play fiddle for Ralph, and once he was screaming in the microphone trying to get the crowd going, or so he thought. I asked Pudge to go up and tell him that the next time he yells at the audience I was going to turn his microphone off."

Curly Ray came to Gary and said, "Look, I disagree with you but it's your place. I was just trying to get the audience into the music." Gary replied, "Look, the audience is already into the music. That's why they come to the Birchmere."

On another show, Gary noticed that Stanley had brought a young musician that he wanted to promote and he was holding back to let the youngster sing. "After the first set, I went to Ralph and told him that the crowd came to see Ralph Stanley, not this kid. Ralph was fine with going back out on stage to give the crowd what they came to hear."

Ray Benson Seifert, (b. March 16, 1951, Philadelphia, PA)

Ray Benson celebrated the 50th anniversary of his band, Asleep at the Wheel in 2021. Although Ray formed the band in Paw Paw, West Virginia, it was opening for Hot Tuna and new-comer Alice Cooper and at an outdoor concert in downtown Washington, DC on August 25, 1970 that would be the band's first gig.

Ray and the band became working musicians playing around the country and in most of the DC clubs including the Emergency, Cellar Door, and the Bayou. He knew Nils, Emmylou, Danny Gatton, the Claude Jones Band and other musicians playing the DC stages in the '70s.

"I'm six foot ten wearing a cowboy hat and I played that first tiny Birchmere joint with the little overhang above the stage. I

© *R. Benson*

almost couldn't fit on that dang stage. By then it seemed that most club owners were pretty sleazy and disgustingly dishonest or incompetent, one of the two.

"So here comes Gary, where the deal you made with him was the deal you got. That's important. And the quality of music they presented. Asleep at the Wheel plays whatever we can within this weird Western swing format. And Gary had jazz, folk and rock acts, and some legendary folks who were no longer in prime doing incredible stuff. That's why we wanted to be there."

Ray was in college in West Virginia when Bill Kirchen came there and performed. "Bill was one of my first guitar influences. Absolutely a mentor. And then we became great friends."

Asleep at the Wheel, based in Austin, Texas since the '70s, counts ten Grammys among their many awards, and continues to bring their trademark Texas country/Western swing music to devoted fans.

Jamieson "Junior" Brown (b. June 12, 1952, Cottonwood, AZ)

"I do a wide variety of music," says Junior Brown. "A delicious mixed-up stew is how I describe it." The country guitarist and singer got his start playing with Asleep at the Wheel and as a solo artist, first charted with "Highway Patrol" and "My Wife Thinks Your Dead" from his 1993 album, *Guit With It.*"

He was one of the first players to return to the Birchmere when it reopened after the pandemic shut it down. "COVID is a lot like country music," Brown joked, "Just when you think it can't get any worse."

Junior Brown with his guit-steel double neck guitar.   © *Oelze*

He designed his "guit-steel" instrument, a combination six-string guitar and steel laptop, and named it Old Yeller. "Michael Stevens built it and one I use now. I can switch from guitar to the steel and play leads." Stevens was the Founder and Chief Designer of The Fender Custom shop.

"The Birchmere has always been good for me because the audiences are all political persuasions and ages and well-suited for the wide variety of music I play. I hope Gary can keep it going," says Brown, who has played the third hall 20 times.

Arthel Lane Watson (b. March 3, 1923, Deep Gap, NC).

"If you call me Mister, I won't talk with you. Just call me Doc," Watson, the 88-year-old legend said in 2011, his last show at the Birchmere. "I earned a living. Everybody does. My talent did it for me, and I didn't invent the talent. The old boy who sits above and watches over us. And to have people who really like you, it is like if I was a carpenter, and you needed me to build a house. I'd get the same feeling if I pleased you."

Audiences responded to Watson's downhome, soulful vocals and deft flatpicking on a wide repertoire of songs from Jimmy Rogers to Little Richard, always astonishing with rapid, clear and often ingenious technique.

(clockwise) T. Michael Coleman and Doc. In dressing room. With Gary. With Jerry Jeff Walker. With Tony Rice.   © *Oelze*

T. Michael Coleman was Doc's bass player: "My association with the Birchmere is three-fold, playing there with Doc Watson and becoming a member of the Seldom Scene and Chesapeake. Instantly we felt at home when we walked in the back door for the first time with our guitars and were greeted by Gary, Linda and Pudge. You would have thought we had been friends for years. I'm positive this was the result of Doc's disarming presence on and off stage. People, including strangers, felt as though they knew him and felt comfortable around him.

"When I decided to leave touring with Doc and join the Seldom Scene, the transition was made easier because I felt so at ease with my new home being the Birchmere... The same courtesy afforded Doc was given to the Scene. Always there with a request for beverages, food and assistance. Gary also was supportive of the Seldom Scene offshoot, Chesapeake, and offered us our first coming-out performance on a New Year's Eve."

Debi Smith toured with Doc Watson, his son Merle and T. Mike. Everybody adored Doc Watson," Smith says, "except the cigarette smokers. Doc absolutely did not want to smell any smoke anywhere. "No smoking" was an absolute rule everywhere in the Birchmere when Doc was around."

***

Tim Finch has been a familiar face on the bluegrass music scene through past performances with his Good Deale Bluegrass band at the hall, often opening for the Seldom Scene. Mike Auldridge played with his band. Today **Savanna Finch** provides lead vocals, harmonies, and original songs for their Eastman String Band.

Chapter 17 – Heart & Soul

One of the Birchmere's secret weapons is K.C. Alexandria. "K.C. is very knowledgeable in all types of music and in charge of operations," says Gary.

At a 2021 show by Wynonna Judd, K.C. suggested she and her band do Lynyrd Skynyrd's "Free Bird" as a second encore song. Returning to stage, Wynonna thanked K.C. for this suggestion and sang it. The next day she phoned sound engineer Bud Gardner and asked him how she could hire K.C.

K.C. with Wynonna Judd in 2021.   © *Oelze*

K.C. was born in Alexandria, VA in 1961. Growing up in a family that appreciated music, he is a multi-instrumentalist who performed in bands in his teens and twenties and can play seven instruments: guitar, bass, flute, harmonica, drums and a few percussion instruments. How K.C. became a Birchmere employee: "I'd drive by the Birchmere sign and either never recognized the people playing there or when I did, they were acts like Ray Charles who were not in my circle of younger R&B

groups. And then one day I saw that Babyface Edmonds was playing, and I thought 'Whoa.'

"I drove into the parking lot and met Gary and John Brinegar outside smoking. They invited me to come in and watch the shows outside the hall in the bar area on the TV screens and that's what I did. The first act I saw in person was the Average White Band. Eventually Gary hired me in 2014 as a stagehand helping acts load in, and I learned operations.

Allen Gorrie and Onnie McIntre, original members of the Average White Band with K.C.   © *Oelze*

K.C. became friends over the years with many acts that have played the hall in the category he calls "grown and sexy." Examples are Boyz II Men, Will Downing, Stephanie Mills, Chanté Moore, Rachelle Ferrell, and many other adult contemporary R&B acts. "The ones coming out of the WHUR "Quiet Storm" radio camp for the 35 years and older R&B fans," he explains.

Eulaulah Donyll Hathaway (born Dec.16, 1968, Chicago, IL)

Lalah Hathaway is the daughter of the late soul singer Donny Hathaway, who had come to Washington DC to study music at Howard University. He met another Washingtonian musician and fellow Howard student Roberta Flack and they recorded together. "Where is the Love" is one of their finest songs. Donny, who struggled with depression, died tragically young at 33 years old when he fell from his 15th floor hotel room in New York City. The Whispers composed a tribute "Song for Donny" in 1979.

In 1991, his daughter Lalah, with saxophonist Gerald Albright, and keyboardist Joe Sample, played two sold-out R&B/light jazz shows at the Birchmere. Michael Jaworek cites this show as a pivotal event for the hall.

The Washington Post's Mike Joyce wrote about her performance: "The daughter of the late Donny Hathaway displayed a big, sultry voice, plenty of poise and often improved upon the recorded versions of the songs she drew from her debut album, relying occasionally on support from Albright."

Lalah has returned annually to the hall since then. Both Sample and Lalah Hathaway later collaborated in 1999 on the successful album *The Song Lives On.*

Lalah's signed poster and with K.C.   © *Oelze*

K.C.'s Credo

"You treat people the way you want to be treated. And when musicians come to the hall, I welcome them. When they return, I welcome them *back home.* They all get treated the same way. I don't care if they are Chaka Khan, or Larry from around the corner. Everyone gets the same respect. I've had musicians tell me, "My God. We don't get treated this well at other places," but I give them what Gary calls "the Birchmere experience."

The 2021 list of Be'la Dona players are Sweet Cherie (Keys/Vocals) Karis Hill (MC/Vocals), Ashley Brown (vocals) Chella (vocals) Shannon Browne (Drums), Tempest "Storm" Thomas (Bass), Claudia "Kool Keys" Rodgers (keys), and Natarsha Proctor (percussion). © *K.C. Alexandria*

Be'la Dona is an all-female 'grown and sexy' go-go band," states K.C. The father of go-go, Chuck Brown had played the hall in the '90s, but it was the Eva Cassidy's show doing her album, *The Other Side.* Those songs were jazz and blues standards and not Chuck's typical funk go-go music. He returned to the hall mere as a guest star with Kindred Family Soul in 2011. Eva was powerful local singer with an angel's voice. She died very young of cancer.

"There have been jazz and R&B bands here that have played go-go music, but Be'la Dona is now in the forefront of the grown and sexy movement," states K.C. "When Gary heard them in 2021, he immediately booked them for two future shows. That was a power move by Gary."

Be'la Dona opened the door in June 2021 for other go-go bands to be considered for bookings. Following them in August was Experience Unlimited's Sugar Bear.

Gregory "Sugar Bear" Elliot is known by his T.C. Williams high school students as a beloved special education teacher. To his fans worldwide, he is lead singer and bassist for the Experience Unlimited, and one of the founders of the go-go music genre.

K.C. Alexandria says: "Over 50 years in the business, his band E.U.'s song "Da Butt" is the most well-known go-go song in the world. Loved and respected by the entire District-

Maryland-Virgina area and beyond. Sugar Bear is a living icon. Grammy nominated and *Soul Train* award winning musician! It was his first performance at The Birchmere with his band and he thanked Gary profusely for allowing him to share his gift with patrons."

Gary with Gregory "Sugar Bear" Elliott. © K.C. Alexandria

Maceo Parker (b. Feb. 14, 1943, Kinston, NC)

Two of K.C.'s all-time favorite Birchmere performers is Maceo Parker, who was James Brown's legendary saxophonist, and Larry Graham, who defined the slap bass technique during his stint in Sly and Family Stone and went on to front his own band, Graham Central Station.

"Maceo was James Brown go-to man, hype man (call and response), and is featured in many songs by Brown throughout the '60s and '70s like "Cold Sweat" and "Sex Machine." He was a humble man when I talked with him and just so appreciative of still being able to play," says K.C. He came aboard the Mothership Connection with Parliament-Funkadelic, and joined as collaborator with Prince in 1999. He blew the sax on recordings by Keith Richards, Bryan Ferry, Living Color, Dave Matthews Band, Red Hot Chili Peppers, Jane's Addiction and De La Soul.

Maceo Parker and Larry Graham.   © Oelze

"Maceo was James Brown go-to man, hype man (call and response), and is featured in many songs by Brown throughout the '60s and '70s like "Cold Sweat" and "Sex Machine." He was a humble man when I talked with him and just so appreciative of still being able to play," says K.C. He came aboard the Mothership Connection with Parliament-Funkadelic, and joined as collaborator with Prince in 1999. He blew the sax on recordings by Keith Richards, Bryan Ferry, Living Color, Dave Matthews Band, Red Hot Chili Peppers, Jane's Addiction and De La Soul.

Larry Graham Jr. (b. Aug. 14, 1946, Beaumont, TX)

K.C. says, "Larry is a deeply spiritual man. His love of people resonates throughout his shows. I worked several with him, the last being in 2017. He is the only performer who together with his–band enters the hall "Mardi Gras" style. The house goes dark. He is announced, and he and the band enter from the front doors and march down the aisles playing percussion. A fellow R&B/soul artist and Birchmere regular Jeffrey Osborne also enters from the front of the house, but by himself."

Evelyn Marie Harris, Louise Robinson, Nitanju Bolade Casel, Alisha Kahil and vocalist/interpreter Shirley Childress Saxton (seated).

© *Oelze*

The famed acapella group, **Sweet Honey in the Rock**, has been a mainstay on the Birchmere calendar for decades. Founded in 1973, "Sweet Honey" travels the globe, performing music rooted in the gospel music, spirituals, and hymns of the African American church. Founder Bernice Johnson Reagan retired in 2004 and in a message to the group's followers she wrote, "Now that I've come to the end of the 30 years of creating the work that has become Sweet Honey In The Rock, I look back in wonder at the journey of this last year where as we celebrated three decades of creating wonderful powerful music. We also took up the challenging work of making a way for Sweet Honey to continue as I stepped down as leader and singer in this incredible community of African American singers and extended family"

From the Birchmere dressing room in 2015 Sweet Honey vocalist Louise Robinson told Kyle Osborne: "In the African-America history, music has been a part of our healing and our survival and our expression. The music we are doing is an amalgam of so many different traditions and conversations about life and light and giving and particularly, love. And we do hope that our music offers hope to those who listen.

"What is so good about the Birchmere is that we live in the area. We have families and friends here. It's like going home."

Maysa Leak (b. Aug. 17, 1966, Baltimore, MD

Maysa is a contemporary jazz and R&B vocalist who first gained recognition as a member of her alma mater, Morgan State University choir while pursuing her degree in classical performance. Passionate ballads, jazzy funk with a rich contralto voice is part of Maysa's recipe of talent. She tells her story:

"My best friend was singing background in Stevie Wonder's female backup group, Wonderlove. She got me an audition with him, and he asked me to join his group. I had a year left at college so I asked Stevie if it was possible if I could finish my degree and then come to California and work with him. All my friends thought I was absolutely crazy. Like, how are you going to tell Stevie Wonder when you're coming to work for him? But he was really cool and very sweet and said, 'Sure. Come out to Los Angeles next year when you finished. So, I did and got to sing background on the music for the *Jungle Fever* film he did.

"Stevie is such a nice man. He's a jokester and prankster and very funny. My experience with him was fantastic. I also taught voice in California. Steve Harvey, the producer, was looking for a new American singer to front a band named Incognito. He asked Stevie to name the singer in his Wonderlove group that he'd leave his kids with, and Stevie picked me. I had no idea that Incognito was a jazz-funk soul group.

"I moved to London and sang with Incognito for four and a half years straight. We played the whole world four or five times a year. And Australia, Budapest, and Eastern Europe, and finally the US.

"Will Downing and Phil Perry were friends who played the Birchmere, so I was excited when I found out Incognito was going there, too. This is as close as we got to my old Baltimore home.

"I started my solo career in 1991. I wasn't able to get any Birchmere gigs for a while, and I got upset when they wouldn't hire me. I think Michael Jaworek didn't believe I could bring in 500 people. But I knew I could.

"He finally gave me a chance when I did my solo album, *A Woman in Love* in 2010. I also rejoined Incognito, so I was able to play both solo and with the band for the past 25 years.

"I'm always excited to play there because I know I'm just going to sound good."

Maysa had played the hall over 20 times as a solo artist and 7 times with Incognito.

K.C. with Maysa   © *Oelze*

The Whispers

Beginning in the early 1960s, the original members of the Whispers were identical brothers Wallace and Walter Scott, along with Gordy Harmon, Marcus Hutson, and Nicholas Caldwell. Today it is Wallace and Walter with Leaveil Degree, a founding member of the Friends of Distinction, who play the hall as the Whispers with a solid eight-piece band of seasoned sidemen. It's a party every time they begin their show with the shout "Put your hands together like you don't care." It is also a show where R&B history transcends nostalgia.

The group has scored 15 Top Ten R&B singles including their best-known songs "And the Beat Goes On" (1980) and "Rock Steady" (1987). Their *Love is Where You Find It* album reached number one in 1982. They've turned the hall into a soulful groove party 16 times.

The Whispers spoke in 2020 about playing the hall. Walter Scott said, "From the first time we played the Birchmere, it became one of our favorite places because it reminded us of our early days where the atmosphere is so congenial. Everybody's so close."

Scott, Leaveil, and Wallace   © Oelze

Leaveil adds, "You really can't see the eyes of people in the bigger venues. At the Birchmere you can actually see the audience's faces. You can see their smiles. You can feel their energy and they give it back to you. We've played some of the big jazz festivals where it was 40,000 people there. It's nice because you have that volume of people, but the intimacy you lose. At the Birchmere any one of us can walk out into the audience if we want to. We can leave the stage, literally walked back to the back of the club and walk back up on stage. That's how great it is. That's what makes it so unique."

Scott reminded Walter and Leaveil what they left out: "And the Birchmere has the greatest food in the country. Theirs is a menu that is not to be messed with. When you add the food to the club, then it don't get much better than that."

Jimmy Hayes, Jayotis Washington, Herbert (Toubo) Rhoad, and Jerry Lawson. © *Oelze*

The Persuasions

The acclaimed a cappella group, first appeared at the Birchmere in the '80s and played regularly for 20 years. Original members Herbert "Toubo" Rhoad, "Sweet" Joe Russell, James Caldon Hayes, Jayotis Washington, and Jerry Lawson perfected their five-part harmonies singing on Brooklyn street corners and subway stations in the early 60s; the group recorded over 23 albums. Frank Zappa gets credit for getting them their first recording contract and that relationship led to the group opening for The Mothers of Invention for a time.

The Birchmere has also been very successful in producing shows that feature artists who can fill many more than 500 seats. The eclectic list of recent outside shows at Constitution Hall, Warner Theatre, and the Strathmore include Chaka Khan, Gladys Knight, Ledisi, India Arie, Patti LaBelle, Preacher Lawson, Mint Condition, Smokey Robinson, Frankie Valli, Colin Hay, Scott Bradley, Preacher Lawson, Youssou N'Dour, and Pentatonix.

The Birchmere presented Chaka Khan at the Warner Theatre in 2019.

Isaak Hayes   **Neville Brothers**

War, The Manhattans, Teena Marie, and Joe Sample with Lalah

K.C.   *© S. Moore*

Chapter 18 – Moose, Pudge, Fly, and Shoe

Gary had help from some big talent in the Birchmere's early days that did not play music. The first clubgoers remember the loveable "Moose," an ex-Marine from Pennsylvania that Gary hired to greet the growing crowds at the door and keep the troublemakers out.

The mighty and gentle Moose. © Oelze

Early clubgoers could not recall Moose's formal name for this history. "*Moose had a real name?*" was one response. "He was a great patron that I liked and hired to help me," Gary says. "His name was Paul Keeler, as printed on a county alcohol permit on the back of the kitchen door, which few patrons saw."

Not simply a bouncer, Moose adhered to local safety ordinances... mostly. "We seated 150 legally at the first location but allowed 200 to enter on most nights," Gary admits. "Moose would hold the door as soon as we were full. And at the end of the night when the music was over, he'd tell them, 'You don't have to go home, but you can't stay here.'"

One typically crowded evening, Moose was working the door when an undercover Arlington police detective arrived. But he did not identify himself. "Sorry, we're full. I can't let you in," Moose told him.

"Well, you'll let *me* in," the detective insisted. Moose called Gary to the door via intercom. The detective then shoved a badge in Gary's face, claiming that he was casing "somebody in your joint" and asked to talk privately.

Gary walked him to the back room, where the detective proceeded to accuse the Birchmere of "blowing his cover" because he was "forced to reveal his identity."

"Look, you know me because I eat lunch here sometimes," yelled the detective. "I don't know who the hell you are," Gary replied, and asked him to leave.

It was true that many Arlington county police and firefighters ate lunch regularly there. Gary was on a first-name basis with most of them. They were also aware the Birchmere never had any police calls at night for fights or other trouble.

"The furious detective returned to his car and made some kind of 'all alert, officer in trouble' call. About six police cars pulled into the parking lot," Gary remembers.

"What's up?" the police asked the detective.

"I want to bust the owner," he fumed.

"Who? Gary?" The Birchmere?"

The police just shook their heads, got into their cars, and left.

Burning Mattress Beer Party

Moose was dependable for fun at the club, if not always for safety. Moose had a mattress in the basement, underneath the kitchen, where he would catch an afternoon nap. One time he left a burning cigarette in his hideaway and came upstairs for the evening shift. Shortly after 6:00 p.m., the Birchmere doors opened, and soon the place was packed.

The cooks discovered his smoldering mattress when smoke began to emerge from under the basement door. Two fire trucks arrived, and Moose helped the firemen pull the smoking mattress up to the backyard to extinguish it

Gary commended the amiable doorman for saving the moment, "I then saw pitchers of beer going out the door and followed them. Outside I saw Moose and the firemen standing around the mattress having a beer party. Meanwhile, the audience enjoyed the show.

"Unfortunately, it's the nature of this business when too much drinking becomes an issue. Moose always kept a half glass of beer hidden under the counter or somewhere else. I often gave him crap about drinking on the job. His answer was always, 'But Gary, I haven't had a whole beer all day.'"

Although Moose had a drinking problem, he was never sloppy at work or rude. Everyone generally loved him for his friendly, warm welcome at the door for the Birchmere's regular patrons. However, his health eventually declined. Gary took him to an emergency room one night when Moose experienced breathing problems. While they were in the ER, Moose's heart stopped.

"The doctor seemed annoyed *with me* because Moose was an alcoholic," Gary recalls. "We finally put Moose on a bus to a Pennsylvania VA hospital for treatment. Very sadly, this was the last time we saw him.

Changing of the Guards

The Birchmere was a lively club and Moose was not easy to replace. Luckily, Gary eventually came across another big bluegrass fan. By day Takoma Park, Maryland native William Edwin Tarbett Jr. was a refrigeration mechanic. Today his wife, Peggy Mai, says, "His nickname was Pudge (pronounced Pudgie) and he was a workaholic who wasn't happy unless he was occupied. He was also the guy who never met anyone he didn't like."

Peggy distinctly recalls her first visit to the music hall. "One day Pudge came home and said, 'We're going out tonight to a bluegrass bar to see the Seldom Scene.' I wasn't a bluegrass fan, but I became one that night. We both became Birchmere regulars after that.

Pudge and Peggy.   © *C. B. Smith*

Soon after, Gary hired the hard-working Pudge as Moose's replacement. Pudge woke at 4 am for his fridge repair work. During the evening, he would watch the door and keep the peace. It was usually after midnight when Pudge headed home. One night he left unusually late. While he sat quietly on the side of his bed, taking off his pants, Peggy woke up. She asked if he was just getting home. Pudge said, "No, I'm just waking up." He pulled his pants back on and went off, sleepless, to his day job.

Seeming unstoppable, Gary described the affable and capable doorman Pudge as someone "who didn't sleep. He lived on McDonald's food and gallons of coffee. He'd drink beer, but drinking wasn't a problem on the job. Pudge got along very well with the acts, especially Birchmere's esteemed Jerry Jeff Walker."

"Once Jerry Jeff asked Pudge to drive him to Silver Spring, Maryland to see a friend. They packed a case of beer in Pudge's truck, and on their way through DC, took a long "pee break " somewhere near the Washington Monument grounds." Gary's understanding is that they finished the beer before they got to Silver Spring.

Pete Kennedy recalled Pudge's special sense of fairness working the door: "The great thing about Pudge was that he treated everybody equally. It was not uncommon to see a major label type from LA or NYC pleading with him at the front door for special treatment, like a front table or something: 'Don't you know that I am *someone* (insert celebrity/manager/agent name).

"Pudge didn't know, and he didn't care. Sometimes Gary would come over to the door and rescue the hapless industry type. But not infrequently, he would turn a blind eye and chuckle while they tried in vain to squirm their way past Pudge. Pretension was not suffered at that venue! Everybody had to wait for a table and keep quiet during the show, or they would reencounter Pudge.

"The Birchmere policy was 'check your ego at the door.' In the hierarchal 1980s world of rock celebrity, it was an oasis where the music was all that mattered, and the inflated egos of stardom were quickly deflated. It was all about the songs."

Hot Rize's banjo player, Pete Wernick, says, "Pudge didn't look especially rough and tough. He was just a sweetheart, nice guy. But if a table was responsible for a lot of sound and chatter, then Pudge would give it a visit. He'd say, 'If I have to come back again, then you're gone.' It was well understood that Pudge meant it."

Pudge's wife Peggy later joined the Birchmere wait staff to free her to take care of their granddaughter during the day. "It was very much a family vibe at the second Birchmere," says Peggy. "Gary ran the place while his wife Linda was the greeter, head waitress, and made sure all the acts were comfortable and happy. Pudge was Gary's right-hand guy, fixing things and helping everyone." Dedicated, congenial staff like Moose, Pudge, and Peggy made it easy for the Birchmere to seem like a second home.

Pudge with Birchmere waitresses (l to r) Terry Mayo, Mary Beth Aungier; Perrie Spaulding (Allen), Kim Fulford, Sesi Warnock, Connie Brandt Smith, Linda Oelze, Carrie Oelze, with Pudge in the center.
© C. B. Smith

On one typically packed night at the Birchmere in 1992 while Telecaster master Danny Gatton performed onstage, Pudge was talking on the kitchen telephone. Gary was standing nearby. Suddenly, Pudge hurled backward against the wall like he was shot. Gary grabbed him, and they both crashed to the floor together.

"It was a massive heart attack," says Gary. "This attack was completely unexpected, although Pudge had a family history of heart problems. Pudge didn't say a word, and as it turned out, he would take his last breath in my arms," Gary sadly recalls.

Gary ran to the mic on stage and urgently asked: "Is there a doctor in the house?" There were two. They tried unsuccessfully to resuscitate Pudge. Someone called 911, and soon the ambulance arrived.

A few minutes later, the paramedic called Gary aside and quietly informed him that Pudge was dead. He was only 53 years old.

The paramedic also told Gary, "If I pronounce him dead here, then you'll have to close the place for an investigation, but I can pronounce him dead on the way to the hospital."

Perhaps an illustration of a different time—and world—back then, but this responder's willingness to bend procedures to accommodate the Birchmere demonstrates Gary's rapport with local emergency services.

Pudge kept a guitar backstage during his occasional daytime breaks. Peggy was not aware he had the instrument; she learned about it when someone told her that Danny Gatton had quietly played it alone the night Pudge died. Peggy gave the guitar to Danny.

The death of Pudge was a painful loss for the Birchmere community. Peggy says, "Gary helped me with the funeral arrangements and was completely by my side the whole way. I warned the funeral staff that we expected a sizeable crowd of mourners at the service. They assured me they had experience with "community leaders" who had died. However, they were not quite prepared for the outpouring from mourners. Nearly the entire line-up of performers at the nearby Gettysburg Bluegrass Festival came to the service, and numerous other celebrities, including John Jennings and Mary Chapin Carpenter."

Mary Chapin dedicated a song, "Halley Came to Jackson," to the memory of Pudge at her Wolf Trap concert later that year. John Duffey, who "didn't do funerals," appeared outside the door of the funeral home that day to honor Pudge. Another special friend, Jerry Jeff Walker, sang at Pudge's eulogy.

On Patrol

When crime began to escalate on Mt. Vernon Avenue, with as many as three-car break-ins a night, Gary began personally patrolling the parking lot several times during each show to protect his patrons' cars.

Gary recounts a disquieting encounter, "I got a heavy-duty security flashlight and a concealed carry permit for a .38 revolver. One night, I stepped out of the Birchmere's back door and saw a guy had broken a car window and was leaning inside the car. I grabbed him by the back of the neck. He drew back on me, and I cracked him in the head with the flashlight. Blood started shooting straight up from his head. I opened the back door of the club and threw him in and constrained him. I asked Pudge to call the police."

When police arrived one of the cops joked to Gary, "Well, nobody has ever delivered us a package like this before." This incident led to Alexandria police officer Mark Uzell's suggestion that Gary set up a regular security detail for the Birchmere. Gary readily agreed and promptly hired Uzell.

From then on, the Birchmere has always employed an off-duty police officer to keep the parking lot safe during showtime. "Having police in the parking lot gives everyone a sense of comfort and security when they arrive.

It helps deter drinking and driving," Gary says, adding with pride, "And we've never had a fight in the three Birchmere halls, ever."

Pete Kennedy and Jon Carroll.   © *Oelze*

However, there was something of a shoving match when a crowd of non-Birchmere folks came to a Marlboro Country Talent contest in the mid-80s and patrons disagreed with the contest results. Pete Kennedy and Jon Carroll were in one of the bands that competed, and Pete remembers "We didn't win. The band that did win sabotaged us by turning our amps up after we did our soundcheck. The judges had to tell us to turn down."

Eminiah Shinar AKA "The Fly"

Gary tells The Fly's story: "In 1981 we moved to the second Birchmere on Mt. Vernon Avenue. We had a month to clean the place, build the stage, and get the sound system up. Staff, friends, and even players, including John Duffey, joined in on the work. One day a street kid came to me and said, 'I'm hungry. Do you have any odd jobs I can do?' I replied, "Well, what can you do?" "I can paint murals," he said, so I asked him to paint a dobro on the wall.

'OK. What's a dobro?' he asked. I showed him the front cover of my 1972 *Mike Auldridge Dobro* album.

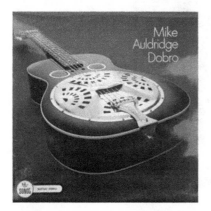 

Album and wall mural.

"The kid takes the album cover, and I lead him to a work table with various paints. Some were acrylic. He takes a measuring stick and climbs up a ladder, and paints a solid red "x" across the wall. And then he slabs a whole blob of red paint and starts adding colors."

By the way, the dobro on that record belongs to Jim McGuire, the famous Nashville photographer. He and Mike both had the same vintage edition model. Jim started his career with a portrait of John Hartford. He went on to do his *Nashville Portraits* series, which now includes more than 1,000 images of America's most influential singers, songwriters, and other country musicians.

"In two hours, the kid had the dobro on the wall. I couldn't believe it. It looked just like the album cover, and he did it all using junk paint. I asked him the cost, and I gave him more than he requested. But nowhere near what it was worth to me."

Gary continues: "We had a tall sign in the parking lot, so I next asked him to paint "Birchmere parking" letters on it. He got some rope and tied it around his waist, and climbed up on the sign. Some neighborhood Latino kids gathered around, calling him "The Fly." And that's how Eminiah Shinar got his nickname.

The Fly.   © *E. Shinar*

"Fifteen years later at the new club, he did the murals. The first mural he painted was the character in tails with the monocle. Then he did the music city map and the jazz and blues guy playing the horn. It's the perfect Americana for what we needed. He painted all the murals on the walls outside and the Seldom Scene mural in the merchandise store. He didn't sketch anything out or run it by me first. I just stayed out of his way. The only thing I asked after he finished was to add the previous Birchmere buildings. I got him pictures of those.

"The Fly hung out at the club and did some work for a while. One night, he showed up when the group, Riders in the Sky, were playing. He was wearing a western outfit with a silly

Howdy Doody cowboy hat on. I told him to get rid of the hat, and I hurt his feelings."

"Gary's comments about my outfit crushed me," Eminiah said in 2020, "because I was thinking I'd be a black man at the club giving tribute to country music, and it would be good for the place. Maybe historic. I told Gary I was quitting after his comments and left. Later, Gary called and told me that it would be stupid for me to quit over a hat, and he didn't want me to leave. Then we talked. I realized he was trying to protect me from ridicule because the hat I wore was a cheap, red plastic hat. So, everything was back to fine, and I stayed working there until I left for Texas much later."

Gary says, "About three years ago, I was thinking about The Fly. The murals were getting dirty and faded. Out of the blue, he called me from Austin. He was doing a mural there and said he was thinking about me, too. I offered to fly him back to refresh the murals, but he asked for a train ticket because The Fly didn't like to fly. He and his wife, Ella Jae, came up. My problem became everybody talking to him while he was doing the refresh painting outside. I had to put a sign, 'Please do not talk to the painter while he paints.'"

On that occasion, The Fly added Ella Jae's name to one of the murals with the number "135" next to it. "That's our favorite seat in the house," says Eminiah, who was working in Jefferson, Texas, on a building mural with a Safari theme when contacted for this book. He is still painting, making and playing steel drums in his two bands, New Light Steel Ensemble (Christian) and Down Home Steel (secular). "I love Gary, and I love the Birchmere," says "The Fly."

Clarence "Shoe" Shumaker

Nicknamed "Shoe,'" he describes his background as "After earning an A.A. from Prince Georges Community College in 1984, I worked as a Technical Illustrator for DOD contractors before going back to school to earn a B.A. from the University of Maryland in 1988. I worked my way through college in a variety of shops until founding my own business, Daybreak Studios in 1990."

© Oelze

Living in College Park, MD, and attending the University of Maryland, Shoe was first introduced to the hall in 1987 by a Birchmere waitress named Jennie O'Neil.

"Jennie was also a musician and commissioned me to do a drawing of the second Birchmere location as a present 'for the Boss.' When Gary got the drawing, he asked Jennie, 'Who's this? And she answered, 'That's exactly what I was hoping you'd say.' Jennie introduced us, and then it just took off from there. We discussed doing monthly calendars. I started doing them once a month—all by hand—delivered them and then I'd catch a show."

Shoe's first drawing for Gary,

When Shoe got a computer, he began to e-mail the calendar drawings to the hall. "Gary has paid me over the years, and I haven't bumped it up that much. I was a fan of Danny Gatton, and I got to see him several times. I was living in Clinton. MD, not too far from Danny's place in Accokeek, MD. My dad was in the service, stationed at Andrews Air Force base, when I was growing up." Other shows he cites as favorites include Keb'Mo', Hot Tuna, and Dave Matthews.

Statue of Pudge that hangs high near the bar.   © *Oelze*

Shoe created the life-size statue of Pudge playing harmonica that hangs near the Birchmere bar. A frequent quip heard among Birchmere regulars is that "Gary loved Pudge so much he had him stuffed."

Here's how Shoe fabricated this statue: "His head and beard are papier mâché. His hands are plastic cast of my hands holding a harmonica. Underneath the clothes are PVC piping and foam rubber. I got the clothes from a thrift shop. I heavily sprayed clear acrylic to stiffen it all up."

Shoe began doing other graphic work at the new Birchmere, including copying Fly's dobro and painting it next to the merch store near the hall entrance. He signed it "Shoe-Fly." Shoe and the Fly have actually never met each other.

Shoe also did the brick wall art for the stage. The hungry i nightclub in San Francisco first featured this red brick wall stage backdrop in the 1950's, which became a trademark of subsequent comedy clubs. The Birchmere process was painting a large canvas completely red, and then painting in the brick outlines in yellow.

Shoe draws small portraits of people for the days when there are no shows. These drawings commemorated the birthdays of each celebrity.

Abe Lincoln, Frederick Douglas, Frank Sinatra, Edgar Bergen, Santa, Douglas MacArthur, Gilda Radner, M. L. King and Bob Marley. © *Shoe*

Chapter 19 – General Management

(l to r) John Brinegar, Gary, K.C., and Bud Powell.   © *Susan Oelze*

Longtime General Manager John Brinegar (1997-2021) is a native Alexandrian who loved the Birchmere from the first show he attended. John explains: "It was David Ball, kind of a one-hit wonder with his 1994 song "Thinkin' Problem." Gary's wife, Linda just happened to be our waitress that night, and I asked her if I could take some pictures. She said 'No photos allowed,' but after the show she said, 'I usually take some pictures of the acts, so if you leave me your name and address, then I'll send you some.' And that's what she did. She did this many times for others like me. That was my first experience at the Birchmere."

Brinegar later got a part-time evening job working the door and progressively added additional tasks like getting food for the acts. Gary encouraged John to continue doing more work for him and eventually offered him the General Manager job.

John recalls, "Back then, Gary and Linda were kind of like the Dolly Parton and Porter Wagoner of the hall. I don't know if Gary will like that description, but that's how I remember it. Gary was doing nearly everything. Booking, the money, the hiring, etc. and his attitude was, 'Whatever's going to be good for our business, then that's what we want to do.' He makes the final decision on everything, but it's more of a 'Let's get there by committee' approach.'

"At first, I wasn't scared of him, per se, but I didn't think I could contradict or even offer constructive criticism. But as our relationship has grown, I've learned how he operates. It's like Gary tells us what he thinks we should do on any given topic and then waits and listens to see which of us or if all of us will try and talk him out of his decision. But it's never 'his way or the highway.' He values others' opinions.

"But even more revealing, and something that impressed me when I became the General Manager, was an early discussion we had in his office. He said, 'You understand the commitment to this work that is needed. But you know we have bands who are the openers, and then we have support acts. Every one of these headliners has opened up for somebody else at some point in their career. I want the opening acts to feel as welcome as the headliners. Let's make it a point to treat everyone who comes here welcome. Treat everybody like you want to be treated yourself.' I knew we were on the same page when he told me this, and I've never forgotten that talk."

Over the years there have been several general managers with a primary role to handle particular wants from the acts. They check the contract riders where special demands are listed. For example, Robert Cray is a wine connoisseur so his tour manager will send a list of the brands he prefers at the time of his show.

Ben Finkelstein is the Birchmere associate promoter. He remembers a grand demand requested by soul singer Solomon Burke: "Burke was a very large man. His rider requested we provide him with a throne to sit on like a large chair. We didn't really have anything. At the time a friend of mine worked in the theater world in DC. She gave me the number for these Shakespeare Theatre Company props department. And we talked back and forth and they ended up lending us a throne. I don't know my Shakespeare. I'm going to say the Henry the Eighth. This big throne, me and our sound guy,

M. Jaworek, C. Adams, Solomon Burke, and Bud Gardner.   © *Oelze*

"We drove over in a van, picked it up, brought it back. Solomon loved it. He ended up taking a picture of what we provided and then included that in his future contract rider, which had to piss off other venues because they had to go and get something really grandiose."

Once John Brinegar got a particular request for an ounce of weed and directions to a nearby Buddhist temple. "There I would get a wooden box of matches, 78 ounces of special water, a certain kind of gum, and other things. I called the tour manager and said, 'The Buddhist temple I can do, but I can't be getting weed. What do you really have to have?"

On Jimmy Dale Gilmore: "Jimmy plays guitar with Joe Ely and Butch Hancock in their band, The Flatlanders. They've been here many times. About 17 years ago, Jimmy gave me one of those little kid's toys. A thumb puppet on a small stand, where you push the bottom and spring makes it move. I got him a pack of firecrackers the next year. One year I bought him a can of Silly String. I was going to give it to him. But then I thought he probably forgot about this exchange thing. I go into the green room, and he says, 'Hey John, I got something for you.' It was a hairbrush. We got to be pretty good friends sharing this little quirky exchange thing. I kind of treasure stuff like this."

Giving acts their space

"Gary has a strict rule about nobody being bothered," Brinegar says. "If you see an artist looking at the pictures in the hallway, give them their space. Don't try to get pictures and autographs and whatever. They need to get their mind together. I tried to make sure everything is done for them by at least five or ten minutes after seven. That gives them 20 minutes to be by themselves before the show starts. I've established over the years that at some point, I can say, 'Look, the only thing that I really need from you is to start the show on time at seven thirty.-There is a digital clock on stage right— almost on Bud's monitor that we all follow. They can see it. I calmly tell the acts, 'The audience has been here since five o'clock. They've been here two and a half hours waiting. I don't want them to have to wait another half an hour.'

"I get the acts trained to know at seven thirty the show is ready to go. I don't really care about the backend. If they want to go two long sets, then that's fine. But let's start on time. So usually, about seven o'clock, I'd begin a 'Seven o'clock, seven-fifteen, seven twenty-five' countdown to kind of get them moving."

On Familiar faces

John continued: "One of the Birchmere differences that separate us from other clubs is that we really appreciate that they're playing for us.

"Since I've been there, it's five o'clock with people waiting outside in line. The front door opens at six o'clock. People get their numbers in turn. And Gary religiously calls the numbers every single night. It's just like clockwork. If Gary goes on vacation, people notice that he's not there.

"Gary is very accessible as far as the customers are concerned. Many people come up and introduce themselves to him and go, 'Hey, are you the owner?' Or, if we're sitting out on the porch smoking a cigarette, people always want to introduce themselves to Gary to tell him exactly how much they love this place."

Phil Perry. © *Oelze*

Shocking Story

Phil Perry is an R&B singer who has played. -regularly since 2011. He sells out consistently. One night, Phil is on stage singing and everyone is having a great time. All of a sudden, he just falls on the floor of the stage. Brinegar thinks "Oh my God, did he just trip over something? He got up and kept going. But everybody's professional. He's getting close to the end of the show, and he falls again.

"He says goodnight. And they started coming down the ramp. I open the door, get them in, and make sure nobody's following them, trying to get in. We get in the green room and sit down, and I ask Phil, 'Man, what did you trip over?'

'Oh, John. I didn't trip over anything. It's my pacemaker. It went off, and it shocks me,' he explains. And while he's talking to me, it shocks him again. He almost flies out of the chair.

"He's sweating, confused, and looking all funny. I'm scared. I ask the band, 'What are we going to do?' The band isn't super concerned. One of them calmly says, 'Oh, this happened before. He's going to be OK.' I say, 'No. We're calling 9-1-1.

"The ambulance gets there, and he ends up staying in the Alexandria Hospital for two weeks. Phil almost died in the green room. The cause was from some frequency in the wireless microphone system that was interfering with his pacemaker."

Dry Lake

"Keith Emerson and Greg Lake—two-thirds of progressive rock supergroup Emerson, Lake were scheduled to appear in 2010. People lined up almost out to the road on show day. Gary gets a call from their tour manager about five fifty-five.

"Greg Lake [vocals, bass] has stage fright. He's having anxiety issues. We're not a hundred percent sure if we can make the show. Shortly after that call, the manager called again to say there would be no show."

Gary went outside to let people know it was canceled. There were hundreds of people waiting outside. A cab pulls up with a couple in the back, and before Gary could say anything, a lady jumps out and tells him how excited she is. They just flew over from England, and it's her birthday. Gary felt terrible as he had to break the news.

Ben Finkelstein added, "The story I later heard is that Lake and Emerson were fighting that night, and just wouldn't go on together."

Flex Stage

Formerly known as the bandstand, the Birchmere's second stage was remodeled in 2012 and officially relaunched as the "Flex Stage." Located to the right of the entrance area, it is an expansive space with a dance floor, intended for dance-oriented shows. It holds 1,000 people when tables are removed. Playing the bandstand is not a second-rate billing because the hall can still do dinners, followed by a seven thirty show in the larger standing room-only area. Serving up a different vibe, the Flex Stage offers the best of both worlds: shows for club-goers who like to listen quietly and those for audiences—and acts-- who like to move.

Some of the high-energy performers who have played the Flex Stage are the Mavericks, Blitzen Trapper, the Carolina

Chocolate Drops, Chris Stapleton, The Waterboys, the Marcus King Band, Link Wray, Celso Pina, Arturo Sandoval, The Bar-Kays, Felice Brothers, Rokia Traoré, Billy Cobham, BRS-549, The Billy Price Band, The Clarks, Colin Meloy, The Commitments, The Dark Star Orchestra, The English Beat, Fighting Gravity, Glengary Bhoys, The Hooters, The Iguanas, Ingrid Michaelson, Jamey Johnson, Jane Oliver, The Avett Brothers, Jane Oliver, Jenny Lewis, The Knitters, Kurt Nilsen, Langhorne Slim, Leftover Salmon, Magnetic Fields, C. J. Chenier, New Potato Caboose, Minnie Driver, Marillion, Paulina Rubio, The Radiators, Raphael Saadig, The Saw Doctors, Slavic Soul Party, Steve Riley, and the Zac Brown Band.

***

One act that almost didn't play the flex stage was Grateful Dead drummer Mickey Hart and his Rhythm Devils band. This 2006 sold-out show attracted Grateful Dead fans who started lining up outside the night before.

John Brinegar recalls: "Three tractor-trailer trucks full of equipment arrives with Hart's crew. By six o'clock, Hart's not even there yet, and they haven't sound checked. Mickey calls and says we've got to hold the doors. Don't let anybody in the stage area until we soundcheck.

"We let people in the back door to eat dinner in the hall and kept them locked in there. Hart arrives and starts the soundcheck, but that's taking too much time. I go to his road manager and say, 'Look, dude. My owner is having a conniption. You got to get the band ready to play. We got a fire hazard at this point.'

"When I report this to Gary, he says, 'I'm going to give them five more minutes, and then we just turn these people loose.' So, the road manager and I go back to the stage.

"Mickey yells back, 'I told you not to bug me. I'll be done when I'm done.'

"The tour manager begins to argue that he's just trying to do his job. Hart fires him on the spot.

"'C'mon Mickey, this is uncalled for,' I say. Hart asks to borrow my cell phone to call *his* manager to let him know that

313

he just fired his tour manager. I tell him 'No, you can't use my phone. We've got a show to do now. It's 8 eight o'clock. We're going to have a riot. Here's the bottom line. You can do a show if you want, or whatever. We have to turn these people loose.'

"So, Gary lets everybody in. Now the room is just packed. So, he does a three-and-a-half-hour show—blindly—without his soundcheck. It was five o'clock in the morning by the time we got out of there *

Neva Warnock   © C. B. Smith

The Record Store

Former staffer Neva Warnock ran the first small merchandize store with another employee, Jean Nelson in the basement of the second Birchmere: "We had about 700 albums," says Neva. "Gary pretty much let me order what inventory I wanted. Bluegrass, mostly. 99.9% vinyl, with a few CDs and 8-tracks. Two t-shirt spinner racks.

Gary adds, "Other clubs didn't have merch stores then, but the demand for second-hand albums gave us this idea when Dick Cerri of the World Folk Music Association suggested we sell some records."

Neva continues: "One night when Commander Cody was playing, he started digging through one of the T-shirt racks, and pulled out a Johnson Mountain Boys T-shirt, and wore that on stage. Richard Underwood was the banjo player for the Johnson Mountain Boys, and when I told him about it the next week, he was thrilled!"

314

Chapter 20 – Promotor MJ & the Back Office

Michael Jaworek in his Birchmere office. © *S. Moore*

"Michael Jaworek might be responsible for bringing more acts to local stages than any promoter in the Washington DC region. An ageless 67, Jaworek has been wrangling talent for Alexandria's venerable Birchmere since 1988, after getting his start in 1972 as a college student. Given that the Birchmere presents one or two artists just about every night of the week, the number of acts he is signed, sealed and delivered is easily in the thousands."

Buzz McClain
Northern Virginia magazine, Jan. 2020

"I think that Michael could do stand-up comedy if he wanted to. He's a very funny guy. If you ask Michael a question, he will answer it. And if you ask him a question relating to yourself and

the Birchmere, he'll answer the question as to whether this is a good time for you to come back to play, or should you wait, etc. He is always available to you. If you ask for his opinion, he'll give it and you can take it to the bank. And he's got a beautiful wife, Debi Smith, who sings with me now and then, and wrote with me. One of my favorite songs is our "Marry Me Again."

Tom Paxton

"Michael does so much research. He is always reading. We call him the encyclopedia of rock and roll. He knows so much about the acts. He knows exactly where they've sold out and the most obscure stuff. Even when he's on the street he'll walk up to a UPS guy, and if he talks with an accent, he'll start talking about the musician that's really famous in that fellow's country. Michael's job is a match made in heaven."

Debi Smith

Michael Jaworek has been nominated many times as "Nightclub Talent Buyer of the Year" by *Pollstar Magazine.* He was a co-founder of the Washington Area Music Awards (WAMA) organization. He received the International Talent Buyers Association "Club Buyer of the Year" Award in 2013.

"There's no question that Michael is the best promoter in the US," states Gary. "That's why everybody in the business wants to hire him. He's very clever. He greets the acts backstage with warmth and humor and is extremely knowledgeable not only about the music industry but in many other fields, like boxing, racehorses, wines, and really, you name it, he knows about it."

Born in Newark, New Jersey, Jaworek started promotion as a University of Illinois student in 1972. He and three friends formed Blues Power to produce concerts.

"The first show we did was Hound Dog Taylor and the House Rockers. We needed to make $500 for their show in the Student Union and ended up making $1,500. Gee, this is easy we thought. Boy, was I wrong," Michael says.

He went on to produce many Chicago blues acts, and after graduation, became a concert promotion advisor for the

Universities of Tennessee and Maryland. In 1985 he joined Chesapeake Concerts, a spin-off of Cellar Door concerts which eventually became Live Nation.

Jaworek cites his former boss as his mentor: the late Sam L'Hommedieu, a native Washingtonian, veteran concert promoter who ran Chesapeake Concerts, lawyer, and businessman. Sam was a partner with Cellar Door founder, Jack Boyle, and later managed the Warner Theater. He served in the 87th Infantry Division and participated in the Battle of the Bulge.

"Sam was extremely ethical, says Jaworek. "In the 12 years I worked for him, I never heard him use a word of profanity. On the contrary, he was a generous soul and never hid behind the phrase, 'It's just business,' which to me always an excuse to do the wrong thing. Maybe the right thing legally, but the bad thing morally.

"At Chesapeake, it became apparent we needed a local club to book shows and around 1988 I cold-called Gary at the Birchmere and told him I thought I could increase and help diversify his business and also help ourselves as well. So, I worked with Chesapeake to help produce shows at the Birchmere, Ram's Head, Painters Mill, and other clubs."

In addition to diversifying the club's acts, Jaworek introduced a method of moving acts that outgrew the Birchmere to larger Washington area venues. "Gary also wasn't doing any shows outside the Birchmere except ones that included the Seldom Scene. Gary wasn't in the business to book the acts to greater glory in larger venues when their popularity outgrew the Birchmere."

Gary was quite fine with Michael's strategic goals. "At the time he commented, 'It can't get much worse" when I gave him my plan," says Michael.

"I said to Gary, 'You can book this as a concert club like the Cellar Door, which was long gone by then, where you could do a variety of genres of performers that fit the geography,' as I put it, 'of the room and the general thrust of a seated concert club.' This meant it didn't suit metal or hip hop, but whether it was R&B, blues, comedy, jazz or whatever, we could successfully present that at some point."

In 1997, Michael came on board in-house and full time when Gary built the third edition of the Birchmere and began booking shows for the hall and shows outside the building, produced by the Birchmere. The old formula for promotion involved plugging the radio stations that played the music genre of the band and taking out expensive ads in the Washington Post and other news outlets. As the Internet and social media matured, the Birchmere developed a website of over 150,000 followers. "We can sell out a show just by blasting the booking on our website," says Michael. "It's much more effective, with huge savings from how we did it ten years ago."

By the time Jaworek began working directly with Gary, he had 15 years of experience in the music business with solid relationships with radio station promotions managers, artists' representatives, and venue administrations. In 2021, he estimates that he's working on negotiations for three to five contracts per day.

Best in shows

When asked about his top two all-time favorites, he answered, "You mean besides the Four Bitchin Babes shows with my wife Debi Smith?" Other than those he cites two: the Rosanne Cash, Rodney Crowell, and Guy Clark show: "It was transcendent. My second favorite is the Vince Gill show when the new Birchmere opened. He played two hours with his band, one hour solo, and then came back and did a fourth hour with his band again. The four hours sped by quickly. Four hours with Springsteen feels like four hours. Those four hours with Vince felt like it moved in minutes."

Overall, he says this: "The important thing for Gary, with his liberality for artists and shows, and myself, as a promoter, was getting to the point where there was an affinity for the place that comes with having a positive experience. Like the Warner Theater, where everyone will come here. The R&B shows work. Presenting ethnic music from Africa or Latin America works. Presenting spoken word artists like **Laurie Anderson** or **Henry Rollins** works, and all in a nightclub with comfort, convenience, and security. That's really the big success story for me."

318

However, sometimes it doesn't go as planned. In 2019, Michael heard through the booker's grapevine that 83-year-old Jerry Lee Lewis, affectionately known as "The Killer" and one of the first rock 'n' roll musicians, had signed with Creative Artists Agency. Jaworek knew that Lewis hadn't been with a major talent agency in some time, and CAA is one of the best there is. Jaworek explains, "I did some research on identifying the responsible agent, meaning to whom all other agents take *their* offer for presentation to whoever is the decider for the act. Fortunately, the primary agent turned out to be an old friend of mine, Blake McDaniel.

"I called him, and we discussed how cool it would be for Lewis to play the Birchmere. Blake knew of our heritage with Johnny Cash and Carl Perkins, who with Jerry Lee and Elvis was Sun Records Million Dollar Quartet and the other legends who have played the club. So, it came down to, obviously, what's the money going to be?

"When Blake told me Jerry's performance fee, I knew that this would be the highest price Gary's ever paid an act. But Lewis is the last man standing of his rock and roll generation, and it would be an event, not just a concert, and for only 500 seat venue—on *all* deals. I took this opportunity to him at our daily 4:00 pm business meeting which also includes associate Ben Finkelstein and box office manager Stuart Wodlinger."

Gary knew this first show on Jerry's tour would be important and wanted the Birchmere to own it. Next, he discussed with Jaworek what the ticket price needed to be to make a Jerry Lee show profitable. Previously, the top fee and ticket price belonged to B.B. King. Gary tacked an additional 35 dollars on a Lewis seat. "I didn't fear that the show wouldn't sell-out although I normally try to keep prices as low as possible. In this case, I thought the public would understand," states Gary.

Jaworek continues: "We sent the offer to Blake, who got the deal done. We put it up for sale on a Saturday in June, and lo and behold, it took off. I won't say it sold out instantaneously, but we sold out in advance of the date. It would be the first show by Lewis at the Birchmere, followed by world tour stops in Nashville, New Orleans, and other TBA. And then sadly, "The

Killer" suffered a stroke, and the planned tour ended. That's the big one that got away."

Jerry Lee Lewis recovered enough in the next months to participate in a recording session for a gospel-themed album, as yet not released. He had only planned to sing and didn't want a piano in the session. His famed producer T. Bone Burnett—who played the Birchmere in 1992—snuck a piano in there anyway. Surprisingly, Lewis ended up playing it. "It was the first time I used my right hand since my stroke," Jerry Lee told *Rolling Stone* magazine in early 2020. He also said he still hopes to perform again one day. "We're thinking about it. Whether it'll come off or not, I don't know. But for now, I'm grateful to simply be playing again. It feels like I'm home."

Willie Nelson, the *Red-Headed Stranger*

Singer-songwriter, actor, and activist Willie Nelson is one of the great Texan songwriters who never played the Birchmere. But he almost did, twice.

Here's the story by Jaworek: "In 1996, Nelson released *Teatro*, a sparse, atmospheric album produced by U2's Daniel Lanois with 10 of the 12 tracks featuring lovely harmonies by Emmylou Harris. Nelson's agent announced a tour promoting the new album with minimal backing players, not his large "Family" group. Gary thought it might feel more like a solo show by Willie and was thrilled.

"We put a "first hold" on a date which let Willie's agents know that the Birchmere was holding a date open and wanted Nelson to play, so we'll work out the details in a contract and confirm. Negotiations were going well when Wolf Trap's booking agent stepped in and put the kibosh on our deal. Wolf Trap blocked the date. To clarify, they had a Willie Nelson show the following August at the Filene Center. Their in-house promoter felt our show in March was a conflict with theirs, even though ours was for only 500 tickets versus their 7,000.

"Wolf Trap successfully convinced Nelson's management that our 500-seat show in March could or would negatively affect ticket sales at a future 7,000-seat Willie Nelson show. Nelson could be playing later in the summer at Wolf Trap. So,

320

the Birchmere lost on this attempt to bring Willie Nelson to our stage."

"It was the same scenario we faced when Wolf Trap blocked Bill Monroe from playing the Birchmere," says Gary, adding, "Only Willie didn't surprise us by showing up unannounced to play our place as Monroe did."

A few years afterward, the Birchmere had a "first hold" on Willie for another tour when they got a request from Justin Townes Earle's agent to play the same date. In this case, it's customary to let the promoter with the first hold know that another performer wants the venue, too. It puts pressure for a firm decision to be made because it's bad form to keep a first hold on speculation regardless of who the performers are.

"What happened is that Willie Nelson's folks took too long to get back to us on a decision, so we booked Justin, which we think is the fair way to do business," Jaworek says.

Food or No Food?

Michael discussed this occasional problem: "Once in a while, we have an act that doesn't want food service going on while they perform. Perhaps it distracts them when the patrons are eating. In this case, we will propose that we offer an opening act where food services can continue until the headliners come on.

"I once had a very respectful discussion with Joan Armatrading, who is a British act, about this. In England, I gathered from her that if you play in a club that serves food, you are playing in a cabaret or dinner theatre. You are at the end of the road in your career and one step away from being out of business. It's not being haughty or copping an attitude. So, we try the opening act proposal. However, if it's a major act and the opening act option isn't accepted, then we just won't serve food when the headliners are on stage.

"Fortunately, we don't have many problems generally with performers. At least 90 percent of the folks on the road are decent people in an unusual business. Sometimes, when a performer's relative gets involved in their management, it can become a problem. Being both the manager and relative can cause a loss of objective perspective. Not always, that's for sure. But, sometimes, yes.

"Most of our artists love playing here. Their supportive audience knows their music. That's an ideal audience. And because we happen to be in a very economically stable environment, the Birchmere sells a lot of CDs compared to many, many other places. And I know that from talking to artists and their management.

"There are major artists that I don't want to do business with. I've been involved in horror shows where the artists "aren't feeling it" and their audience, who gave them their career, have to suffer for that. But if they deliver for the audience, even if they're not a human person backstage, I can tolerate them. But I have played shows where boy, I couldn't wait until those three hours of performance were over, but rarely at the Birchmere."

Don't Get Me Wrong

Michael Jaworek's biggest Birchmere miscalculation occurred in 2017. His only consolation is that every other promoter in America who became involved with this show also lost money.

"It was a triple bill with Kirk Franklin, Ledisi and special guest PJ Morton, called 'The Rebel, the Soul & The Saint Tour.' It was a mixture of gospel [Franklin] and secular R&B [Ledisi and Morton], which didn't work with audiences. Had it been 100 percent gospel or 100 percent R&B then it might have sold out. But it stiffed when we combined the two, selling only a third of Constitutional Hall. Kirk called me afterward to apologize but I told him no one was at fault for the show's poor sales. "The shows we've done with Ledisi have always done well at the Birchmere and Strathmore. But together we just misread the situation."

Jaworek calculated that his career shows have made money 83 percent–of the time, but for the ones that don't, losses are usually minimal.

On Ben

Ben Finkelstein has been Michael's right-hand booking associate for 22 years. They share adjoining offices adorned with wall-to-wall posters of shows they've brought to the Birchmere and at other larger venues produced by the Birchmere.

Ben attended James Madison University in 1993. "I was working at the radio station there and also booking acts. Michael Jaworek was at Chesapeake Productions, and we met when we both worked on presenting singer-songwriter Ani DiFranco in a concert, which sold out. After I graduated, I got

Ben at Work.   © *S. Moore*

a call from my father that a guy at the Birchmere was looking for an assistant. And that was Michael Jaworek."

Jaworek describes his work and relationship with Ben: "Although I am more of a gambler and optimist, Ben is much better on detail than I am, which is very, very good and helpful to me. And he remembers things I sometimes forget. In spite of all the research, the shows are always a calculated risk. We are in a very dynamic business. I like to say, the only difference between us and a stockbroker is that they wear $2,000 suits and we wear tee shirts and blue jeans.

"Ben has knowledge of the more current music world, especially in the jam band space, which adds to our base of knowledge. His input sometimes will affect me in terms of changing my mind on a show or a deal point. I say to him often, 'That's good counsel Ben.'

"For fifteen years we worked in a small room that is now one of the dressing rooms near the washer and dryer. I was at one end of a table and he was at the other. No windows. And we still work physically close together. It's amazing that we get along so well, but we do. I respect him."

Chapter 21 – Wonderful World

Local DC interest in international music, especially Celtic acts, was strong at the Birchmere's inception. Irish bars like Gallagher's and Ireland's Four Provinces were busy nightly. The Birchmere took advantage of DC's transnational tastes.

As one booking agent, Alison Lee, said in 1985, "Irish acts can draw a good crowd playing the club even if they're unknown because people will assume that they are good if the Birchmere hires them."

Celtic artists played the Birchmere beginning in the early '80s. In order of appearance, the early acts included the following:

De Dannan	Spirit of the West
Touchstone	Liam O' Flynn
Tannehill Weavers	Battlefield Band
Kevin Burke	The Dubliners
Boys of the Lough	Luca Bloom
Silly Wizard	Capercaillie
Joe Burke	Mary Black
Archie Fisher	Nightnoise

Maura O'Connell (b. Sept. 16, 1958, Ennis, Ireland).

Maura began playing the hall in 1983 as lead vocalist with the traditional Celtic band De Dannan. The late Senator Ted Kennedy was one of her big fans; his secretary would call Gary to arrange for Ted to see Maura whenever she performed.

Maura O'Connell (above with Jerry Douglas). © Oelze

When Maura crossed paths with the New Grass Revival, she became more interested in roots and country music. She would return to the club many times as a solo performer with sets that featured a favorite standout rendition of "Summerfly," a song by another Birchmere regular, Cheryl Wheeler. Maura won a Grammy nomination for her 1989 *Helpless Heart* album.

And speaking of Ted Kennedy, Gary was talking with the Senator outside after one O'Connell show at the second Birchmere when Ted stepped back and nearly stumbled over a short three-foot wall around the front of the building, constructed as part of the city's flood plan when nearby Four Mile Run creek would frequently surge. Gary grabbed him and saved him from falling backward.

A friend of Gary's drove by just at that moment and later joked, "As long as I lived, I never thought I'd see you hug Ted Kennedy."

In 1992, Maura O'Connell sang at Kennedy's wedding to his second wife, Victoria at their home, and then played the Birchmere that night. "It was a beautiful day and we were treated royally like honored guests and not some band that came in the back door," said O'Connell. And that evening

Kennedy, with his new bride, were seated at the Birchmere enjoying Maura's show.

Ian Dawson Tyson (b. Sept.25, Victoria, Canada)

Canadian folk singer Tyson was scheduled to follow Maura the next week. Ian lived in Alberta, Canada, and by then had written many renowned songs like "Someday Soon," a hit for Judy Collins, Moe Bandy and Suzy Bogguss, and "Four Strong Winds," named by CBS as "the most excellent Canadian song of all time." He had also divorced his wife and musical partner Sylvia (Fricker) Tyson, who continued to perform at the Birchmere with her band, Great Speckled Bird. She was also an acclaimed songwriter with songs like "You Were On My Mind," an international hit for the We Five.

As Ian & Sylvia, the duo was managed by Albert Grossman whose other famous clients at that time, were Bob Dylan and Peter, Paul, and Mary. Noel "Paul" Stookey also played the Birchmere as did some of Grossman's other notable clients: Odetta, Gordon Lightfoot, Richie Havens, and Jesse Winchester.

However, on this 1992 Birchmere booking, Tyson phoned from the border with a problem.

"Gary, my paperwork is screwed up and I can't cross into the US," Tyson explained.

"Don't worry, and don't go anywhere. I'll try and help," Gary assured him.

Because Ted Kennedy's secretary had become friendly with Gary, he turned to her.

"Now, I have a problem, and maybe you can help me," Gary asked. When Kennedy heard about Tyson's problem, he dispatched an aide to fly to the border and help Ian get to the Birchmere.

Before the show, Ian asked Gary, "Just how in the hell did you get that done?"

Gary casually said, "Oh, I just called my friend Ted Kennedy and asked him to let my buddy through."

Ian responded in wonder, "Well when you have a big gun, shoot it."

Ian Tyson.   © *Oelze*

During the 1960's Ian & Sylvia were popular at the Cellar Door night club. John Duffey was doing a weekly gig with the Country Gentlemen at the Shamrock club across the street from the Cellar Door and Ian & Sylvia would routinely take in a Country Gentlemen set when in town. A great friendship developed between the Gents and Ian & Sylvia, especially Duffey's bond with Ian Tyson. In turn, Duffey would always try and see Tyson at his Birchmere shows. John was impressed by Tyson's "Four Strong Winds" and wrote a song, "The Traveler," which he hoped would be as popular.

In 2021, the 88-year old Tyson was living on his southern Alberta farm with his beloved horses. A favorite autographed poster in the Birchmere hallway shows Ian on horseback, all four hooves off the ground.

Pentangle was a pioneering and influential British band that created an unique fusion of folk, jazz, blues, baroque, and medieval styles. Largely acoustic, the original band performed and released a series of classic albums from 1968 through 1972; later line-ups of the group were active starting in the

80s. Pentangle's first line-up was John Renbourn, Bert Jansch, Jacqui McShee, Danny Thompson, and Terry Cox. The band played the hall several times starting in 1986; at that show Jansch and all of the original members were still with the group, although Renbourn had been replaced by Mike Piggott. Renbourn and Jansch, both legends in their own right, forged careers as solo artists; each played the hall individually several times and teamed up for a duo show in 1991.

Gary says, "John Renbourn played many times solo. He, with Arlo Guthrie and Charles Esten, are the only three players who offered money back when we had a bad turn out. Esten played a show during the COVID-19 pandemic where the audience was thin and he contributed his entire salary back to the Birchmere."

© *B. Gardner*

Fairport Convention. Few bands can be credited with creating an entire genre, but arguably, that is what Fairport Convention did, kicking off a durable folk-rock genre that blended British folk traditions with the energy of rock and roll, delivered by multi-vocalist-and-instrumentalist groups that covered traditional folk ballads and penned original songs that sounded like they were traditional folk ballads. *Liege & Lief* originally released in 1969, was Fairport's first album completely devoted to British "electric folk," and has remained influential for over 50 years. Although many gifted musicians have passed through the Fairport ranks over the years, including Richard Thompson and the legendary late Sandy Denny, the current line-up--Simon Nicol (the last of the original group) Dave Pegg, Ric Sanders, Chris Leslie, and Gerry Conway--has been the longest lasting.

Fairport Convention has returned to the hall multiple times, going back to 1998, drawing on a rich catalog that encompasses decades of material, old and new. At their 2013 show, they led the audience in a singalong of a traditional drinking song, "The Happy Man."

© Oelze

Richard Thompson (b. April 3, 1949, West London, UK)

Thompson is one of the most prominent founding members of seminal British folk-rock band Fairport Convention. He left the group in 1971 and embarked on a solo career, with a period of collaboration (1974-1982) as a duo with his wife Linda, who has also played the hall as a solo artist.

A Birchmere favorite, he has been coming to the hall since the 1980s, playing often sold-out shows selected from a career's worth of original songs like "1952 Vincent Black

330

Lightning," "The Dimming of the Day," and "Meet on the Ledge." His live shows are also an occasion for his droll wit: during one show in 2015, when the audience applauded his guitar playing in mid-song, he commented, "It was nothing really, just a few warming-up exercises." During the same show, he played "Guitar Heroes," performing in the styles of guitarists—like Django Reinhardt, Les Paul, and James Burton—who influenced his own virtuoso guitar technique.

The depth of his musical background was also on display in 2004 during his "1,000 Years of Popular Music" show, a selection of songs that spanned the 13th Century to the present, from his album by the same name. The record was inspired by a magazine editor's invitation to name the top 10 songs of the last millennium.

Thompson returned again to the Birchmere in 2021 for two nights and told Keith Loria in a Special to *the Fairfax County Times:* "I've been playing in bands since I was 12, so it's just been crazy and without question the longest I have ever gone without being on stage [because of the pandemic.] It's been a long 16 months and I am just thrilled to be going back on the road. This will be one of my first gigs and I'll be playing some new stuff and see how the crowd responds."

Billy Bragg (b. Dec. 20, 1957, Essex, UK)

British singer-songwriter, political activist, and author Billy Bragg started out in England's punk scene in the early 1980s, creating and honing a singular sound influenced by folk music, punk and rock and roll. As his career progressed, his songwriting became infused by his fierce political activism.

Bragg has brought his unabashed political passion and musicality to numerous shows at the club throughout the 2000s. His sets have showcased both original music and covers, as well as songs that are bit of both: Bragg was asked by Nora Guthrie, Woody's daughter, to set some of her father's unrecorded lyrics to music. Collaborating with Wilco and Natalie Merchant, the results were the critically acclaimed *Mermaid Avenue* albums (1998-2013). During a three-night residency in 2019, he greeted the audience with "Welcome to the 7:30 Club!"—a gentle poke at the Birchmere's early hours and a reference to another famous DC venue, the 9:30 Club.

John Mayall OBE (b. Nov. 29, 1933, Macclesfield, UK)

The roster of young British blues players who John Mayall enlisted in his band, the Bluesmakers, includes Eric Clapton, Mick Taylor, John McVie, Mick Fleetwood, Peter Green, and Harvey Mandel.

On his first Birchmere visit in 2010, he told the *Alexandria Times:* "In England and in Europe in general, we didn't have the racial divide that America had so we appreciated American black music far more than in their home country. All the blues players and jazz players who would come over to Europe, they were treated like gods. That really was a very big influence in fact, the fact that we had access to these wonderful musicians. I worked with John Lee Hooker quite a lot in the '60s and Sonny Boy Williamson and T-Bone Walker, all these people who are long gone now."

John Mayall during soundcheck in 2010. © *Oelze*

Mayall played the hall several times, including a celebration of his 80th birthday tour in 2013. He told Kyle Osborne "I take the history of the blues very seriously. As a performer, it's my duty to be honest about what I do and share that with other musicians. We enjoy playing the Birchmere. We are always pleased to see it on our calendar and look forward to being here."

***

In the '80s Gary and Michael began working with embassies in DC to help spread the word for a growing number of world music shows. The embassies would use their mailing lists to promote the dates. The eclectic additions to the calendars added flair to the increasingly diverse music. A few of the shows that spotlighted international musicians at the Birchmere include:

o   Altazor Traditions (Latin America)
o   Balalaika Festival with Russian and Ukrainian folk artists
o   Bulgarian Balkana with the Trio Bulgarka
o   Cesaria Evora (Cape Verde)
o   Donovan (UK)
o   Guitarist Egberto Gismonti (Brazil)
o   Hawaii Hapa, Charles Ka'upu, Healani Youn (hula champ)
o   *Muzsikás* with lead singer Marta Sebestyen (Hungary)
o   WETA Welcomes Vertina from Finland
o   Youssou N'Dour. Senegalese music known as mbalax

Donovan's first show at the second Birchmere in 1996 and returning in 2004.   *© Oelze*

© Oelze

Peter Kenneth Frampton (b. April 22, 1950, Kent, UK)

Frampton came alive for four great shows in 2006-2009. His "Wind of Change," "Show Me the Way," "Do You Feel Like We Do" and encore, "Jumpin' Jack Flash," were exciting crowd pleasers. The first show was in support of *Fingerprints,* his 14-track release of instrumentals that pays homage to two inspirational guitarists, Django Reinhardt, the gypsy jazz innovator, and Hank Marvin, lead guitarist for UK's The Shadows.

Marvin plays on one of the tracks, as does Charlie Watts, Bill Wyman, Warren Hayes, and many others including guitarist John Jorgenson, a Birchmere alum with Desert Rose Band shows since the '80s.

Both Jorgenson and Frampton are Djangophiles. John's jazz ensemble is the John Jorgenson Quintet.

Chapter 22 – Gatton, Rice, and Burton

Danny Gatton can play anybody's music. No one can play his. And there's the rub: What do you do with someone who has no patience with boundaries and therefore obliterates them, who slips jazzy octave solos into a country tune, or finger-picks the blues bluegrass style, or plays complex chords where others might settle for single notes? In the age of specialized music, where it's easier to promote something that is blatantly one thing, how do you sell someone like Danny Gatton who is all over the map? Richard Harrington from his 1991 *Washington Post* magazine profile "The Fastest Guitar in the East."

"Danny always seemed to be around. I'd call Danny whenever I needed someone to fill in for a night. He always stayed around after the show for a couple of beers. We'd talk about cars. He

called them "old tins." He loved old cars more than music. Nobody could play an electric guitar better than Danny."

Gary Oelze

Daniel Wood Gatton Jr. (b. Sept. 4, 1945, Washington, DC).

Raised in the blue-collar neighborhood of Anacostia, Danny Gatton combined jazz/rockabilly/country/and rock and roll on his preferred '53 Fender Telecaster guitar in astonishing performances. An appellation used by journalists, but never friends and fans, was "the world's greatest unknown guitarist" because Danny never achieved commercial or financial success, despite his flabbergasting guitar skills.

During one of his early Birchmere soundchecks, Danny's guitar thundered through his Fender Deluxe amp. "It was rattling the walls," Gary recalls. "I should have known better, but I asked him if he could turn it down."

"Sorry, Gary. I can't get the feel of what I want to hear if I turn it down," Danny explained. To accommodate Gary's request, he didn't adjust the volume knob but faced his amp to the back wall of the stage. This was a customary move for Danny and other loud guitarists in smaller venues. It still rattled the walls, but it took the edge off...slightly.

"Many musicians would have just told me 'screw you, this is what I do,' but Danny was always a class act. A nice guy and super-fun, on and off stage. And kind. I remember his condolences when Pudge died. He was playing that night. And also, his grief when Billy Windsor, his singer, manager, and close friend passed away."

Pete Kennedy played frequently with Danny at the Birchmere. When Pete and Mike Auldridge formed a band called Front Porch Swing to play live gigs to support their 1982 record, *Eight String Swing,* they invited Gatton to play bass. Pete asserts that "Danny was discouraged with his career and had quit playing at this time, perhaps by the record industry's lack of understanding of his 1978 *Redneck Jazz* project." Pete believes his invitation to play again helped get Danny back in action. After a few gigs, Danny stopped showing

336

up for the Front Porch Swing dates and returned to gigging with his regular crew.

Kennedy, Preveti, and Gatton acoustically. © *Oelze*

Pete with bassist, John Preveti, also persuaded Danny to play an acoustic show at the Birchmere in 1985.

Danny's last commercial album, *New York Stories,* was recorded at the Birchmere in 1992.

Gary tells this story: "Well, when that album came out, Danny was in the dressing room after a show for an unusually long time. My wife, Linda, went to check on him. She found him sitting in a chair alone."

"Danny, what's the matter?" asked Linda.

He replied, "Well, I'm getting old and fat. Hell, Linda, I think I'll just go home and shoot myself."

Linda didn't take him seriously. Looking back today, Gary admits, "We've all said things like that, and others have told us that they heard Danny say this on other occasions. I've also heard over the years from some that he had depression they were aware of, but I never noticed it."

Danny had a big, beautiful barn-turned-garage next to his Newburg, Maryland home where he worked on his many cars. In the fall of 1994, Danny and his brother, Brent, were in the process of restoring a 1949 Mercury model that Gary owned. "They were going to help me chop the top me chop the top, lower the rear end, and take off all the chrome so it more closely resembled actor James Dean's '49 car," Gary remembers. It was in that garage on October 4, 1994, where Danny took his life. He was 49 years old.

Gatton on stage in 1988.   © *Oelze*

Danny's Tribute

Beer-bottle slide.   © Oelze

After Danny's death, his wife Jan held an auction to raise money for herself and her daughter, Holly. "Jan was losing her government job before Danny's death, and money was always tight in the Gatton household," says Gary. "I saw my Mercury listed in the auction announcement and called Jan asking, 'Hey, are you selling my car?'"

Jan wasn't aware it belonged to Gary, so she began to apologize. Gary stopped her. "It's okay. Just sell the car," he whispered. Gary wanted to help Jan, given the sad circumstances of the passing of a great friend of the Birchmere, and one of the finest guitarists the whole world almost knew.

One thousand $65 tickets sold out immediately for the Birchmere's tribute concerts, held on January 8 and 9, 1998.

All proceeds went to daughter Holly's Virginia Tech college fund. The Fender music corporation, *Guitar Player* Magazine, WMZQ-98.7FM and BASF Tape sponsored these shows.

Maura Kennedy fondly remembers: "They also had a silent auction with items donated by performers. I especially liked a beautiful dress that Emmylou Harris donated. I put the first bid on it but before long it was beyond my means. I didn't have much money. At the end of the night, my husband Pete handed me the dress."

Danny's first appearance on an album "Bobby Charles Invades the Wells Fargo Lounge." Gary has a signed copy in his office"

Vince Gill said he first heard stories about Danny's guitar abilities at his Birchmere shows in the early '80s and went to see him at a DC bar one night after he finished his sets. Gill says, "I can't remember the name of the bar, but I played on stage with him, and I understood why he was appropriately nicknamed "The Humbler" --- for good reason. Another time I played Wolf Trap and afterwards the band went with me to see Danny. And all I remember was he kind of chuckled after I played and then just began to destroy everything and everybody. There was a whole lot of guitar coming out of one man.

"It's so funny about guitar playing. People kind of want to liken it to a gunfight competition, and I've never felt that way. I was just inspired by anybody that played. Some play subtle, beautiful, or they played a lot like Danny—unbelievable jaw dropping and all that kind of stuff. I know many that are much better guitar players than I am, and I'm perfectly comfortable with that. But everybody likes to say, 'Oh, well, he smoked him.'

"I got to play with Danny and Albert Lee on a 1993 TV show out of Nashville called *American Music Shop.* "I remember that Albert and I were on stage watching Danny and we just started laughing. We thought, God, how can anybody do that? But what I remember is that my sweet Mom, who turns 95 in a couple of weeks, called me. She said, 'I saw you on TV last week and you did a good job son. But that boy with the slicked-back hair, he is just crazy or too loose.'"

Gatton's origins and influence are the subject of the 2021 documentary, *Anacostia Delta* featuring appearances by 30 DC musicians, including his friends and disciples Anthony Pirog, Barry Hart, Big Joe Maher, Billy Hancock, Bobby Spates, Tom Principato, Bruce Swain, Chick Hall, Chris Hall, Chris Battistone, Chuck Underwood, Dan Hovey, Dave Chappell, and Dave Elliott.

David Anthony Rice (b. June 8, 1951, Danville, VA)

"Tony was the best musician I ever met" says Gary. © *Oelze*

Tony Rice's father, Herbert Hoover Rice, was an amateur musician and expert welder. Herb's work took the family from Virginia to California, where he co-founded a bluegrass group, the Golden State Boys. Herb's sons Wyatt, Ron, and Tony were in the band.

Growing up in Los Angeles, Tony Rice's main guitar influence was guitarist Clarence White of the Kentucky Colonels and later, The Byrds. Fellow LA musicians and friends like Ry Cooder, Herb Pedersen, and Chris Hillman reinforced Tony's devotion to bluegrass.

"Tony's timing is what he really got from Clarence," says Hillman. "Tony *swings*. That's the best thing I can say about him." Roy Orbison once declared that Tony was one of the best singers he ever heard.

In 1970, banjo master J. D. Crowe asked Tony to sit in with his group at Crowe's regular Holiday Inn gigs in Lexington, Kentucky. Crowe had been playing banjo since 1954, most notably with Jimmy Martin's Sunshine Boys. At that time, Rice had been talking with Country Gentleman Eddie Adcock about joining his. "newgrass" band, II Generation, but decided to go with J.D. Crowe's New South progressive bluegrass band.

Their 1974 debut album was a top seller for Rounder Records. Although both Rice and Skaggs had left by the time J.D. and the group started playing the Birchmere, regular shows with the New South helped the Birchmere immensely.

"In reuniting the New South band, I called Tony. He was living in Sausalito, California with record engineer Billy Wolf." Gary explains, "They had broken up with their wives and were having a pity party for about a year. I asked Tony if he'd participate and he said 'Sure, I'll come and do the show,' so I sent airline tickets. He hadn't been with the New South guys for a long time, and when they arrived at the Birchmere for practice and tuned up it was boom, magic.

Gary told Tony that he needed to get out of California and offered to put a band together for him. "He agreed and I got his brother Wyatt, Jimmy Gaudreau, and Mark Shatz for the band. This group was The Tony Rice Unit. I also hired Billy Wolf to run sound at the Birchmere at that time.

"I had a spare bedroom at my house, so Tony moved in with me for the first six months. He called me "Rajneesh," who was an Indian mystic who opposed traditional morals, so not sure if that was a compliment. My nickname became "Raj" over time.

"His first Birchmere show was enormously successful, and we all had a meeting afterward. Tony had this woman with him, and she was supposedly his business manager. I was suggesting that Tony get out on the road and do some dates, and this person kept interrupting me about how she needed to be involved. And I finally looked at her and said, 'I don't see any reason for you to *be* involved. You're not in the business, and don't know what the hell you're talking about.' She threw her notebook at me and walked out."

(l to r) Jimmy Goudreau, Bill Emerson, and Tony Rice. © *Oelze*

Tony told his biographer Tim Stafford about this time: "Gary Oelze had taken me under his wing to work a lot at the Birchmere. He served as my business manager for a while, too. I owe a lot to Gary for moral support. His friendship was a healing for what I had been going through with my break up with Leela. Things started to happen. I really felt good about being alive."

Gary began booking Tony: "He started getting busy and doing the things he wanted. He had all his money come to me and my accountant audited it. I had to control the money because Tony knew he'd spend it all. I helped Tony get a boat in Florida and he eventually moved down there. I didn't take a dime. I did it because I loved the guy, and thought he was one of the best musicians I ever met in my life. Certainly, he was the best guitar player."

Ben Eldridge, John Duffey, Mike Auldridge, and Tony Rice. Tony would fill-in for John Starling when he missed gigs.   © Oelze

When the Tony Rice Unit became really popular, Gary called Nashville's top talent agent Keith Case, the most important booker of acoustic music artists in the history of Music Row, and brought Rice to meet him. Case happily took over his management, adding him to his other famous clients like Ralph Stanley, Nitty Gritty Dirt Band, Suzy Bogguss, Guy Clark, Townes Van Zandt, John Hartford, and other luminaries. Case passed away at the age of 79 in 2019.

One night in 1987, the Tony Rice Unit played a bill with The Seldom Scene at the Birchmere. Afterward, Tony—with Billy Wolf, Mark Shatz, and others—bought a couple cases of beer and a large stash of reefer and held an all-night recording party at Track studios. They cut "Greenlight on the Southern," "Walls," and "Songs for A Winter Night." Tony later said that that was some of the best music he ever cut, if not *the* best: "That stuff came out of the all-nighter. It was a good time to do it. Yeah, we were raring to go, especially Mark Shatz. He was a ball of energy. He could record 24 hours a day."

The Seldom Scene's Dudley Connell says, "Tony's right hand almost looked like it's it is double jointed. All that cross-picking stuff that he did so fluidly was just amazing. A lot of people have tried to emulate his style, but you know, there's only one Tony. Right?"

In the earlier days, Tony would sit in for John Starling when his duties as a physician kept him from making the Seldom Scene gigs. This happened about ten times, and mostly at the Birchmere. Mike Auldridge especially enjoyed these nights because Rice added such gorgeous guitar solos to Mike's instrumentals.

When Starling decided to leave the Seldom Scene, there was a discussion about bringing in Tony to replace him. The band members loved that idea, and John Duffey imagined how they might increase their asking price if Tony came aboard. The inclusion of Tony Rice would have changed things for the Scene since he was so famous. But Starling hung on a few more years, and Phil Rosenthal eventually got the gig in 1977.

Billy Wolf commented in Rice's authorized biography: "When Tony would sit in with the Seldom Scene, it was like they would stand up straight suddenly. Duffy was a showman, but many times we forget the skill he had as a mandolin player. Duffy took a lot of liberties, and when Tony was in the band, he would play his butt off. They never sounded like that. Tony is one of those musicians who is greater than the sum of the parts when he sits in with someone. I worked Seldom Scene gigs once a week for I don't know how many years, but it was a treat with Tony. That would've been a special band, and he really did consider joining them."

Lincoln History

Gary Oelze has an extensive library in his home. He prefers history and has at least 20 books on Abe Lincoln alone. Tony Rice got deeply involved in biography while he stayed with Gary, specially about our 16th President.

Gary introduced Tony to his 1965 book, *Twenty Days. A Narrative in Text and Pictures of the Assassination of Abraham Lincoln,* by Dorothy Kunhardt.

Tony in disguise.   © *Oelze*

In Tim Stafford and Caroline Wright's biography, *Still Inside: The Tony Rice Story,* Tony said, "The more I read, the more fascinated I became. I ended up reading and buying more books and wanting to photograph places like Ford's Theater. Things like that I really took an interest in."

What fascinated Rice were the subtleties and lesser-known details of history that weren't the things he was taught in school. For example, John Wilkes Booth wasn't just a deranged madman but also the most popular actor of his day.

"That's how the instrumental song "Port Tobacco," came about," said Tony. "I wrote that song about John Wilkes Booth, hoping someday that he would somehow hear it." Gary adds, "Tony even joined the Surratt Society, a group devoted to the Lincoln assassination history."

In his biography, Tony said, "John Jennings and I were palling around with Mary Chapin Carpenter before she became famous. I met her through Gary Oelze. We were drinking beer after a show one night, and I told her. 'You know what? If anybody could write a good song that would present John Wilkes Booth in the light of reality, it would be you.'"

In 2020, Carpenter continued Tony's story: "Tony Rice is one of my most favorite artists. And one of my favorite singers in the days he was singing. An iconic, genius musician on the

346

planet. To be able to see him up close at the Birchmere was an extraordinary experience. In those days. Gary and his amazing staff would lock the doors when the audience was gone. We would sit around at the tables, just chilling out, late at night. And they were also so kind to allow me to just sit and hang out with them. I just worshipped what Tony Rice did. His music in the wider realm of bluegrass is just about my favorite of all time.

"There was a period of time when Tony was living with Gary and Linda, and being sort of a local for a little bit of time. And he was a real history buff then. One night I have this memory of him turning to me and saying, 'Do you know anything about John Wilkes Booth?' I sputtered something whatever every school-age kid in America would have known about Booth in that moment. I remember this somehow that I think Tony was like going around to various places that had some connection to the assassination.

"And he said, 'Why don't you write a song about John Wilkes Booth?' And in that moment, I thought maybe, the way he just kind of tossed that off. And it was like, huh. There was no Internet at that time. And I just started reading everything I could about Booth. And then I wrote the song and I called it "John Wilkes Booth." I played it for John Jennings.

"We did an acoustic guitar demo of it. And then I handed it to Tony and said, 'Here's your song,' never dreaming—truly never dreaming—that he would ever connect to it in such a way that would make him want to record it. But he did. When that happened, it's sort of like I was done. If I never wrote another song again for someone that would be enough. It was that special to me and it remains that way."

Tony recalls in his biography: "I bet it wasn't two days later she and Jennings came to the club after everybody left and put on a cassette over the sound system. It was "John Wilkes Booth." I said, 'Damn, how in the world did you do this so fast?' and Chapin said, 'I went to the library.'"

This song appears on Tony's album, *Native American*. It's not a romantic outlaw ballad, like Woody Guthrie singing about Pretty Boy Floyd, but more of an effort to paint an accurate, sorrowful picture of the tragedy of losing Lincoln just when the country really needed him, and the complexity of his misguided assassin. In the album liner notes, Tony wrote, "Speaking on behalf of Mary Chapin as well as myself, neither of us could condone such a criminal act as the one committed by John Wilkes Booth." Chapin never recorded the song herself.

Tony with Gary's Maltese dog, T. Wilkes.   © *Oelze*

Gary had just put his dog to sleep when Tony first moved in with them. Tony bought this little Maltese dog for Gary as a gift. Gary named the dog T Wilkes— the T stands for Tony. Today Gary has another Maltese he calls Wilkes Two.

Rice's legacy includes the albums, *Manzanita, Roses in the Snow* (Emmylou Harris) *Skaggs and Rice, Still Inside, Mar West, Backwaters, Cold on the Shoulder,* and *Church Street Blues.* Many think *Native American* was the album where Rice beat back some of the depression from which he intermittently suffered. His longtime bandmate on dobro, Jerry Douglas, said: "It's a favorite album because it seemed so much fun to listen to, his voice was strong, and his collaboration with Billy Wolf was at its peak."

Tony with Mike Auldridge and Jerry Jeff.   © Oelze

The Tony Rice Unit packed the Birchmere often and always received critical acclaim from the press for their experimental "spacegrass" music. With Jimmy Goudreau on mandolin, Tony's brother Wyatt on rhythm guitar, and Todd Phillip's walking bass lines, the superb quartet was brilliant. In 1988, Ronnie Simpkins, now with the Seldom Scene since 1995, replaced Phillips. Alison Krauss played regularly with the group in concert for about a year but never appeared on the albums.

The call-and-response of Rice's low-note, rapid guitar riffs with Gaudreau's lovely mandolin lines were thrilling. The Unit played its last show at the Birchmere on New Year's Day,1996.

Rice retired from performing as multiple health issues, including the loss of voice and dexterity, made performing difficult. In 2015, Rice was quoted as saying, "I am not going to go back out into the public eye until I can be the musician I was, where I left off, or better. In 2013, Tony Rice received the International Bluegrass Music Association's most tremendous honor and was inducted in the IBMA Hall of Fame by Birchmere Sam Bush and Peter Rowan. "Of all the second and third generation bluegrass artists who have influenced our music's direction, no one has been more important or more influential than our friend Tony Rice," said Rowan. Sam Bush, who first heard Rice and brought him into the Bluegrass Alliance band in 1970, added that "Tony Rice is arguably the greatest guitarist in the history of music. His timing, tone and licks are the gold standard of bluegrass guitar—imitated but never duplicated."

Clarence White's Guitars

The late Kentucky Colonel, Clarence White, never played the Birchmere. The closest he came was in a Virginia hillbilly bar, Lulu's, with his brother Roland in the early '60s. They'd both head to the Shamrock after those gigs to catch a ride with Eddie Adcock back to his mother's house to jam and drink all night long, according to Adcock. The last time Clarence played the DC area was in 1973 at Georgetown University's McDonough Gym with The Byrds. White was killed five months later, struck by a drunk driver while loading up his gear after a Palmdale, California gig. He was 29.

White's 1952 Fender telecaster electric guitar was acquired by Marty Stuart. The unmistakable sound has been enjoyed by thousands of Birchmere fans at Marty's shows.

Tony Rice was nine years old, a guitarist in his dad's band, when he met Clarence White in 1960 at a radio show. He saw White's dilapidated guitar with no name on the headstock and asked him what kind it was. "It's a Martin," Clarence told him. It was a repair candidate that White had bought for $25. He let Tony play it.

Rice told the late writer, Art Dudley: "It felt like a million bucks to a nine-year old kid." The guitar was a herringbone Martin that White gave up in 1965 to raise cash to buy his Telecaster. When Rice started playing with ex-Kentucky Colonel's fiddler and bassist, Bobby Sloan in The New South in the early 70s, he decided to track down who owned White's D-28. It was Joe Miller, an ex-UCLA football player, whose family owned a chain of liquor stores in Pasadena.

Tony called information for "Miller's Liquors," and the operator asked, "Which listing you want? There are 20 of them." Tony called the first number and reached Joe.

"Do you have Clarence White's guitar?' he asked.

"Yeah, it's upstairs under my bed," Joe answered.

"I'm Tony Rice. Do you know who I am? I'd like to buy the guitar. Would you sell it?"

Joe replied, "For you, yes."

Tony called this guitar "The Antique." It is heard on all of his recordings.

James Edward Burton (b. Aug. 21, 1939) Dubberly, LA)

Washington DC TV reporter Mark Segraves shared Birchmere memories when he interviewed guitarist James Burton. It was a 2018 benefit for the Marine Corps Scholarship Foundation and James Burton's only hall appearance. "Like most of us I remember the original Birchmere location and started going there to see the Seldom Scene. I've seen a number of great shows there over the decades. As a local reporter, Gary and Michael have always been very good to me, opened up their doors to me several times, and connected me with some of the artists who pass through.

"The best example of that would be guitar legend James Burton. Burton was playing with Ricky Nelson's sons, Gunnar and Mathew, and Skunk Baxter. When I arrived with my crew for the interview there was nobody there from the management company. Gary brought me where they were setting up and there was James Burton. I walked over and introduced myself. He didn't even look up at me. He grumbled and said 'I've got to go do this interview. It will take two minutes. They only ask about Elvis and Dylan, and then I'll be right back.' Gary walked us into a back room. We sat down. I told Burton I would be as quick as possible. Burton started laughing. He said 'Take all the time you need' and I did. We talked for almost 40 minutes. We did a Facebook live interview and I took questions from people on line. Gary sat there the whole time listening. It was a great night."

Mark's conversation with Burton began with an introduction: "Tonight's concert includes a long list of rock and roll heavy hitters, but none bigger than James Burton, who has played with just about every rock and roll superstar since the 1950s, including Ricky Nelson, John Denver, Bruce Springsteen, and the King of rock and roll, Elvis Presley

Mark Segraves, James Burton, and Gary.   © M. Segraves

Burton replied "You know I played with two: Elvises. Elvis Presley and Elvis Costello. They were both fantastic."

On his records: "I've probably played on thousands of records. I got a call to play with Barbra Streisand one time, but I was working on a project. So I never had another chance to work with her."

On Ricky Nelson: I first started with Ricky in 1956. He came in doing a song called "My Gal is Red Hot." And we started playing together. We were good friends. I went and did a TV show called *Shindig* with Johnny Cash in 1964. I never really had the opportunity to go back and play with Ricky. We last worked a show together in Las Vegas at the Sahara hotel. I was playing for Jerry Lee Lewis and Ricky opened the show. Jerry Lee closed the show. Ricky and I hung out for a couple of weeks. That was exactly one year before he got killed in a plane crash. And yeah, that was very sad."

On Chet Atkins: "I began playing guitar when I heard Chet Atkins, Merle Travis, and Les Paul. They were great players. And of course, Chet was my hero. He was just amazing player. I love his tone and everything. I wanted to play like Chet. I wanted to play like Merle Travis and Les Paul. I woke up one day and said, no, it's not going to work. There's only one Chet,

Les, and Merle. I got to do *my* thing. So, I wouldn't be a cotton picker. I became the chicken picker."

On Danny Gatton: "Danny came to my hometown of Shreveport when I opened my rock and roll café. He came with Jerry Donahue and we opened the club We had much fun playing. He did the beer bottle trick. He does all these little tricks. I did the same thing when I was 13. Danny was just a great player and a good guy. We worked together. He was a monster."

"I love Vince Gill. We're all family. You know, eventually I worked in a band called Pure Prairie league with Bryan Berline in LA. And I played on "Amie" when they recorded that record.

"And then Elvis called me and asked me to put a band together for him."

Gary asked Burton if he'd come back in the future and James agreed he'd like to. They've been in touch, so the Birchmere is hopeful for a return engagement.

Emmylou Harris (b. April 1947, Birmingham, AL)

(clockwise) Emmylou with staffer Chris Adams, w/ Buddy Miller, signed poster and w/ John Starling and John Duffey. © *Oelze*

Burton added, "On Emmylou Harris: "Wow. What a sweetheart. We did Gram Parson's albums live. Gram wanted to be a country singer. Emmylou was a background singer for him. And Gram unfortunately passed away. Emmylou's husband, Brian Ahern, produced a record for her. But we didn't get to go on tour with Gram. He passed away."

Gary asked Burton if he'd come back in the future and James agreed he'd like to.

© *Oelze*

Leo Kottke (b. September 11, 1945) Athens, GA)

"There are so many other great guitarists to mention who have played here, Gary says. " John Fahey, Peter Frampton, George Thorogood, Steve Vai and others." Another special player is Leo Kottke. Considered a master of the acoustic guitar, inspired by the Delta blues style of Mississippi John Hurt, Kottke has been fingerpicking the Birchmere for over 40 years.

In an early 1982 show, the *Washington Post's* Mike Joyce wrote "Hot shot guitarists are everywhere. Some are faster than Leo Kottke. Others share his fondness for dancing in syncopated melodies but no one creates the special textures and sonorities that defined the cocky style better than the guitarist himself." Bud Gardner commented that "Kottke doesn't do a sound check. He also doesn't use monitors. He sits in the middle of the stage and just plays. He is laid back and personable. He tells me 'it's not rocket science.'"

Chapter 23 – These Magic Moments

Birchmere special events are routine. Around 2003 it began to be regarded as the premiere club for seasonal shows in the DC area. In the first week of December that year, comedian Larry the Cable Guy started the month off, sprinkling Christmas jokes into his act on a Tuesday. Folk-singing icon Judy Collins, appeared on Wednesday accompanied by the Georgetown University Chorale. In the next week, the acapella singing group, Rockapella, showcased a holiday album and began their evergreen annual holiday tour, and country singer Suzy Bogguss featured cuts from her Christmas album in her set. Maggie's Music presented their "A Celtic Christmas" that month, repeated the following year.

Other holiday shows have included Christmas with Aaron Neville & his Quintet, Christmas in Hawaii with Jake Shimabukuro, The Aimee Mann and Ted Leo Christmas Show, and Good for the Jews: 'Putting the Ha! In Hanukkah' Tour! with Jared Stern, to name just a few. But none are as outrageous or as quickly sold out as the as the annual Christmas shows by John Waters proving that even the edgy and unexpected have a place at the holiday table.

John Samuel Waters Jr. (b. April 22, 1946, Baltimore, MD)

"People wouldn't consider me a traditionalist." says American filmmaker, artist, and author John Waters, "But doing my annual show at the Birchmere, followed by my Christmas party at my Baltimore home are my two traditions."

The tickets for John Waters' first Birchmere show, built around the erotic possibilities of Christmas, went on sale in July, 2009 for his December show. Is Santa erotic? Can you have sex in a chimney? His irreverent and hilarious musings are the metaphorical cherry on the top of the Birchmere diversity cake.

The COVID-19 pandemic forced him to cancel both events after a decade, but he vows to return in 2021. "I cancelled 39 speaking engagements in 2020. I look forward to my annual Birchmere Christmas show as the last performance I do each year and then I'm home."

Waters became a hometown Baltimore—and subsequent international cult hero—when he wrote, directed, and produced the outrageous 1972 film, *Pink Flamingos*. It starred his high school friend, Glen Milstead, who debuted as beloved drag queen, Divine. The plotline is simple: it's basically crazy people competing to be "the filthiest people alive." It's graphic, offensive, disgusting, and cool fun. Spoiler alert: Divine eats fresh and authentic dog poop at the end, earning this brilliant film's tagline, "An exercise in poor taste."

One of the first showings of this innovative and unorthodox art film was at the University of Maryland at College Park. Waters went on to create other cult films, *Multiple Maniacs*, *Female Trouble*, and *Polyester* to name a few, as well as his mainstream 1988 film, *Hairspray*, which became a successful Broadway musical, remains in continuous production, and spawned a Hollywood musical remake.

From his Baltimore home in 2020, he discussed his fondness for the Birchmere: "I love pulling into the parking lot.

It's so exciting to do my one-person show at such a diverse club. The posters on the wall, the friendly staff like Bud and John who take care of me, and the food. It's the only place I play where I also eat.

"Michael Jaworek stops by every year to say hello. My sister likes to come here for shows. And I think it was my assistant, Ian, who encouraged me to do the Birchmere in the beginning. I write every word of my shows and they are always different year to year. It takes me about two months to create one, and a few weeks to memorize it because I never use notes," says the friendly Waters.

Cathy Fink and Marcy Marxer

The Washington Area Music Association has recognized this musical duo with over 60 Wammie Awards for folk, bluegrass, and children's music.

Cathy says, "The Birchmere has been generous to the roots music community. They have partnered with Marcy and I on several fundraisers to help our mutual music pals Kate Wolf, Grace Griffith, Dave Giegerich and many others. Their partnership in these fundraisers made a huge difference to these folks and their families. I don't want this aspect of their membership in the community overlooked."

Pete Kennedy says, "Cathy Fink has always had the ability not only to come up with great ideas but to then follow through and actually make them happen. She also has the wide connections in the roots music world to put together a great cast for a tribute show. Her ability to pick up the phone and line up artists like Bill Kirchen, Robin & Linda Williams, Claire Lynch, Robbie Fulks, Pete & Maura Kennedy, The Bumper Jacksons, Mark Schatz, Dave Giegerich, Lynn Morris, Marshall Wilburn, Rickie Simpkins, Patrick McAvinue, Dave Chappell, and Mike Stein, year after year, guaranteed a great series of tributes to Hank Williams, dubbed "The Hillbilly Shakespeare" because of his unvarnished depiction of life's most tragic and joyful extremes. It takes a performer with depth and life experience to put Hank's songs across, and it takes an audience that shares that depth of understanding and empathy to fully plumb the greatness of his work. The Hank Tributes were, consistently, examples of a perfect Birchmere night."

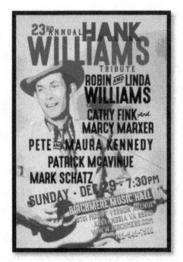

Poster designed by Dick Bangham.

Mike Seeger.   © *Oelze*

Mike Seeger, (b. Aug. 15, 1933 in New York City)

Cathy and Marcy, with Mike Seeger, launched the Annual Mike Seeger Commemorative Old Time Banjo Festival series that continued annually for a decade. Pete's half-brother grew up in the Washington, DC area while both his musically accomplished parents worked with the Federal government to preserve music, his father with the Resettlement Administration, and his mother, with the Archive of American Folk Song at the Library of Congress.

Mike launched his early group, the New Lost City Ramblers in 1958 but also made his name as a music historian. He made over 30 documentary recordings of old-time Appalachian and other traditional music, and another 40 records with the likes of John Hartford, Ry Cooder and Robert Plant, to name a few. Additionally, he created instructional DVDs on Southern banjo styles. Seeger performed not only on the banjo, but on an array of traditional instruments in the first three Birchmere banjo festival shows. He passed away in 2009.

Additionally, he created instructional DVDs on Southern banjo styles. Seeger performed not only on the banjo, but on an array of traditional instruments in the first three Birchmere banjo festival shows until he passed away in 2009.

Performers who also contributed music to this banjo festival series were Sam Gleaves, Roni Stoneman, The Ebony Hillbillies, Tony Trischka, Kaia Kater, Michael Miles, Cheick Hamala Diabte, Bob Carlin, Dan Gellert, Bill Evans, Adam Hurt, Evie Ladin & The Old 78's, and others.

In 2013 the Birchmere presented the "New York Banjo Summit," a "gathering of 5-string masters" featuring Bela Fleck, Tony Trischka, Bill Keith, Noam Pikelny, Richie Stearns, and Eric Weissberg,-with Russ Barenberg (guitar), Jesse Cobb (mandolin), Alex Hargreaves (fiddle) and Corey Dimario (bass).

Gary keeps a very special banjo head in a secret drawer somewhere in the Birchmere. It's an autographed treasure.

Signed banjo head by Tony Trishka, Bela Fleck, Eric Weisberg, Earl Scruggs, Ben Eldridge, Dr. Ralph Stanley, Bill Keith, and Doug Dillard.
© *Oelze*

Cathy and Sir Paul.   © *C. Fink*

Picture Yourself

Cathy Fink remembers a 2007 memory far away from the Birchmere at the Staples Center in Los Angeles: "I was a Grammy Trustee that year for the 49th annual awards and was able to sit in the front section with nominees for the TV show awards. Marcy Marxer and I also were MCs of the pre-televised awards that year. During the commercial breaks, I ran around looking for Alison Krauss, who we'd known since her early days at the Birchmere and folk festivals. She's such a wonderful

360

person and, of course, has a house full of Grammy Awards. I never managed to find her but walked past Sir Paul a few times. So, during one break, I started a conversation with him about the song "Everybody Dance," which he had written for his young daughter. Marcy and I love that song.

"As we spoke, his bodyguard/bouncer kept telling me to go away. Paul ignored him, and so did I. But we were getting close to the end of the break. So, I asked the bouncer guy to take our photo, which Paul was up for. The bouncer guy took a blurry picture and cut off the top of my head. I sent the pic to photographer pal Irene Young, who replaced the top of my head using another photo of me. Meantime, the break was over, I wasn't in my seat, and I had to crouch on the floor as Taylor Swift sang from a platform in the crowd. My friends in the bleachers were watching me and my yellow shirt all over the place!"

Paul McCartney's album *Memory Almost Full* was nominated that year but did not win. However, Birchmere alum performers who did win a 2007 Grammy Award include:

Bluegrass: Instrumental, Ricky Skaggs and Kentucky Thunder
Contemporary Jazz: *The Hidden Land,* Bela Fleck/the Flecktones
Country Album: *Taking the Long Way*, Dixie Chicks
Country Instrumental: "Whiskey Before Breakfast," Doc Watson
Jazz Instrumental, *The Ultimate Adventure*, Chick Corea
Male Country Vocal: "The Reason Why," Vince Gill
Pop Instrumental Album: *Fingerprints,* Peter Frampton
Traditional Blues: *Risin' With the Blues*, Ike Turner

Ida Lewis Guillory (b. Jan. 15, 1929, Lake Charles, LA)

Before she became Queen Ida with her Zydeco band, she was a full-time mother of three and a part-time bus driver. Ida grabbed a button accordion when her kids left the nest and began playing in her brother's soft-rock trio. She learned Zydeco music. The name comes from the Creole pronunciation of the French word for beans, "les haricots," and the music is a blend of blues, rhythm and blues, and the music of the

Caribbean and French Creole and Native inhabitants of southwest Louisiana.

Queen Ida in 1986.   © *Oelze*

A *San Francisco Chronicle* free-lancer profiled her in 1975 and Queen Ida was crowned. By 1986 her Bon Temps Zydeco band was playing 200 concerts a year and she had the first of her three Grammy nominations.

© *Oelze*

Glen Travis Campbell (b. April 22, 1936, Billstown, AK))

The multi-talented Campbell—singer, songwriter, session musician," actor, TV star, and winner of a Grammy Lifetime Achievement award—brought his "goodbye tour" at the hall twice in 2012 for two nights each time. He was suffering from dementia and this would be his last year as a performer.

In Dave McKenna's *Washington Post* review of the show, he noted Campbell "is a different sort of player these days, too. He began his career as a guitarist for the Wrecking Crew, an esteemed studio session outfit in Southern California, and as part of the house band of "Shindig," a TV show that introduced pop bands to the masses. (He worked alongside Leon Russell on both ventures.) But even in his prime as a front man, Campbell never let on that he was aware of how awesome his musical gifts really were.

"These days, Campbell is not a precise picker. In his solo on "Galveston," as on several tunes, he struggled to find the right spot on the fretboard. He hit blizzards of wrong notes all around the song's timeless melody, then suddenly worked his way to where he'd been trying to get all along. Yet his solos, imperfect as they were, were fascinating. The abstract playing gave his iconic material an aura of jazz or parody."

***

Gary: "I was a huge fan of Glen Campbell in the '60s and '70s. For a while many folks didn't know he was in The Wrecking Crew. The book about those LA session musicians has some very funny stories about Glen recording with Sinatra and so many others. His "Gentle on My Mind" became a hit, so he went out on his own. His follow up "By the Time I Get to Phoenix" was ranked number 20 on BMI's Top 100 Songs of the Century.

"Whenever Glen talked on TV or wherever, that's him. It's not phony. He was just a nice person. When I first met him, he asked me if Roger Miller ever played the Birchmere. I told him yes, so he began telling me Roger Miller stories. Of course, everybody in Nashville has a Roger Miller story, but, the one Glen liked went like this:

"A young kid wanting to be a songwriter came to Nashville and asked Roger for advice.

"Roger said, 'Don't carry your change and your pills in the same pocket.'

"'Why?' asked the kid.

"'Because I just took thirty-five cents.'

© *Oelze*

"His last tour was very sad. His dementia was worse than most people realize. His children did a wonderful job helping him. They protected him and didn't want the public to know how bad he was.

"I remember another lead break on one song and, God, it was amazing. And when he got to the end of the break, he just started it again because he didn't remember that he had done it."

Roy Linwood Clark (b. April 15, 1933, Meherrin, VA)

Washington DC-apprenticed Virginia native and *Hee Haw* TV star, with hit songs like "Thank God and Greyhound," and "Yesterday When I was Young," Roy Clark did his first hall show in December 2008. From the age of 11, he grew up in the

Highlands neighborhood of Washington, DC where his father worked nearby at the Navy Yard. Roy learned banjo and his first appearance was on local TV channel WTTG in 1949 at the age of 16. Throughout his career, he would cite the influences of musicians in Washington he listened to in his teen tears.

His third Birchmere show in 2011 was the most memorable, with a special moment for the audience, too—and for one particular fan, Rick Frank.

Frank, a Fredericksburg, Virginia banker, had a close friend named Ray Rainwater, a very successful businessman who lived in Lorton, Virginia. Ray had managed his brother, Marvin Rainwater, a rockabilly and country artist in the late '50s.

Marvin's hit song was "Gonna Find Me a Bluebird." He was a quarter Cherokee and wore Native American-inspired stage attire. Ray knew many country stars like George Jones and Patsy Cline , and when Rick said he was seeing Roy Clark, Mr. Rainwater said, "You know, I got Roy Clark into show business, I bought him a guitar when he was a teenager, and arranged for him to be on Arthur Godfrey's TV talent show." Rick responded "Right," sarcastically but followed up by contacting Clark's manager. He listened and gave Rick his cell phone number with instructions to call him when they arrived at the Birchmere.

(l to r) Ray, Roy, and Rick backstage. © R. Frank

Roy Clark began his set but then stopped the show announcing: "Bring the house lights up please. We have a celebrity in the house. This man got me my first break in show business, bought me my first guitar, and got me a gig on the Arthur Godfrey show. Ray Rainwater, please stand up."

Rick thought, "Son of a bitch. Ray was telling me straight." He went backstage after the show and listened as the old friends talked excitedly "I barely got a word in." Marvin was able to get Clark on the Godfrey TV show because he, himself, had won the talent contest in 1955 earning him a recording contract with MGM. Rainwater died in 2013 at the age of 88.

Ryland Peter Cooder (b. March 15, 1947, Los Angeles, CA)

In 2015, writer and friend of the Birchmere, Charles David Young, had a short bucket list of favorite performers he'd never seen that included Ry Cooder, a multi-instrumentalist (best known for slide guitar), and named one of *Rolling Stone's* "100 Greatest Guitarists of All Time." Charlie says "I was excited to see his name pop up on the schedule for the Birchmere that fall as part of a group including Ricky Skaggs, his wife Sharon White and her father, Buck White.

"It turned out to be one of the best and most timeless concerts of the untold dozens of shows I've seen at the latest incarnation of the venue. As either Ricky or Ry announced at one point, 'None of the songs we will play tonight was written after 1965."

"Using a number of vintage instruments and equipment, the evening was a bit like time travel, and the setlist was pure Birchmere-perfect Americana, with songs ranging from early Dillards, Kitty Wells, Louvin Brothers, Flatt & Scruggs and Blind Alfred Reed. One song would give us a Hank Williams country blues and the next a Black gospel celebration.

"The icing on the cake, as often happens at the Birchmere, was the whole supergroup coming out to tables for a chat and signing session after the show. I'd met Ricky a few times before, but I finally got to meet Ry and thank him for all the years of great music."

In 2020, Ricky Skaggs cited this show as his favorite Birchmere appearance.

Bellydance Superstars

Birchmere associate promoter, Ben Finkelstein recalls when Miles Copeland, brother of Stewart Copeland, and manager of the Police, assembled The Bellydance Superstars & The Desert Roses tour in 2004. "Miles was calling a variety of promoters to see if they'd be interested in booking them. Most of the agents were clueless. Then he calls Michael Jaworek who immediately said, 'Sure, let's do it.' And it was amazing. We've done it pretty much every year since, and that was also one of the most exciting backstage acts we've seen." For Ben and Michael, it was very pleasant because their office at that time adjoined the dressing room.

Her calendar graphic. © Oelze

Psychic Phenomenon

Famous psychic and *New York Times* bestselling author, **Sylvia Browne** appeared once in 2013 in "An Evening of Insights and Live Readings." One non-fan of Browne posted a comment on this show: "I love the Birchmere, and it actually pains me that they're allowing that awful fraud to do a show in their building. I am secretly hoping it's a trap and they're going to toss her in the Potomac when she shows up."

When asked if the mind-reader's show was good or bad, another patron answered "Medium."

Raul Francisco Martinez-Malo Jr. (b. Aug. 7, 1965, Miami, FL)

Born to Cuban exile parents and raised in a home rich with American, Latin, and classical music, Raul Malo formed The Mavericks in the late '80s with high school friend Robert Reynolds. Although they came together based on their mutual love of traditional country music, the band got its start playing the Miami alternative and punk rock clubs.

By the early '90s, The Mavericks signed with a major record label and throughout the next three decades, earned a devoted fan base for their infectious, genre-busting mix of country, Latin, pop and rockabilly music, picking up a Grammy and various Americana, CMA, and other awards along the way. The band dissolved twice in the early 2000s, reforming in 2012.

During the hiatus, Raul—whose soaring, expressive voice drives the signature sound of The Mavericks--launched a solo career as performer, songwriter and record producer that continues today.

Rolling Stone observed: "Malo possesses a voice that vibrates through a listener's entire core—to say nothing of what it does on an emotional level. Equal parts Orbison and Pavarotti, Malo, then, is regarded as one of country music's most respected singers."

Raul with Bud Gardner.   © *Oelze*

Raul has released six solo albums and been involved in an array of projects as singer, songwriter, and record producer, including a 2005 album with the supergroup, Los Super Seven, featuring the likes of John Hiatt, Delbert McClinton, Joe Ely, Lyle Lovett, and members of Los Lobos and Calexico (among others). Since 2012, The Mavericks have toured and recorded, including their first all-Spanish album, *En Español,* in 2021.

In a 2020 interview with Mark Engleson for the concert review blog, *Parklife DC,* Malo looked forward to his upcoming show at the club:

"The Birchmere has really been like a home away from home. It's one of my favorite venues. It's been there forever. They're such great advocates of music and musicians. You get there and they treat you right. It's nice, you don't have to get a hotel room. You can hang out there. They feed you. Not only that, but professionally too, it's always a pleasure there. It always sounds great. They've got their guy who does a great job. I have a lot of going memories going back 15, almost 20 years I've been playing there.

Engleson asked Malo if he would be going solo for the date. He humorously replied, "These are my solo shows. I go out by myself. I tell stories and whatnot. It's like a Mavericks show, just a lot lamer."

He also discussed how he worked solo versus with the Mavericks: "I play to the room and go with the vibe of the night...you can't do that with a band. We can call certain songs and we can do certain things. But not with the freedom like by yourself, where you can do whatever you want. I like that. It's also scary, too. It's good to get out of your comfort zone."

As both solo artist and front man for the Mavericks, Raul Malo has appeared 18 times at the Birchmere.

Gary adds, "Raul is one of the greatest singers to play the hall. He can sing anything."

The Biggest A-hole

A non-scientific poll was taken among the Birchmere staff in 2020 asking who was the most "challenging" performer that played the hall. Sometimes the question was worded, "Who was the biggest A-hole?" The winner is:

James Hugh Calum Laurie CBE (b. June 11, 1959, Oxford, UK)

Actor Laurie played the misanthropic doctor in the TV series, *House.* Birchmere fans know him as a talented jazz and blues pianist who headlined in 2012 and 2013 as "Hugh Laurie with his Coppertone Band."

Laurie was listed in the 2011 *Guinness World Records* as the most-watched leading man on television and was one of the highest-paid actors in a television drama, earning $409,000 per episode.

The Birchmere staff couldn't talk with him directly. They would have to direct questions like, "When would you like to eat dinner?" to his manager. The manager, standing next to

Hugh, would repeat it to him, verbatim. Hugh would respond, and the manager would parrot his answer back to the staff.

In the House: Hugh Laurie.   © Oelze

It turns out that Laurie agrees with the Birchmere staff. Since the late '90s, the actor has frankly acknowledged his battle with depression. The affliction, he said in an *Evening Standard* interview, "affects everything—my family and friends." In the article, Laurie admits to having been "a pain in the arse to have around... miserable and self-absorbed."

When asked if Laurie is welcomed back at the Birchmere, Gary answered, "Of course. His performance was great. He played some songs we've never heard before in the hall, like Bessie Smith's "Send him to the 'Lectric Chair" and Jelly Roll Morton's "I Hate a Man Like You." The crowd loved him. What's not to love?"

Michael Jaworek adds, "My own interactions with Laurie were limited, although I was able to talk with him one-on-one since our conversation wasn't about Hugh. It was about Dr. John and other New Orleans musicians. Laurie is an example of people who have problems, but who find a niche in any occupation where they can function even though they're difficult. Beethoven and Mozart, from what we've read, were also no fun to be with."

Chapter 24 – Birchmere Pops

One of the highly praised, and according to BMI, most-played pop records in musical history is "You've Lost that Loving Feeling" by the Righteous Brothers. Original Righteous Brother Bill Medley has sung this song twice at the Birchmere. Glen Campbell played guitar on the original recording, and thought it was the greatest record he ever played on as a session musician. Here is an abbreviated selection of the popular recording performers who have graced the Birchmere stage.

"Herman."   © Oelze

Peter Blair Bernard Noone (b. Nov. 5, 1947, Urmsted, UK)

Peter Noone was 16 years old when he walked into a London recording studio and recorded the Carol King-penned, "I'm Into Something Good" with his band, Herman's Hermits. The band had a great run in the mid-60s, adding "Mrs. Brown, You've Got a Lovely Daughter," "I'm Henry the VIII, I Am," and another dozen hit songs to their resume. Noone brought these songs with him to the Birchmere for over 20 years. Once in 2004, he changed up his regular set by playing several British Invasion songs he passed up at the time, including "Love Potion No. 9" by the Searchers, "Dandy" by the Kinks, and "For Your Love," a hit for the Yardbirds.

He often ends his shows with one of his early songs, "There's a Kind of Hush" and lets the crowd finish singing the line... "all over the world."

Elaine Page   © *Oelze*

Elaine Jill Paige, OBE. (b. March 5 1948, Barnet, UK)

When the "First Lady of the British Musical Theatre," Elaine Paige, embarked on her debut American tour in 2013, she appeared at the Birchmere.

Paige started her career as a cast member of the 1967 UK *Hair* tribe in the role of Sheila, singing "Easy To Be Hard." The roles of Eva Peron in *Evita* and Grizabella in *Cats* were originated by Paige. Shining in a red sequined dress, Paige played a beautiful Sunday evening concert in March to an elated Birchmere audience. Highlights included "As If We Never Said Goodbye" (*Sunset Boulevard*), "I Knew Him So Well," (*Chess*), "Don't Cry for Me Argentina" (*Evita*), and the signature and pervasive "Memory" (*Cats*).

Sally Olwen Clark (b. Nov. 15, 1932, Surrey, UK)

Petula Clark started out as a child actor in film and theatre, but she is best known as a singer who had a series of upbeat international hits that exemplified the spirit of the swinging mid-60s, including "Downtown," "I Know A Place," "Don't Sleep In The Subway," and "Sign of the Times."

Journalist Ken Roseman was there at Clark's November 2018 Birchmere concert. He says her show "included all of those greatest hits, plus The Beatles' "Blackbird" and John Lennon's "Imagine." At 86 years old, Clark still had the energy of a performer half her age. Her Las Vegas-style show was fantastic. I'm glad I got to see a legend like Petula Clark in the intimate Birchmere setting."

© *Oelze*

Alfred Giovanni Boe, OBE (b. Sept. 29, 1973, Blackpool, UK)

English tenor and actor Alfie Boe, is best known for his role as Jean Valjean in *Les Misérables*, his reprise of the role in the *25th Anniversary Concert* of the same, as well as other musical theater appearances in *Finding Neverland* and Baz Luhrmann's *La Bohème.* Boe, who has sold over a million albums in the UK, was full of pop song surprises at his first Birchmere show in 2012. He opened with Tim Buckley's "Song to the Siren," and loaded his 16-song set with two Stones covers, Fred Neil's "Everybody's Talking," Dobie Gray's "Drift Away," and Greg Allman's "Midnight Rider." He added "Neapolitan Arias," and a few other classical-styled tunes from his *Storyteller* album. and, of course, the emblematic "Bring Him Home" from Les Misérables

His diverse show paid tribute to two of the hall's favorite performers, Ralph Stanley ("Rank Strangers") and John Prine ("Hello in There"), his two encores. A bonus highlight was his enthusiastic drum solo during an Elvis medley.

"Having Alfie Boe at the Birchmere was a big deal for the club," Gary comments. Boe returned the following year for two more shows.

Stephen Louis Bilao III (b. Dec. 19, 1944, Palo Pinto, TX)

Steve and Ray.   © Steve Tyrall

Steve Tyrell has been popularizing classic pop standards for a modern-day audience for five decades. His American Standards albums have achieved top 5 status on Billboard's Jazz charts. He made his Birchmere debut in 2004, the same year he won a Grammy for producing Rod Stewart's album, *Stardust: The Great American Songbook Vol.*

376

"Steve has played for us 10 times since 2004 and he is a wonderful entertainer," says Gary.

A few other popular artists who played the hall include:

Nancy Sinatra　　　**Donny Osmond**　　　**Wayne Newton**

Don McLean　　　**Michael Bolton**　　　**Lisa Marie Presley**

Another popular feature.

Never before seen by half the audiences: The six-foot mural in the women's restroom.   *Painting by Eminiah "The Fly" Shinar*

Chapter 25 – Send-Ups

Sometimes comedy isn't pretty but it's certainly no stranger to the Birchmere. Duck Breath Mystery Theatre was a fledgling San Francisco comedy group when they first played the Cellar Door in 1980. In their audience was a National Public Radio producer who suggested they contribute some material to the station. When they did, their notoriety grew and they became an early comedy group to play the Birchmere in 1986. Duck Breath and the Star-Spangled Washboard Band first brought comedy to the Birchmere.

Duck Breath Mystery Theater.   © *Oelze*

Roger Dean Miller Sr. (b. Jan. 2, 1936, Ft. Worth, TX)

On his first solo tour in 1991, singer-songwriter Roger Miller forgot some words to his song, "England Swings" at the beginning of his Birchmere set. He apologized to the audience by joking: "I hate to forget things these days. But what's good about having Alzheimer's is that you get to meet so many new people. You can hide your own Easter eggs. And you get a new car every day."

Roger was kidding, as usual. When he arrived that afternoon, he asked to talk with Gary.

"Gary, you've got to do something about that dog outside," he insisted.

What dog?" asked Gary.

"It's outside in the parking lot. He started humping my leg when I tried to get in the door."

"So, what did you do?"

Roger replied, "I told him to hurry up."

Bada-boom.

"King of the Road."   © Oelze

Novelty songwriter Sheb Wooley ("Purple People Eater") was Roger's cousin's husband and bought him his first fiddle when Miller was a boy. His song-writing inspiration was Hank Williams. Roger stole a guitar at age 17. When caught, and to get off the hook, Miller joined the Army. There, his Sargent happened to be Jethro Burns' brother, who convinced him to head for Nashville. There, Roger eventually became the millionaire songwriter of his much-covered 1964 crossover hit "King of the Road" and other offbeat songs that showcased both his songwriting prowess and his mischievous sense of humor.

Gary on Roger: "Before his big song-writing hits, he was Minnie Pearl's fiddle player. His humor was addictive, and other Nashville songwriters used to follow Roger around because everything he said was a potential song. He was like a musical Robin Williams. Roger's first single, "Dang Me" was a number one hit in 1964."

However, Miller once quipped, "The human mind is a wonderful thing. It starts working before you are born and doesn't stop working until you sit down and try to write a song."

"In 1985 Roger wrote the music and lyrics to a Broadway show called *Big River* about the adventures of Huckleberry Finn. When he was asked to write the score, he had never read the book and said he had only seen one play in his life. When rehearsals began, he was told they needed more songs, so he wrote them immediately."

One year after his solo Birchmere performance Roger discovered a tumor beneath his vocal cords. He had previously written a song about his life-long cigarette habit called "Dad Blame Anything a Man Can't Quit." He died of lung cancer at age 56.

Paula Poundstone (b. Dec. 29, 1959 Huntsville, Al)

Comedian Paula Poundstone has played the Birchmere for 17 years, selling out multiple nights with each engagement. "I love the Birchmere," she said. "It's a cherished place, and the only venue I do three nights in a row because I can unpack and enjoy the excitement of sleeping in for two mornings.

"I stay in nearby Crystal City. The first time I left my hotel in the morning, I turned right and started walking, looking for a coffee shop or something. And nothing but tall buildings for blocks. The next year I turned right and walked even further. I was like Lewis and Clark. Nothing. Finally, about two years ago, I had this crazy thought. I'll go left, and sure enough, I found a strip mall with a Barnes & Noble. I have never been happier."

She has served for years as the national spokesperson for the American Library Association. On many occasions, she has split the profits from her merchandise sales with the Friends of the Alexandria Public Library and other libraries on her tour itineraries. She observed: "It's funny that we think of libraries as demure places where dusty, bun-balancing, bespectacled women shush us. The truth is libraries are raucous clubhouses for free speech, controversy, and community."

Paula Poundstone   © *Oelze*

"We love Paula," says Gary. "She starts talking with the audience from the stage, inventing comedy on the spot by asking them questions. It's spontaneously funny, but the humor sticks with you in a personal way long after the night is over. Her shows are always different since she isn't doing routines. Her fans return every year because the material is always fresh."

Known for her colorful, oversized zoot suits and loud ties and for smart observational humor, Paula was the first woman to host the White House Correspondents' dinner in 1992.

One factor that influenced her improvisational approach to humor is that she couldn't memorize the material she wrote. "I have a skeleton in my head, but no fat or skin on it. I love talking to the audience, and I must be the luckiest performer in the world. I always land something or somebody that takes off.

"I seek out the faces in the audience who appear bored or not especially happy. I become more interested in someone who is looking like they don't want to be at the show. Somehow that attracts me. The truth is, once I get the person talking, it may turn out that wasn't their feeling at all. I was misreading their body language because that's not my area of expertise."

She becomes charming on the subject of her fans. "There's one dear person who comes to see me every year at the Birchmere I call "the framer." Framing pictures is her profession. The first time we met, we took a picture together. The next year she came with that picture framed, and we did another photo together. We do this every year, so we now have a print of a photograph of an image, et cetera, of us together holding a picture of ourselves."

Another audience member became a devoted fan when Paula discovered from the stage that he worked in the U.S. Patent office. His occupation became grist for that night's act. "But afterward, he started sending me photocopies of patents that were rejected, including one for a machine with a fake hand patting a baby to put it to sleep. I think I saw that on The Three Stooges one time," Paula laughs.

Suzanne Westenhoefer (b. March 31, 1961, Columbia, PA)

She began telling jokes as a barmaid in Secaucus, New Jersey to a receptive bar clientele who loved her comedy. She hit the road as a comic in 1990, and became the first openly gay comic to perform on television, appearing on a 1993 Sally Jesse Raphael TV segment titled "Breaking the Lesbian Stereotype... Lesbians Who Don't Look Like Lesbians." A year later, she became the first to have her own HBO comedy special.

Michel Jaworek recalls, "By 1991 she had played Lisner auditorium. Her agent called and we thought if she did well at Lisner then she should do well at the Birchmere. We hired her and it was a success.

"Gary and I were standing near the monitors at the end of her first Birchmere gig when a man— one of the few males at the show—came up to Gary and asked if he was the owner. Gary nodded and the man said, 'I'd just like to say how much those of us in the [gay] community appreciate being able to come someplace that isn't "ours" to see a show like Susan's.'

"It's called show business," says Gary, who is proud that the Birchmere became LGBTQ-friendly early on.

For some people, speaking unscripted for 75 to 90 minutes is a terrifying thought. For Susan Westenhoeffer, it's like "Bring it on."

© *Oelze*

Westenhoeffer says, "I think there was a real hunger for gay comedy then in the '90s so I picked the right time to start. The Birchmere is my favorite place to play. It's fantastic. Many of the people who were coming to see me then were driving three or four hours from Virginia and Pennsylvania to the club. I was doing something that no one else was doing at that time. I was going to these quote-unquote "straight audience clubs" and demanding to be taken seriously, which sounds funny coming from a comic. I wasn't getting up and making apologies for being gay. Like, I can't help it. I'm gay, but I'm still a nice person. Rather I was saying 'I'm gay. It's up to you if you don't like it. I'm amazing. I chose to be gay. I could have been anything, but I won the lottery.' This kind of attitude was unheard of in 1992."

Her success helped open the Birchmere doors to other LGBTQ performers including the Queer Queens of Qomedy hosted by Poppy Champlin with Carol Leifer, Dana Goldberg, and Kinsey Sicks over the years. Kate Clinton, who billed her act as "Say Yes to K8!" appeared in 2009.

Russell always quipped that most of his jokes and songs are very topical and have "a shelf life shorter than cottage cheese."

Nonetheless, his January 5, 2013 Birchmere show included parodies of Vice President Biden, and Senators Rand Paul and Mitch McConnell. He asked the crowd to shout "Darwin was wrong" when he mentioned their names while spoofing them.

Take Offs

Another much-loved comedy show over the years is the annual World Famous Pontani Sisters present "Burlesque A'Pades in Loveland," (among other names) hosted by "Mr." Murray Hill and featuring an everchanging cast including Angie Pontani, The Evil Hate Monkey, The Maine Attraction, Cleveland's Own Pinch & Squeal, PLUS Cherry Bomb, Ginger Leigh & Goldi Fox of the Peekaboo Revue.

"It's burlesque, a little circus-like, and very funny. The audience has been loyal to these performers," says Gary.

Joseph Marcus Ruslander (b. Aug. 23, 1932, Buffalo, NY)

The future political satirist Mark Russell moved to the Washington DC area with his family in the 1950s, and was accepted into George Washington University. But he joined the Marines instead.

Mark Russell   © *Oelze*

When discharged, he became the bar manager at the Carroll Arms Hotel in the shadow of the Capitol, and gradually began playing piano around town, developing his political humor act. He is best known locally for his long tenure performing at the Shoreham Hotel. His later PBS Specials and TV appearances made him a legendary political satirist.

He also referenced then-President Obama's vow not to negotiate the debt ceiling crisis with the Republicans with the question, "I wonder if he's going to negotiate with the Chinese when they cancel our credit and turn off our utilities." The lyrics of his song parody that summed up these particular bits was—to the tune of "Auld Lang Syne"—"For old acquaintance be forgot, let's shake hands and just be friends, till we meet again in two more months, and screw the people once again."

Larry the Cable Guy

Spoiler Alert: Larry the Cable Guy is not a real person. He is a character played by **Daniel Whitney**, (b. Feb. 17, 1963,

Pawnee City, NE), actor, comedian and former radio personality. His catchphrase—and title of his autobiography—is "Git-R-Done!" He played the Birchmere in 2003. Gary Oelze's favorite Larry joke isn't family-friendly, but here are three other examples.

© *Oelze*

- This is a song I wrote about my girlfriend. She cheated on me with another man. It's called "I Can't Get Over You till You Get Out From Under Him."
- One year my dad bought my mom a mood ring. Them things work pretty good. When she was in a good mood it was blue and when she was in a bad mood it made a red mark upside my dad's head.
- I was living with a girl for eight months, until she found out I was there.

Caroline Gilchrist Rhea (b. April 13, 1964, Westmount, Canada)

Prior to her February 2007 show, comedian Caroline Rhea visited injured soldiers, and donated tickets at Walter Reed Army Medical Center. She started her stand-up career in 1986, and by the time she entertained the hall she was best known as Aunt Hilda on the TV series, *Sabrina, the Teen-aged Witch.*

Rhea's comedy style is endearing; her persona is a humble Canadian woman who grew up thinking bronze was the top award in the Olympics. On stage she said "Some celebrities are intimidating but I'm the kind of celebrity where fans say to me 'I've gotta go.'"

"I went to the big fancy University of Arizona. One of the jobs I had was being a cater waiter. I'd pass out food at events. Over Passover I was a seder cater waiter. That had to happen sooner or later. Once I saw an alligator. Ok. I'll stop."

At 44, she had her daughter the year before the show. "I had like a million sonograms so I started my own website, "MyTubes."

Signed poster and with Bud Gardner.   *© B. Gardner'"*

Robert Klein (b. Feb. 8, 1942, Bronx, NY)

Singer, actor, and stand-up comedian Robert Klein appeared at the club in 2007, accompanied by a pianist. And yes, he performed the blues parody that closes most of his shows, "I Can't Stop My Leg."

He had hosted *Saturday Night Live* twice, and had a Tony nomination for his starring role in Broadway's *They're Playing Our Song*. His Birchmere show coincided with promotion of a multi-disc DVD compilation of his HBO specials dating back almost 30 years. "It's about time!" Klein quipped when he learned these discs were being released.

Gary, Kathleen Madigan, Kelly Pilchard, and Susan Oelze. © *Oelze*

Kathleen Madigan (b. Sept. 30, 1965, Florissant, MO)

Beginning in 2009, comedian Madigan has played the hall nine times. "I always give homeless people money, and my friends yell at me, 'He's only going to buy more alcohol and cigarettes.' And I'm thinking, 'Oh, like I wasn't?'"

Kathleen Madigan has been working the road doing up to 300 shows a year at theaters and clubs, benefits for service people, and corporate events.

Gary says, "One of the reasons she stopped playing here is that she likes to do two shows a night, and we don't do that." Other comedians who have appeared include Felipe Esparza, Tom Pappa, Donell Rawling, Preacher Lawson, Gad Elmelah, Ralphie May, Rob Schneider, and Piff the Magic Dragon.

Roseanne Bar in 2004: "She played only one show and we all expected her to be smart-assy," said Bud Gardner. "But she wasn't. She was sweet and friendly to everyone, and very funny." © Oelze

Chapter 26 - Jazz Hands

One important music promoter in Washington, DC in the early 1970s was the late Bill Washington. He founded Dimensions Unlimited. His 1973 Dimensions Unlimited Freedom Festival at RFK stadium brought out 55,000 people to see Funkadelic, Mandrill, Rare Earth, and Buddy Miles. Bill made money on this event when similar festivals at that time lost money.

He promoted successful black artist-oriented shows at DAR Constitution Hall and the Capital Centre. However, five of his ten large venue shows, including Stevie Wonder, lost money in 1982. Dimensions Unlimited continued to decline in the Washington DC market.

The 1,200-seat Howard Theater had closed in 1968 in the aftermath of the riots following the assassination of The Rev. Martin Luther King. It reopened in 1975, but closed again in 1980. Moreover, there weren't many club-level venues available for R&B acts.

But there was the Birchmere. Michael Jaworek says, "We had been reliably featuring R&B and funky jazz artists for some years when we got the chance to book Joe Sample and Lalah Hathaway in 1991. Mike Joyce heralded this show in his Washington Post review titled "R&B at the Birchmere: "The Birchmere, a citadel of bluegrass and acoustic music, opened its door to two sold-out R&B shows Monday night featuring singer Lalah Hathaway, saxophonist Gerald Albright, keyboardist Joe Sample and an impressive backup band."

Jaworek continues: "Our double bill of Sample and Hathaway for two nights became a tipping point, as the saying goes, for the Birchmere. We perceived at that time that this show put us on the front page of the African American community. By the 1990's Gary and I were reliable people with a listening club open to a wide variety of genres. The Cellar Door was long closed. Their management was doing mainly rock shows at the Bayou and larger venues. The 9:30 Club was doing alternative rock and later new wave. There wasn't as much competition for us, and the Birchmere became a significant player in this marketplace. The artists' agents valued us."

"The combination of these acts being well-known in the area and popular helped break through any reservations their audiences may have had about coming to the Birchmere, feeling secure, feeling safe, and perhaps feeling some ownership of a venue as people do when it presents the music they love."

© *Oelze*

Joseph Leslie Sample (b. Feb. 1, 1939, Houston, TX)

Keyboardist and composer Joe Sample is a founding member of the Houston-based quartet the Jazz Crusaders. He brought his Jazz Crusaders, once to the hall, and his trio six times. On one of those shows, Sample nicked his finger on a broken key during sound check. Gary was relieved when it was a minor cut, and the show went on.

This piano is now safeguarded in an inner room of the hall among other collected treasures. One is a rare 1969 Hammond B-3 organ with original Leslie speaker that Rock and Roll Hall of Famer Gregg Allman made an offer to take home with him when he played in August 2015. The Hammond organs that Gregg played were an important element of the Allman Brothers' signature sound. But Allman left empty-handed as the Birchmere wanted to keep this organ around in case an act needed it.

Patti, Bud, and Tuck   © *B. Gardner*

William Charles "Tuck" Andress (b. Oct. 28, 1952, Tulsa, OK)

Patricia Cathcart "Patti" Andress (b. Oct. 4, 1945. San Francisco, CA)

Tuck and Patti were already classical musicians when they met and married in 1978. They next spent ten years polishing their jazz music together and released their debut album, *Tears of Joy* in 1988 on the prestigious *Windham Hill* label.

"It was like a hurricane hit us when that album came out," says Tuck. "And we were gone for 11 years out of the month on the road for the next few years and the Birchmere was one of our first stops. And when we get there the first time on October 15, 1989 and see the posters of everyone we've ever loved, and it was it was like 'Oh, my God. We are playing here?" We have the good fortune to be on a stage like this?'"

Former sound engineer Billy Wolf remembers Tuck and Patti: "I did sound for them a half dozen times. I love them.

Truly, they are dear people. They liked interacting with the audience. Patti had ear monitors and she asked me to put a mic on the audience so she could hear their reactions and feel a symbiosis with them. The Birchmere was rather unique then, with audience members about two feet away from the performers looking right at them. I thought Tuck and Patti were remarkable in how they used that proximity. Some artists were scared of the closeness."

Patti remembers, "I loved champagne and I knew the Birchmere wasn't a "champagne" place. But every time we came back to play, Gary would have champagne for us."

An excerpt of Joe Brown's 1992 review of their Birchmere show in the *Washington Post* reads "In the guitar & vocal, husband & wife, jazz & pop & new age & you-name-it duo Tuck & Patti, Tuck Andress is the virtuosic guitar orchestra to Patti Cathcart's soul-stirring solo choir. On the road—they appear at the Birchmere Tuesday & Wednesday—the pair can travel lighter than just about any band in the business: Andress brings along only two guitars, a rack for electronics and monitors; Cathcart always has that exquisitely deep, husky, gospel-trained voice with her, of course."

Tuck & Patti brought a diverse audience to the Birchmere. Says Patti: "We had a folk crowd, jazz fans, R&B fans and walked in a different kind of world where we were accustomed to mixed audiences because that was just kind of the nature of our appeal and the fact that we were an interracial couple."

One other distinction is that they were pioneers in linear mixing their own sound while they were performing. This is another reason they had the respect of Billy Wolf.

Gary adds, "They are warm and friendly, and wonderful talented people. They helped the Birchmere immensely."

© *Nick Kalivretenos*

Armando Anthony Corea (b. June 12, 1941, Chelsea, MA)

Jazz composer, keyboardist, and bandleader, Chick Corea played in the late 1960s Miles Davis band and contributed to the birth of jazz fusion music. He next formed Return to Forever with McCoy Tyner, Herbie Hancock, and Keith Jarrett.

Corea has played three times, fronting three different groups: the Chick Corea Trio with Carlitos Del Puerto and Marcus Gilmore (2018); the Chick Corea Elektric Band featuring Dave Weckl, John Patitucci, Eric Marienthal and Frank Gambale (2016); and The Power of Three: Chick Corea, with Stanley Clarke, and Lenny White (2009).

Corea is credited with composing five songs that have become jazz standards. "Windows," "La Fiesta," "Armando's Rhumba," "500 Miles High," and "Spain." He has been nominated for 60 Grammy awards, winning 25 times..

At his 2016 show, Chick came back to the stage after the audience left and performed for over two hours by himself as the staff cleaned up and prepared to close.

Alfred McCoy Tyner (b. Dec. 11, 1938, Philadelphia, PA)

In addition to his playing with Chick Corea's Return to Forever, McCoy Tyner's remarkable career includes his acoustic piano work with John Coltrane, his NEA award as Jazz Master, and five Grammy album awards.

At 71 years old, he played one show in 2010, accompanied by saxophonist Gary Bartz. The *Washington Post* review by Mike Joyce noted: "A standing ovation greeted pianist McCoy Tyner at the Birchmere on Friday night...Thundering left-hand chords, chromatic sweeps and teeming crescendos often surfaced, with Tyner simultaneously serving as pianist, percussionist and orchestrator...And the audience was back on its feet some 90 minutes later, cheering a quartet performance that consistently affirmed Tyner's commanding technique and might."

Stanley Clarke (b. June 30, 1951, Philadelphia, PA)

Also, a founding member of Corea's Return to Forever band, Clarke has headlined the hall six times. Birchmere staffer K.C. Alexandria says "Stanley is a genius at what he does but he presents it with so much ease. On the day he signed my bass he came surrounded by a band of young prodigies. His drummer was 18. Stanley hooked into the mainstream when he put in with George Duke on the *Mothership Connected* album. I'm from the jazz album generation and when you finally meet these guys, they turn out to be the coolest, most encouraging people. When I asked him to sign my bass, he said 'Sure' but joked 'I'm not letting anybody write on *my* bass.'"

Clarke refined the **Larry Graham** killer-slap bass technique. Founder of Graham Central Station, Graham played bass for Sly and Family Stone and has done six shows since 2010.

Ottmar Liebert (b. Feb. 1, 1959, Cologne, West Germany)

This praised Flamenco guitarist first appeared with his band, Luna Negra, in 1990. His first album, 1989's *Nouveau Flamenco*, was recorded for less than $3,000 on an old analog machine in a shack beside a gravel pit in Santa Fe, New Mexico. It became the best-selling instrumental acoustic guitar album ever, establishing Liebert's modern-flamenco style. Liebert has returned to the Birchmere 20 times since his impressive debut.

Ottmar Liebert   © *Oelze*

"Instrumental music is like a book," Liebert explained, "because you have to imbue it with meaning. Songs are like a movie where you don't have to do anything but let it wash over you. The audience for instrumental music has to be active in a way.

"I began at the Birchmere 30 years ago, opening for a singer-songwriter from Santa Fe named Sara Kaye. It was a kind of a weird bill because she was singing, and then I came on. I've always enjoyed returning. Michael Jaworek, a very funny guy, welcomes me. We have a kind of ritual where he comes and says, 'Well, we're still standing.'"

Liebert has played the hall with his regular trio, a nine-piece band, and as a solo performer. He has a catalog of 33 award-winning albums.

"And now I would say there are fancier jazz clubs in the country like the Triple-A in Seattle and others, but when the lights go out, there is nowhere better than the Birchmere."

When Liebert was a teen in the '60s, he watched a local German TV show called *Beat Club*. It showcased Cream, The Doors, Jimi Hendrix, and other rock acts that greatly influenced him. Coincidentally, like the Birchmere, these acts performed live in front of a plain brick wall.

"I knew then that I wanted to play electric guitar. However, I lived with my family in a small apartment, and the loud sound would be a problem. As a compromise, I bought a nylon string acoustic guitar to learn. It was my Trojan Horse," says Liebert.

"But I ended up learning classical music and Flamenco, which is the music of the Gypsies. Many people think of Flamenco as Spanish music. It is really a mishmash of rumba, which was brought to Spain by sailors from the Caribbean who were influenced by the slaves' music. And from Tonga, the traditional music of Polynesia that early English explorers like Captain Cook discovered.

"So, there is a vast black component in this music. I would say something like seventy percent of it is Arabic, Northern African Arabic, and then you've got this whole Caribbean and Islands part of it. And if you listen to rumba, Tonga, reggae, and salsa, there is no emphasis on 'the one' [first beat]. In fact, there is a famous reggae drum beat called the 'one drop,' because nothing is happening on the first beat in Flamenco music."

On one tour, Liebert brought a video screen and his laptop. "I had this slideshow of images from around the world that I had taken. I would just play whatever song I wanted to, and people always thought the slides were connected to my music. Synchronicity was something that everybody's brain was creating. At least 20 people would tell me afterward how coordinated everything appeared."

Dore "Herb" Alpert (b. March 31, 1935, Los Angeles, CA)

"I prefer playing the Birchmere to the much larger venues. Being very close to the audience, it's a real experience," Herb Alpert told music writer Mike Joyce when he began playing the club in 1996 at the age of 61. It was his first tour in 20 years when he joined up with another jazz trumpeter, Hugh Masekela.

A classically-trained musician, Alpert's first success came as a songwriter; he penned Sam Cooke's "Wonderful World." Inspired by a mariachi band at a bullfight in Tijuana, Mexico, he turned his Tijuana Brass band into a 14-platinum album phenomenon. With his business partner, Jerry Moss, he transformed his garage-based A&M record label from a $200 investment into a $500 million-dollar payday when they sold it to Polygram Records. Alpert's '96 show was with jazz pianist Jeff Lorber, promoting their *Second Wind* album.

Albert has appeared with his wife, vocalist Lani Hall, several times since 2011, and as this book goes to print they are scheduled to perform together in 2022.

In with the In Crowd.   © *Oelze*

Ramsey Emmanuel Lewis Jr (b. May 27, 1935, Chicago, IL)

At 75, jazz legend Ramsey Lewis brought his "Electric Band" to the Birchmere for his only show in 2010. He had hit the charts with his first album in 1956. Ten years later, his *The In Crowd* album earned him international acclaim.

Bud Gardner recalls: "We rented a Bösendorfer, one of the largest acoustic grand pianos we ever had. The band did a brief sound check. Mr. Lewis walked in, took the stage, played an incredible show for 90 minutes, and walked out the back door. One of the things I've learned is that the more accomplished the acts are, the nicer they are."

Herbert Jeffrey Hancock (b. April 12, 1940, Chicago, IL)

In 1964, Herbie Hancock joined the "Second Great" Miles Davis Quintet. Hancock's electric keyboard wizardry helped Miles eventually record *In a Silent Way*, regarded as Davis' first jazz fusion recording. *Washington Post* writer Mike Joyce wrote about Hancock's only Birchmere appearance in 2007: "Jazz piano poetry or keyboard-driven funk? Herbie Hancock was almost always in a mood to party at the Birchmere on Sunday night. Leading a new, horn-less quartet, the renowned jazz musician and composer opened the concert by moving from a blues-tinted allusion to "Butterfly" into a propulsive arrangement of "Actual Proof," riddled with hammered piano chords and electric keyboard flourishes. What followed wasn't exactly dinner music, either: A tricky take on "Watermelon Man" that jumped back and forth between an old-school funk groove and an exotic odd meter.

Herbie Hancock backstage at 2007 show.   © *B. Gardner*

"Amiable, chatty and occasionally roaming the stage while playing a portable electric keyboard, Hancock emphasized a vibrantly kinetic sound over and over again."

George M. Duke (b. Jan. 12, 1946, San Rafael, CA)

The great pianist played both the bandstand and the music hall, beginning in 2004. Duke is beloved among jazz fans, and by Frank Zappa devotees. From the dressing room in 2005, Duke talked to Moses T. Alexander for the pilot episode of his TV show *The Greene Room: LIVE*:

"For whatever reasons it's like family in DC. I love me some DC. What contributes to my longevity is that I try and keep the music real, no matter what the style is. I love DC because I can play what I want as long as I can give them some "Dukie Stick,"

"Reach For It," or "Sweet Time." Then I'll be cool. They won't fuss and then they'll leave me alone and let me do what I want."

On this occasion Duke was promoting his *In a Mellow Tone* album, which was a departure for him. He said, "I've never done a record like this where half the album are jazz standards and the other half I hope will become standards"

Duke first gained prominence on the 1969 album, *Jean Luc Ponty with the George Duke Trio.* Ponty, who played the Birchmere in 2007 and 2018, earned fame as Frank Zappa's electric violinist. Duke would be in Zappa's band for two years, and credits Frank for introducing him to both the synthesizer and his own singing talents. That's Duke singing Zappa's masterpiece, "Inca Roads."

When asked how he would like to be remembered, Duke ended his green room discussion by replying, "More than likely, by what they [fans] think, rather than what I think. I just do what I do, so let others make that decision. Having said that, if it were up to me, then 'a great musician' and 'a nice guy.'"

Duke with Bud Gardner in 2006. © B. Gardner

Other Frank Zappa-related musicians playing the Birchmere include his son, Dweezil with his Zappa Plays Zappa band (four times), guitarist Steve Vai (twice) in 2005 and 2007, Vinnie Colaiuta, one of Zappa's drummers, backing Herbie

Hancock, and Tom Fowler, bass player, who played the music hall in Ray Charles' orchestra.

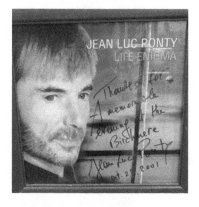

Jean Luc Ponty in 2001.   **Dweezil Zappa** in 2015.

Candy Dulfer
is a Dutch saxaphonist, who began her Birchmere shows in 2007, returning six times. She has performed and recorded with Maceo Parker, Pink Floyd, Tower of Power, and Van Morrison.

Other jazz artists over the years include: Gato Barberi, Hugh Masekela 75th Birthday Celebration (2014), The Blue Note 75 All-Stars, Jeff Lorber, Kenny G, Najee, Pieces of a Dream, Preservation Hall Jazz Band, Rachelle Ferrell, Robben Ford, and many others.

Chapter 27 ~ Hooray for Hollywood

Michael and Kevin   © Oelze

Michael Bacon (b. Dec. 22, 1949, Philadelphia, PA)

Kevin Norwood Bacon (b. July 8, 1958, Philadelphia, PA)

The Bacon Brothers were the first act booked at the Bhall who were better known for award-winning connections to film—Kevin in *Footloose, Apollo 13, and A Few Good Men* among many others—than their music.

The Bacon Brothers—Michael, an Emmy-winning composer and Nashville songwriter, and singer/actor/icon Kevin—have sold out the hall 27 times since 2007. Blending country, folk-rock, and soul music, both brothers sing and play guitar, with Michael adding classical cello. Their band includes Paul Guzzone (bass, backing vocals), Joe Mennonna (keyboards, accordion), Tim Quick (lead guitar, mandolin, backing vocals), and Frank Vilardi (drums).

"We enjoy playing the Birchmere and we always enjoy trying to work new material in," says Kevin, adding with a little self-deprecation, "People want you to play your hits and when you don't have any hits it is even more challenging. But it's nice that our audience has songs that they want to hear. I wish we had the facility if somebody held up a sign, we could just play the songs they request."

Folks not familiar with the Bacon Brothers music might only be interested in the celebrity brother's film fame. "Kevin lives in a bubble when we tour. We don't do the merch table meet and greet, although I would like to," Michael Bacon admits. The duo takes measures to keep the focus on their music.

Far more than just a famous name, the brothers have serious musical chops. Michael is an award-winning, gifted film composer who has scored hundreds of films and TV shows including *D Day Remembered, The Trials of J. Robert Oppenheimer, The Jewish Americans,* and *Losing Chase,* starring Helen Mirren (Golden Globe winner) and Kyra Sedgewick, directed by Kevin Bacon.

The Bacon Brothers are both strong songwriters, evidenced by their enthusiastic returning audiences. And after many appearances, they finally started incorporating "Footloose" in their set although Kevin didn't sing it in the movie.

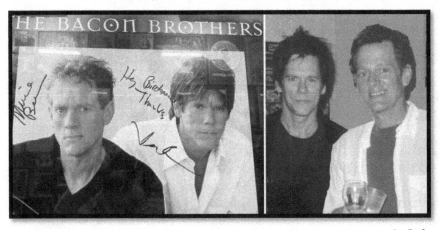

© *Oelze*

© *Oelze*

Charles Esten (b. Sept 9, 1965, Pittsburgh, PA)

From a 2020 article by Keith Loria in the *Fairfax County Times:* "Alexandria's own Charles "Chip" Esten has had quite the versatile career in the entertainment business since graduating from T.C. Williams High School in 1983.

"He started his career as an improv specialist on *Whose Line is it Anyway?*" made women swoon as tortured heartthrob Deacon Claybourne on the country music drama series *Nashville,* and has developed a strong following among the tween and teen sets for playing the devious Ward Cameron on Netflix's big summer hit, *Outer Banks.* Esten also appeared in *The Office* TV show as Josh Porter.

Esten's Birchmere debut was in 2014 and three years later he was able to release a new recording every Friday for a year and tour with his *Nashville* co-stars Clare Bowen, Chris Carmack and Jonathan Jackson.

He told the *Washington Post's* Angela Haupt about his Alexandria musical roots: "My mother got me guitar and piano lessons. I was in Fairlington [a neighborhood four miles from the Birchmere] banging away on a piano, trying to imitate Bruce Springsteen's albums. But it wasn't until I came to Nashville [to film the show] that I was able to really dig in. I always felt that I was starting from behind. But I loved writing so much, and I had a bunch of songs — I was just stalling and never pulling the trigger. Finally, it occurred to me: Why not release them as singles?

Gary notes "During the COVID pandemic, Esten played a concert and returned his fee as a contribution to the Birchmere."

© *Oelze*

Steven Frederic Seagal (b. April 10, 1952, Lansing, MI)

Known for his macho movie roles and numerous nominations by the Golden Raspberry Awards for worst actor, worst supporting actor, worst picture, and his win for worst director for his 1995 film, *On Deadly Ground*, Steven Seagal is actually a pretty good guitarist.

Bud Gardner recalls when Seagal played in 2006 with an impressive band, Thunderbox, to promote his second CD, *Mojo Priest*, featuring blues players like Hubert Sumlin, Bo Diddley, and James Cotton. *Blues City Magazine* put Seagal on the cover, called him a natural talent, and cited his guitar playing as "exceptional."

"Seagal came up to me after his show and said, "I'm taking you out for a steak. I've had a run of shows where the monitor sound was terrible. But you've reinstalled my faith in live music. Tonight, was one of the best shows in my life." Seagal took Gardner to Ruth Chris Steak House for dinner.

"I had heard all these horror stories about Steven Seagal and how difficult he could be," Gardner says, "but to me, he was very nice. We went out to eat with his band, and it was a cool night. His show was pretty good also, as he has a vast collection of guitars formerly owned by famous guitarists like Albert, BB and Freddie King, Muddy Waters, and Jimi Hendrix. Seagal played many of these guitars on the stage."

Woody Harrelson with Three Kool Cats.   © *Oelze*

Woodrow Tracy Harrelson (b. July 23, 1961, Midland, TX)

Here's an actor who won an Emmy for his role in the TV show *Cheers* and followed it up with decades of versatile and acclaimed film and television roles, yet few are aware that his talents also include music. Harrelson brought a six-piece brassy band and a tight harmony group named Three Kool Cats in to play in 1991. He was happy and humble, trying to rock the crowd with covers of "Jailhouse Rocks," "So Fine," and other classics.

Music critic Mike Joyce ended his review of the show as "the songs radiated a disarming frat house spirit and energy before they drifted forgettably into the night."

Jane Lynch (b. July 14, 1960, Evergreen Park, IL)

Signed drumhead promotion in a corner of Gary's office. © Oelze

The sixth and final season of the *Glee* TV show wrapped up in 2015, and multi-talented star Jane Lynch honed her cabaret act and hit the road. One of her first stops was the Birchmere, appearing with fellow Second City alum Kate Flannery. TV fans will remember Kate as Meredith, the alcoholic redhead on *The Office.*

When Lynch took the stage, she greeted the audience with how happy she was playing the legendary hall "a stone's throw from the Auto Zone" (the car parts store is adjacent to the hall entrance on Mt. Vernon Avenue).

One stand-out funny number in her set was "Blood on the Coal," a song written and performed by Christopher Guest, Michael McKean, and Harry Shearer in the folk music mockumentary *A Mighty Wind.* Lynch co-starred with actor/director Guest in this and two of his other films, *Best in Show* and *For Your Consideration.*

Randall Stuart Newman (b. Nov. 28, 1943, Los Angeles, CA)

"Like a Band-Aid for a broken neck," Randy Newman quipped on stage at the Birchmere after chugging from a bottle of water.

410

Newman, inducted into the Songwriter's Hall of Fame in 2002, began as a songwriter in 1962--"Mama Told Me Not To Come" was his first hit composition for Three Dog Night in 1970--and he developed into a gifted composer of film and TV scores, as well as songs covered by a Who's Who of other artists. His own, often controversial, work generated such well-known tunes as "Short People," "I Love L.A.," "and "You've Got a Friend in Me." Working mostly as a film composer since the 1980s, his credits include scores for all four *Toy Story* films, *A Bug's Life*, both *Monsters, Inc.* films, *The Natural* (1984), *Pleasantville* (1998), *Meet The Parents* (2000), *Seabiscuit* (2003), and *Marriage Story* (2019).

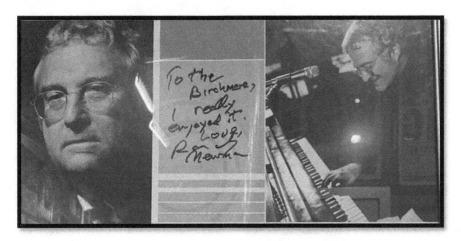

Newman's sold-out shows presented a wide emotional range from "You Can Keep Your Hat On" (featured in the-film *9 1/2 Weeks)*, "Lost Without You" about a couple facing a wife's death, the bittersweet "I Think It's Going to Rain Today," and grim yet hilarious "Political Science." His piano playing evokes a ragtime feel, brilliantly employed in the score for the film, *Ragtime.* One of his finest songs, "Sail Away," was described by *Rolling Stone* writer Stephen Holden as presenting "the American dream of a promised land as it might have been presented to black Africa in slave running days."

Throughout his shows, Newman demonstrates a true enjoyment of entertaining and interacting with the audience.

Roger Catlin posted this introduction in his review in *The Vinyl District* for Newman's 2017 Birchmere show: "At 73, Randy Newman is still writing sharp and funny political songs, elaborate and cynical set pieces about the state of the world and, in between them, the kind of stark songs that unexpectedly rip your heart out. At a wide-ranging, 2-set, 33 song panorama of his work of the past half century, fans responded to his oldest, most enduring numbers but were just as knocked out by the newest things, as collected on his new Nonesuch collection *Dark Matter.*"

© *K.C. Alexandria*

Kiefer William Frederick Dempsey George Rufus Sutherland (b. Dec. 21, 1966, Paddington, UK)

The Kiefer Sutherland Band formed in 2016 and performed their original country music at the Birchmere in 2018, promoting their first album, *Down in a Hole*. Actor Kiefer sang lead vocals and played guitar. The *Guardian* newspaper wrote, "You have the first Hollywood hobby act unshackled by convention and with a real shot at greatness."

K.C. remembers, "We were surprised because no one knew he could sing, and then we were impressed that he could sing and play guitar and was pretty good at both. He came across like the acting was one thing he knew, but playing music was where his heart was." Down to earth and humble is how K.C. remembers him. "Most acts relax in the dressing room, but he went out back and sat on the picnic table, had a drink and a cigarette."

His DC visit included a Saturday afternoon enjoying Cole Porter tunes at a performance of the American Pops Orchestra.

Stuart Wodlinger with Snuffy Walden.   *© Jay Schlossberg*

William Garrett Walden (b. Feb. 13, 1950, Louisiana)

Box office manager and merch store guru, Stuart Wodlinger shared the above photo. Says Stuart: "My friend Jay Schlossberg sent me this picture of Snuffy Walden when he opened for Eddie from Ohio in 2019. I much appreciate Snuffy for his success as a touring and session musician and for the Emmy nominations and awards for numerous scores he wrote for television series like *The West Wing, Roseanne, Thirtysomething, Friday Night Lights, Ellen,* and many more."

Billy Bob Thornton (b. Aug. 4, 1955, Hot Springs, AK)

Billy Bob Thornton brought his six-piece band The Boxmasters to the hall in 2015 and 2019. Long before he found stardom in roles like the mentally disabled Karl Childers in his Academy Award-winning film, *Sling Blade,* the actor played in garage bands, so he knows his way around a music stage. He looked like he was enjoying himself delivering a combo of well-known cover songs like "Hang on Sloopy" with a few of his own compositions like "Smoking in Bed" and "Everybody Lies."

Gary tells this story: "Billy Bob was a fan of Tony Rice and invited him to one of his shows. Tony, his wife, Pam, Bud Gardner and I went in his tour bus. Pam asked Billy Bob to "do" Karl [the murderer in his film, *Sling Blade*].

Billy Bob. © Oelze.   As Karl in Sling Blade.

He smiled and said he'd rather not. But after further coaxing, Billy Bob put his head down for a moment, and then raised it and became Karl. It was chilling. He stayed in character for about 15 minutes and talked about eating French fries with mustard and whatever else we were chatting about."

Patrick Foster wrote in his *Washington Post* review: "The most surprising thing about the Billy Bob Thornton show was not that only a modest crowd turned out to hear the actor do his rock 'n' roll thing, but that he was pretty good at it."

John Corbett (b. May 9, 1961, Wheeling, WV)

Emmy and Golden Globe winner John Corbett, best known as "Chris in the Morning" on *Northern Exposure,* long runs on *Sex in the City, United States of Tara,* and *Parenthood,* both *My Big Fat Greek Wedding* films, and dozens of other film and TV appearances, is also a Billboard-charting country musician with two albums under his belt. Corbett and his band played a sold-out show in July 2006; between solid renditions of country-rock numbers from his newly-released album *John Corbett,* he regaled the audience with details of his private tour of the White House earlier in the day (which included meeting the Bush family dog, Barney), arranged by his partner, now wife, actress Bo Derek.

© *B. Derek*

© *B. Gardner*

Beatrice Arthur (b. May 13, 1922, New York, City, NY)

Actress Bea Arthur, TV's *Maude* and Dorothy in *Golden Girls,* brought her 25-city tour show with friend and piano accompanist, Billy Goldenberg, to the hall in 2005. Calling her performance "a closet full of memories," she was celebrating 50 years in show business. She told stories about her fellow actors and sang her favorite songs.

Staff recall that she required a proper chair to sit in and a spotlight. The Birchmere doesn't use or own a spotlight, so they had to rent one.

Kevin Michael Costner (b. Jan.18, 1955, Linwood, CA)

Buzz McClain attended actor/director Kevin Costner's 2008 sold-out show. He wrote "Kevin and Modern West were clearly prepared to impress the remarkably well-behaved audience (no shrieking) for nearly as long as one of Costner's cinematic epics. He led a six-piece rock band that featured "explosive solos" from Teddy Morgan, the indie Americana favorite from the Pistolas and the Hacienda Brothers, on electric guitar."

Gary remembers that "Buzz got me a little bit in trouble with Kevin when I brought him backstage to meet the actor. Buzz took out his reporter's pad and started asking him questions. Kevin was a little annoyed and let me know. But that's what makes Buzz a great reporter."

Tim Robbins (b. Oct. 16, 1958, West Covina, CA)

Actor Robbin's breakout film role was baseball pitcher Ebby Calvin "Nuke" LaLoosh in the 1988 film, *Bull Durham*. He co-starred with Kevin Costner, and future partner, Susan Sarandon, who attended Catholic University in Washington, DC. This kicked off a decades-long acting, directing and screenwriting career that garnered industry nominations and awards for such acclaimed films as "The Shawshank Redemption," "Dead Man Walking," and "Mystic River." Robbins came to the hall to promote his only album *Tim Robbins & The Rogues Gallery Band* (2010), a collection of songs he had written over the past 25 years that he ultimately took on his only world tour.

Tim's dad, Gil Robbins performed with Tom Paxton and was a founding member of the Highwaymen who played the Birchmere once in the early days. The Highwaymen are famous for their recordings, "Michael Row the Boat Ashore" and "Cotton Fields."

Amelia Fiona Jessica Driver (b. Jan. 31, 1970, London, UK)

Actress Minnie Driver played in 2004, promoting her debut album, *Everything I've Got in My Pocket* and returned in 2007. Although known as a successful movie actress, with an Oscar nomination for her role in 1997's *Good Will Hunting*, she began a music career as a teen and went on to release three albums. Reviews of her musical act were mixed. Rashod D. Ollison in the *Baltimore Sun*, "After a while, the singer's breathy vocals and the gauzy, glacially paced acoustic-folk music begin to blend. Although Driver is a fine singer (her vocals are hypnotic at times), she isn't very nuanced."

Jeffrey Warren Daniels (b. Feb. 19, 1955, Athens, GA)

Actor Jeff Daniels, is known for a career on film (dozens, including *The Purple Rose of Cairo, Terms of Endearment, Dumb and Dumber, Pleasantville*), TV (*The Newsroom, The Looming Tower, American Rust,* among others) and stage (most recently playing Atticus Finch on Broadway in *To Kill a Mockingbird*). But he also has a musical side, writing and recording six folk-flavored albums with proceeds benefiting The Purple Rose Theater, performing live shows that serve up his music with a helping of comedy, and musically collaborating his son, Ben. During the pandemic in 2020 he did a very successful virtual show for the Birchmere.

418

Chapter 28 – Beatle-esque

When Beatles producer Sir George Martin appeared in 1997 to promote his book, *Summer of Love: The Making of Sgt. Pepper*, the packed house was privy to previously unheard sound tracks from the making and mixing of that historic album, as well as an extraordinary revelation: "I was with John Lennon in his Dakota apartment in the '70s. I had spent the night there. We were just rapping about old times, and he suddenly came out with 'You know I wish we could just do [record] everything again.'"

Martin replied, "Oh come on John. Not everything."

John insisted, "Yes, everything."

"You mean you don't think we did anything right?" Martin asked.

"Most of what we did was crap," John shot back.

"You can't say that," said Martin. "What about "Strawberry Fields?"

John looked directly at George and replied "*Especially* Strawberry Fields."

Martin added that this was how John Lennon operated. "He always dreamed of things he couldn't have achieved."

Gary remembers: "A man brought a Sgt. Pepper's album in for Martin to sign after his presentation. It was already signed by all four Beatles on the front cover, but Martin would not sign it on the front. He autographed the back cover."

Martin thought that the Beatles would have recorded even greater things if they had stayed together, but their growing individualism wouldn't allow that. "They submerged their egos into being the Beatles, and they got tired of that. They wanted to be themselves." Martin said in his presentation.

Tim Kidwell was running sound that night, with Sir George and his wife, Judy, were together next to Tim in the rear house sound booth for part of the presentation and Sir George also on stage. Martin used a projection screen to show the track settings that illustrated the music clips, for example, what tracks Ringo was drumming on, where Paul played piano etc. Tim says: "The Beatles and Martin used one four-track recording machine to mix tracks to a second machine, so they could reduce four tracks down to other tracks and send to the second deck. Astonishingly, they were able to achieve such sonic miracles on that album."

Tim adds proudly, "One of the greatest compliments that I ever received was after this show. Sir George told me, 'Wow. You made me sound brilliant. The sound tonight was perfect.' I was awestruck."

(l to r) Rich Pagano, Frank Agnello, Will Lee, Jimmy Vivino, and Jack
© *Fab Faux*

The Fab Faux

Rolling Stone magazine writer David Fricke described this group as: "The Fab Faux invigorate the artistry of even the Beatles' most intricate studio masterpieces with top chops and Beatle maniac glee." His story's byline called The Fab Faux, "The greatest Beatles cover band without the wigs."

The band's drummer and vocalist Rich Pagano talks about the Birchmere: "Before the Faux, I was on the road with a band called Marry Me, Jane. We weren't able to get a date at the Birchmere. Still, we were told it was historical, more singer-songwriter-centric, and a better music listening room. The Fab Faux played the 9:30 club and the Hamilton before Michael Jaworek contacted us. We did a few stripped-down shows [without horns and string section], and we loved it."

Sean Lennon on stage and near his tour bus with Linda Bangham
© Dick Bangham

Sean Taro Ono Lennon (b. Oct. 9, 1975, New York, NY)

In describing Sean Lennon's 2006 show, *The Washington Post's* Dave McKenna wrote "Musical ability is nature, rock is nurture. Sean Lennon's brief and serene Sunday set at the Birchmere seemed to provide clues as to what his father, the Beatle John, might have been like had the elder Lennon also had two parents who loved him."

Sean was reserved backstage. However, Washington DC cinematographer and artist, Dick Bangham and his wife, Linda, found him very cordial when they met him outside his tour bus. Lennon was on the road to promote his second album, *Friendly Fire.*

In the dressing room with Bud.   © *B. Gardner*

In a review of *Friendly Fire* in *Pitchfork* magazine, Stuart Berman wrote, "John and Yoko's son returns with his first album in eight years, a record steeped in baroque piano-bar melodies, foreboding Jon Brion string arrangements, and a palpable sense of empty-bed despair."

His guitarist was Cameron Greider, son of political writer William Greider. Cameron played a licensed John Lennon model of the famed Epiphone Casino guitar that both John and George once used.

Writer Dave McKenna mentioned that Sean also liked the Birchmere's artichoke dip, but noted that he only played 45 minutes on stage. "That's short by today's standards, but for those keeping score, it's longer than the Beatles' first Shea Stadium concert," Dave observed.

Julian's signed poster promoting his Photograph Smile album.

Julian Charles John Lennon (b. Apr. 8 1963, Liverpool, UK)

At his only appearance in 1999, eight years after his Constitution Hall debut in Washington DC, John Lennon's oldest son seemed to love the Birchmere.

"He was happy and friendly and asked me to show him around the place. I gave him a tour, and he was very interested in everything here," said John Brinegar.

his show and remembers, "Julian was great. He played piano and guitar. He sounds like his Dad, but he has a much lower-register voice. His show had a little funk in it. He was good. I saw a show he did in Europe earlier, and his backup band was Tears for Fears."

Patrick Foster commented in his *Washington Post* review, "Seeming at last comfortable with himself and the fact that no one expects him to write something on par with "Strawberry Fields Forever" every time out. It seemed the fans of the Birchmere wouldn't care if he dropped his last name altogether."

Current 1964 line-up is Mac Ruffing (Paul), Tom Work (George), Mark Benson (John) and Bobby Potter (Ringo).   © *S. Moore*

1964: The Tribute

First, *Beatlemania, the Broadway musical,* successfully ran from 1977 to 1979. Then came national tours and a movie called "loathsome, "cheap, and disingenuous" by the *New York Time*s. Ultimately, the Beatles' Apple Corps sued the producers of *Beatlemania* for copyright infringement.

"The Broadway show spurred the Beatles tribute band industry," says Mark Benson, who plays John Lennon in 1964: The Tribute, "but we had no idea when we started this act in 1985 that 36 years later, we would have played Carnegie Hall 14 times, the Red Rocks amphitheater in Colorado 15 years in a row, or sold out the present Birchmere also 15 times. Now, it's no longer just a baby boomer show; there is no age limit for who comes to see us."

The band uses wigs, clothing, and vintage instruments and amplifiers to create the illusion of the Beatles in the early sixties. When they began, Benson, also a guitar tech, made a replica of Lennon's black Rickenbacker guitar to use on stage. "There weren't any re-issues back then, and I couldn't afford a vintage one," he says.

The original line-up sadly changed in 2010 when Mark's buddy, Gary Grimes, who started the band with him, died of brain cancer. The current group is Mark Benson (John), Mac Ruffing (Paul), Tom Work (George) and Bobby Potter (Ringo).

They typically get a Birchmere staffer to recruit someone from the audience or backstage to "announce" them from the stage, like Ed Sullivan did on TV. Mark explains, "We ask them to say 'Ladies and Gentlemen. How many Beatle fans do we have here? We welcome you to sing and clap along. You're all expected to scream, please. Welcome what *Rolling Stone* magazine calls the number one Beatles tribute band, 1964." One recruit was writer Buzz McClain.

Mark Benson with Stephen Moore in 2021. "I enjoyed meeting Mark and discussing his career impersonating John Lennon for 3 plus decades," says Steve, who saw the Beatles in 1964 and 1966. © *S. Moore*

When asked who the most noteworthy "announcer" was, Benson said, "It was Sid Bernstein, the first concert promoter to bring the Beatles to the US. He produced their first Carnegie Hall show and told us that there were so many radio and news people at that show that he never did actually get on the stage.

"When he arrived for our soundcheck, the Carnegie Hall house manager was there and said, "Mr. Bernstein, you probably won't remember me, but I was a 17-year-old stagehand when you brought the Beatles here. I just want to welcome you back. Sid choked up, and his eyes watered. It was such a cool reunion. When Sid 'announced' us at our first Carnegie Hall show in 2003, he was 95."

Marshall Howard Crenshaw (b. Nov 11, 1953, Detroit, MI)

Pre-fame, acclaimed singer-songwriter Marshall Crenshaw got his start playing John Lennon in West Coast and touring companies of *Beatlemania*. (He has another connection with Beatles tribute acts, having worked often with Rich Pagano of the Fab Faux.) When Crenshaw burst onto the music scene with his eponymous 1982 debut album—called the year's "most gorgeous singer-songwriter debut" by *Rolling Stone* and still on their list of best albums of the 1980s—critics took notice. His well-crafted songs and infectious pop energy invited comparison to both the Beatles' early sound and to one of the group's own influences, Buddy Holly, who Crenshaw went on to portray in the film *La Bamba*. In the ensuing years, he has released multiple albums and, among his many collaborative projects, was nominated in 2007 for both Golden Globe and Grammy awards for writing the title song of *Walk Hard: The Dewey Cox Story*. He first played the Birchmere in 2004, returning 9 times, including a 2011 30th anniversary celebration of his musical career.

Frederick LaBour (b. June 3, 1948, Grand Rapids, MI)

Also known as Too Slim in the Western music group "Riders in the Sky," LaBour played an essential part in launching the "Paul is Dead" urban myth of 1969. He was a sophomore journalist at Drake University when he answered the phone in the college newsroom. He explained what happened next to Peter Ames Carlin in his book, *Paul McCartney: A Life*: "I was speaking to a guy who kept insisting Paul McCartney was dead. It was really spooky, Labour said, recalling how the voice at the end of "Strawberry Fields Forever" sounds like someone is saying 'I buried Paul' and why is Paul the only Beatle wearing a black carnation on Magical Mystery Tour and why is his back turned to the camera on the rear cover of *Sergeant Pepper*?

Labour made a few notes hung up and shook his head. Ridiculous, but he had a bit of the prankster in him, so by the next morning, he had an idea. He talked it over with his friend, John Gray. I told John, "I'm just going to kill him. I'm going to make the whole thing up," which is exactly what Labore did, stringing the caller's clues together with a wider variety of eerie observations he made up out of whole cloth.

With fellow student John Gray, Fred wrote a satiric article, in his school newspaper The *Michigan Daily* titled "McCartney Dead; New Evidence Brought to Light." Various "clues" were offered to explain Paul's demise. Supposedly, Paul had died three years earlier in a car crash, the subject of "A Day in the Life," with lyrics "he blew his mind out in a car." The article was illustrated by a gruesome picture of a decapitated head, and was picked up by national newspapers on both coasts. According to Beatles historian Andru J. Reeve, it owns the distinction now of being "the single most significant factor in the breadth of the rumors spread."

Radio broadcaster Robbie White is heard on Takoma Park, MD radio station WOWD hosting his "Forbidden Alliance" music program. A Beatles historian himself, Robbie brought his copy of Carlin's book for Too Slim to sign after a Riders in the Sky Birchmere gig. Robbie reports that other Riders were laughing when they saw his college picture.

And now you know why Too Slim's bio on the Riders in the Sky website includes his other credits as a janitor, industrial galvanizer, puppeteer, hay stacker, burlesque show emcee, sportswriter, wildlife manager, electric bass man, and *rumor monger.*

Riders in the Sky

Longtime Birchmere favorites Riders in the Sky are a Western musical group that hearkens back to the Golden Age of "singing cowboys," replete with smooth harmonies, cowboy garb, lots of hilarity, and some genuine yodeling skills. It is their humor that arguable makes them "Beatle-esque" in addition to Too Slim's "Paul is Dead" connection. Ranger Doug has cited *Mad Magazine* and Monty Python as early comedic influences. Their 40-plus album discography includes an album recorded live at the Birchmere in 1984.

They also wrote and performed music for Pixar movies, and won two Grammy Awards in the Best Musical Album for Children category for *Woody's Roundup: A Rootin' Tootin' Collection of Woody's Favorite Songs* and *Monsters, Inc. Scream Factory Favorites.*

Riders in the Sky's Woody Paul, Ranger Doug, and Too Slim.
© *Oelze*

The British Invasion 50th Anniversary Tour

This 2016 show was hosted by Peter Asher. Performers included Chad and Jeremy, Billy J. Kramer, Denny McClain (Wings), Mike Pender (The Searchers), and Terry Sylvester (The Swinging Blue Jeans). Gerry and the Pacemakers were booked for this show, but Gerry took ill. Terry Sylvester replaced him.

Peter Asher and Jeremy Clyde returned together in 2020 to share songs and stories of their careers. One magic moment was hearing the first tape of McCartney singing his composition "World Without Love." He wrote it while staying at Peter and his sister Jane's parents' house for Asher to record with his singing partner, Gordon Waller. Paul and Jane were a couple then. The tape is just Paul singing and playing the Asher's' family piano.

Gary on the Beatles

"When they began, The Beatles were playing this authentic wonderful music that reminded me of the Everly Brothers, Carl Perkins, and music I grew up with. My theory now of why they became so popular is that they were still playing rock and roll but the younger people needed their own heroes. And the

Rolling Stones were playing American blues. That's what the British Invasion did: Remind the world why this American music is so important."

Peter and Jeremy.   © *S. Moore*

Chapter 29 – Working Five to Live

© Oelze

Dawn Williams was born and raised in Alexandria. She started at the Birchmere as a waitress in March, 1995. She tells her story: "I had never been there before. I knew it because my father owned a barber shop across the street. Gary's wife, Linda hired me as a waitress. The first night I worked was the first time I'd ever been inside the door. I was 24 years old.

"Riders in the Sky was the act on my first day at work. They did a daytime matinee show for kids and an adult show that night. The movie *Toy Story II* had just come out and they were part of the movie promotion because they had a song, "Woody's Roundup" on the movie soundtrack."

"The other big shows I recall in my first weeks working the hall were Jerry Jeff Walker and the Dixie Chicks. The short list of celebrity patrons I've served over the years include Kyra Sedgwick, Billy Crudup, Mary Louise Parker, Paula Patton, Michelle Obama, Linda Carter, Lou Rawls, John Riggins, and Patrick Ewing.

433

The second Birchmere menu signed by the original Seldom Scene.
Courtesy of David Smith

"Barbecue and chicken sandwiches, burgers, nachos, and salad. That was about all we served when I arrived. Yeah, it's definitely gotten better. It is very fair to say that the clients here, now and back then, were incredible. It was always a really nice, safe, and happy place to work. People are well-behaved There were certain nights when I started that it would get a little rowdy, but nothing major. If we had Dave Allen and the Blasters in there, then you knew you were going to get some heavy drinkers.

"Our busiest time is from six o'clock until show time. We still have to make our rounds, but we're out there anyway. A lot of times I just stand against the back wall and watch the show. I'm close to my section. I've worked back in the back with the bands periodically. I've worked in the office with Ben and Michael. I sometimes bartend now. I've done just about everything that there is to do around here."

Moments to Remember

"The Danny Gatton tribute with all the players on stage for two nights just stopped me in my tracks. It made me realize, just what a gem of a job I have. I've remained friends with people that I started working with and keep in contact. I've had servers that have worked here for 15 to 20 years.

"People feel like they're coming home when they walk in the door. We all try and remember their names, what they eat and drink. It makes them feel good. Everybody just loves it. There's always a familiar face. They say "Gosh, how long have you worked here? I've been coming here for 20 years. You've always been my waitress.'"

When asked what's different about food service at the Birchmere, Dawn explains, "It's very difficult for all of us on the floor. It's not like waiting tables at any other restaurant, where each server has a maybe four or five tables and people come in, eat, and leave and you turn over the table again.

On a busy, sold-out 500-person night, each server has about 50 to 60 seats in their section. The people arrive within the first 15 minutes. They all get there at one time. So, you really have to get their drinks out, and get their orders quickly into the kitchen. The kitchen staff have a production line and usually get the food out within 15 minutes of placing the order. The kitchen staff arrives in early afternoon and they have everything ready to roll at six o'clock when we open."

Dawn oversees between 16 and 20 waitresses/waiters with up to five bartenders. "I get to call this place my "job. I would never wait tables in any other place. I'd never work in a restaurant anywhere else."

Smokin'

The Birchmere menu is tasty, serving American cuisine with a Southern accent. Clift Thompson is the head chef: "We have our own smoker to cook ribs and chicken and pulled pork. We make our own potato chips. There are very few things that are frozen. We make the batter and bread our own catfish. We make the red beans and rice. We make the salads fresh. We make the pizzas fresh. Everything's pretty fresh. It's been like this since we opened the current Birchmere."

Dawn adds, "Some people walk in and say, 'I can't see the menu. It's dark. Just give me a burger.' But we stopped doing hamburgers a long time ago because people want good hamburgers cooked medium or rare, for example, and we can't

435

do temperatures for custom orders. There are certain things you just can't do and feed 500 people at one time. Our goal is to have everything ready by a quarter to six."

Head chef Clifton Thompson stands next to the barbeque smoker.
© *S. Moore*

Drinkin'

"We definitely have our stories of people getting drunk in here or coming here drunk. It's the love of the music that gives us a different vibe here. You're not getting people coming to stand around, party, and dance all night. You really do learn to come to the Birchmere to enjoy the fact that it is a listening room. Over the years, I've seen people come here for the first time and didn't understand this. Then they come back and they love the fact that it's like this.

"I've seen many acts that I think are just incredible, but my personal favorites are Emmylou Harris, and the late Hal Ketchum, who could sing anything. He could sing the phone book. I loved Hal before I started working at the Birchmere. That was a real treat for me when I started, because I actually got to know him. It was the same with Emmylou Harris, who my parents liked also."

Hal Ketchum was a favorite.   © *Oelze*

Dog on the Run

Dawn says, "One thing everyone who works at the Birchmere needs is a sense of humor, because things can get crazy here." One colorful dining story involves an encounter between a woman who was the sister of a very powerful Washington, DC businessman. (Names withheld to protect the innocent), manager John Brinegar, and Mark Uzell, the parking lot police security officer.

The unnamed woman and her date came to a show with a small dog she had smuggled in her purse. Once seated and served, she let her pet out. Manager Brinegar was surprised to see the dog sitting on the table and eating from the woman's plate. As the story goes, Brinegar calmly went over and politely told her that she needed to take the dog outside.

Gesturing for her to follow him to the door, John walked ahead, and she trailed him, hurling obscenities and even trying to kick him from behind. Officer Mark Uzell arrived just as the indignant woman seriously threatened the Birchmere manager. "I'm going to get my gun and shoot you," she yelled.

Officer Uzell ordered, "Ma'am, you're under arrest."

As Mark led her outside, she began swinging her purse—with the poor dog inside—at Officer Uzell's head.

437

Mark called to Brinegar who was standing nearby, "Help me here, John."

"You'll have to deputize me first," John joked.

John grabbed the bag and tried to hand it and dog over to the woman's date. He backed off, protesting, "No thanks, I'm out of here."

Officer Uzell then deduced that the woman was in such a state that calling an ambulance was a better solution than arresting her. When she fainted, it definitely became clear that was the necessary action. She was taken to a hospital.

What started out as a funny story took a sad turn when it was later revealed that the woman likely suffered from mental illness. A few weeks after the incident, a lawyer called John. The woman's influential brother wanted him to come testify at a competency hearing to tell his story to the judge as evidence of how "confused" she really was. John respectfully declined.

Complaints

Clubgoers have posted complaints over the years. One is "Why not just let everyone take their seats when the doors open? Why give out numbers?" Gary answers: "The numbered entry allows the waitstaff to start taking orders from the "first come" folks." Gary monitors inside progress with pauses in calling numbers to expedite an orderly, efficient way to serve all the customers before the show begins. The performers also appreciate the timely service because it eliminates the chatter and distractions of the food service by the time the show starts.

"We have to serve full dinner and drinks to 500 people in 90 minutes," Gary says, adding "McDonalds can't do that."

Another question is why can't I buy a reserved ticket? Why does the Birchmere make me take off work and get in line outside for hours so I won't get a bad seat?

Gary answers: "There *are* no bad seats in the place. Besides, the closest seats that the early birds seek aren't the best because they're *too* close to the stage. I call it "crotch row.""

For many, waiting outside augments the community feeling they seek at the Birchmere. The die-hard fans are evergreen in their support for their favorite performers. For example, the first ten folks for a Marty Stuart show might go back ten-plus years together and look forward to their fan reunion outside on line.

H2O Problem

Gary addresses the water issues that have flowed through the years. "People ask for water. In the beginning the waitstaff were running around serving water. We don't make any money carrying water because we need to serve the food quickly. So, we started putting pitchers of ice water and glasses on the tables.

"Now there was noise during quiet songs with people pouring water out of the pitcher. Both the audience and the acts complained. And at the end of the night, we had to wash a hundred pitchers and five hundred water glasses. The kitchen staff didn't like that very much.

"I thought, 'I'll put a stop to this. You want a glass of water. You can buy bottled water for two bucks.' People told me this might not work, and they were right. I had people call the health department and downstate government, complaining. Former CNN broadcaster Bernard Shaw got in my face one night, moaning about paying $40 for a meal and then me charging him for water. Every restaurant gives you free water, he argued. I told him truthfully, 'Bernie. We are a music hall. There's nothing here for free.'"

The county backed Gary up that no law compels the Birchmere to provide free water. One day Gary saw water holder belts in a restaurant supply catalog and happily bought them. Now the servers keep five water bottles in their belts and they pass them out to anyone who asks for water and charge them $2.00. Problem solved. Right?

"Not really," says Gary. "Now, people complain about plastic bottles and climate change."

Wait!

Teresa O' Brien began working at the Birchmere as a waitress when music was first introduced. Teresa is one of the most devoted Birchmere fans. "Working there was the greatest experience of my life," she says. She donated all of her photos to the hall for this history project. Teresa lives today in her hometown of Dublin, Ireland.

Teresa has kept close with friends over the years who were the early Birchmere waitresses.

Teresa with Peter Rowan and Emmylou Harris.   © Oelze

(l to r) Former waitresses Theresa O' Brien, Linda Oelze, Mary Beth Augier, Carol, and Peggy Mai in front – with Rodney Crowell center.
© C.B. Smith

440

Don't Forget the Lights

David Beebe running the stage lighting.   © *S. Moore*

In the back of the hall, next to sound engineer Justin Kidwell's soundboard, sits David Beebe, the Birchmere lighting director, working the Avolites Pearl expert lightboard. Every patron has heard his smooth voice because he also introduces the acts.

Beebe starts the discussion on a common phrase heard among stage lighting professionals: "If you notice the lighting during a show, the lighting guy is not doing his job." Everyone knows the sound, but 95 percent of the people don't know 'running the lights' exists. They think it's all done by computers," Beebe says.

David was born in Wichita Falls, Texas in 1963 but his Air Force dad took the family to Germany three months later, and next to Colorado, Nebraska, and Virginia. During high school in Burke, Virginia, he started his career managing a band, running the sound, learning technical skills and eventually, running the lighting for another band.

Beebe landed a job at the now-defunct Jaxx music club, where he met Bud Gardner, now director of sound production at the Birchmere. Gary hired David in 2004.

Beebe says, "There wasn't much lighting here when I came. Some front and sidelights, and cheap moving lights. We had no lights in the back of the stage, which creates all the drama of effects. A band named Asia came in and begged us to put some lights up in the back. They had some extra ones to offer. So, I did and Gary noticed and said 'Those look great. What do you need?' And next, we added ten LED lights at the back of the stage. So, we had those for a couple of years and it improved the show."

Gary told Beebe in 2012: "Build your dream system" and the Birchmere upgraded all the lighting in the music hall. "We've progressed to different moving lights since then and we added the mirror ball.

"That idea came from a band who plays here called Carbon Leaf. They brought one. We liked the look of it."

When Beebe is in action, it appears that he knows the music of the acts he is lighting. But how is that possible? When asked about this, he answers "It's hard to describe how I do it. I estimate I've seen 15,000 concerts in my lifetime. In my early professional life, it was mainly rock and heavy metal, but I was raised on Kris Kristofferson-type music. I like all kinds of music."

Beebe is riding along with the music. He's using his imagination. He's jamming.

"Yes, they call this busking," he explains. "If acts come in with a certain way they want the lights, I try to ask questions if I'm able. I try to do what they want but it's their show not mine. I clarify yet make suggestions. If they say 'I want this song in blue,' I'll ask 'You want the *entire song* in one shade of blue? And they might realize that doesn't make sense.

"One smooth jazz player started telling me from the stage, what lights to use—while he was playing. He was less then professional in how he complained." Here's an example for why some acts bring their own sound and lighting guys.

Beebe is also the manager of Birchmere's social media. You can find it at www.birchmere.com. He cites Arlo Guthrie as one of his favorites. "Arlo tells great stories. They are great even if you've heard him 20 times, as I have."

Chapter 30 ~ Taking Care of Business

"The Birchmere is a venue I've always been proud to have in our town and, although of course I don't like to lose anything as a competitor, I never felt like we were wronged by someone choosing to play there. People clearly love to go there. A great independent venue is good for all us independents. It means we ain't going anywhere. I don't know Gary that well, except that he's always owned the place and it's still open. That's quite a feat these days."

Seth Hurwitz
Owner, I.M.P. • 9:30 Club
Lincoln Theatre • The
Anthem • Merriweather Post Pavilion

"Everybody knows how to run the Birchmere. They've been telling me how to do it for 55 years," says Gary. "However, I've never liked being called the Birchmere owner. I own the corporation that operated all three clubs, so I prefer to be known as manager and operator.

"There weren't many rules when I started in this business. New York City's Bottom Line club began music the same year as I started managing the Birchmere restaurant—and closed in 2004 despite Bruce Springsteen's offer to pay their back-rent.

"DC's Blues Alley began one year before I started managing the Birchmere restaurant in 1966. It closed for 18 months but reopened in 2021. They've had three owners over the years.

"I knew Cellar Door owner Jack Boyle. He once kept his bar outside of the club on a patio. Inside is where you sat up close and listened to the music."

One Model Shop

The business model for the venue is a familiar one for many music halls. The current hall employs managers and staff in five main divisions: booking, general management, box office and merchandise, dining services (waitstaff and kitchen staff).

They operate semi-autonomously, with Gary overseeing all things Birchmere. His easy-going "all in the family" management style puts less emphasis on supervision while inviting staff to be involved in the decision-making process. This vibe helps keep employee morale high.

The ticket prices are correlated to the performers' fees. The place makes no profits on selling tickets. The food and drink sales are what keeps the Birchmere in business and keeps the lights on.

Gary says, "People think it's easy to run a club like the Birchmere. It is anything but easy to attract national acts night after night and maintain a high level of artistry. I've heard how so-and-so is going to start a new club and put us out of business at least a dozen times. Many new clubs come into this market. I've always found the best way to proceed is to concentrate on what we are doing and not what others are doing. We take pride in presenting premiere entertainment. That's our secret."

Second Coming

The Birchmere was forced to move after the razing of its original location, reopening in 1981 at 3901 Mt. Vernon Avenue. Original building owner William Hooper died at his home in Lusby, Maryland after a heart attack in 1980. Gary negotiated with his widow, Edith, to own the Birchmere name.

Gary also took on a group of about twenty "Friends of the Birchmere" as investors. These were staff, patrons, and business associates, all of whom were loyal bluegrass fans who enjoyed the association with the club. In the end, benefits were primarily just being part of this select group.

The new landlord of the Mt. Vernon Avenue building leased it to Gary. However, it wasn't long before friction between the landlord and Gary emerged. Gary recalls, "The landlord became reluctant to make building improvements. Then came his request to use the club when the Birchmere was closed. "This was stunning. He wanted it for his own private parties. I told him that I own all the licenses and such use would be illegal. Besides, who is going to run the place for these parties? He answered, 'You will.' I told him that's not going to happen.

"Despite all this, a five-year lease was renewed in 1992. However, problems increased, as did the rent. My accountant introduced me to Ralph Capobianco, the owner of King Street Blues, an Old Town Alexandria restaurant. When lease renewal time came around in 1996, I asked Ralph to negotiate a better lease with the landlord. After two months, Ralph told me he couldn't get anywhere with the landlord and negotiations failed.

"I couldn't make the numbers work. I didn't want to re-invent the Birchmere somewhere else and continue these leasing battles. I was thinking about retiring and heading back to Kentucky to go fishing," Gary admits. It was widely publicized in the DC newspapers that the Birchmere might be closing.

The third Birchmere from the air. © *Oelze*

Third Time Up

Providentially, the city of Alexandria called Gary suggesting a prospective new home for an expanded Birchmere. It was

Berkeley Photo, an aging, abandoned Kodak photo processing plant located two blocks up the street. A city representative told him they didn't want the Birchmere to leave the city.

Gary: "I invited Ralph to accompany me to visit this space. He brought along a friend, Jimmy Mathews, an entrepreneur and experienced developer. We took a look. It came loaded with electrical power, water, space, and ample parking. And, at 56,000 square feet, it was three times bigger than our Mt. Vernon location up the street."

Mathews went to Kodak headquarters in North Carolina and negotiated an agreement. He bought the building and lot. "Jimmy Mathews saved the Birchmere," proclaims Gary.

Mathews proposed a three-way partnership on the new space: Ralph would handle the food service; Gary would continue the music operations and Jimmy would own the building and lot and be the landlord. They agreed.

Next, Gary formed the present corporation, with Ralph as a partner. The Alexandria city council claimed credit for keeping the Birchmere in the neighborhood. *The Washington Post* headlined this news as "Old Music Club Sings a New Tune: Alexandria's Best-Known Music Club Sheds its Skin."

Gary continues: "Jimmy bought a Bobcat Excavator and ripped out the building's guts and began designing the space. He spent 15 hours a day for a year, configuring and rebuilding. We collaborated on the music-related construction like sound, dressing rooms, audience seating, and sightlines.

"Jimmy could see benefits in expanding the services—especially the food and the bar—to take advantage of the larger space. At this time the Birchmere only served beer and wine, so we applied for a liquor license. With an expanded kitchen, we could also do catered private events. A brewery was installed and successful for a few years. It became difficult to operate so we later sold it."

Gary wanted the design of the new music hall to be wide instead of deep, which would keep everyone close to the sturdy new stage and afford excellent views of the performers. A state-of-the-art sound system was installed. The brick background on the stage is actually painted canvas which helps eliminate reverberation.

Meanwhile, Jimmy designed an enormous kitchen, and brought in a great barbeque smoker. He recruited the chef, kitchen staff and brought in restaurant consultants to help write the menus. It was Jimmy's hard work that significantly improved the food service. Ralph disappeared during this building renovation phase, for reasons that were personal.

Gary and Ralph   © *Oelze*

"I liked Ralph," Gary says. "He was a character. I never met a person who knew Ralph that didn't think he was a grand guy.

A favorite story of Gary's illustrates how Ralph ticked: "We both used the car wash up the street. One day Ralph asked me how much I paid to get my tires black and shiny?

"I said, 'Two bucks. How much do you pay?'

"Ralph boasted, 'I get them done for free.'

"'Well, how do you do that?'

"He answered, 'I tip the guy 5 bucks.'

"That was Ralph. Always trying to beat the system, or at least thinking he had. But it's fair to say that his very up-front personality touched almost everyone he met in some way.

"He enjoyed being thought of as the Birchmere owner, complete with vanity car plates that read "Birchmere." My

Ralph problem became serious as his lack of attention to the club's day-to-day management responsibilities increased. Finally, he told me he didn't think he or I needed to be there on-premise that much. He suggested we take turns. I said, 'No way. We have to be here.'

"That's when it dawned on me that there can only be one captain of the ship. What sparked my creativity was concentrating on the music and how we could strongly present and improve it. His wife Lisa used to joke that 'Ralph loved to start restaurants but he hated to run them.'"

Sadly, Ralph suffered a massive stroke in 2009 that left him blind and in a wheelchair. He passed away a year later at age 64. Gary settled with Lisa and became the sole owner of the corporation. Gary says, "I was planning to only continue as manager/operator for another five years when we launched the present Birchmere. But I'm still here. Jimmy actually owns "The Birchmere" and when I decide I can't run it anymore, then Jimmy will be the one who figures out how to carry it forward. I'm confident it will continue."

Chapter 31 – Sound Masters

Billy Wolf visits a 2021 Steve Earle soundcheck.   © *S. Moore*

"Billy Wolf is a beautiful soul. He took us under his wing on November 1, 1996. It was the day after Halloween. We had done a gig at a bar the night before and we spent the whole day recording at the Birchmere. Eighteen songs, in two-track stereo, just live on a stage with no overdubs. And we ended up putting 15 of those out. That was essentially our first album.

Billy became our mentor and gave us such good advice. He was jaded enough from the industry that he scared us clear of some entangling alliances that we could have fallen into. He was so good to us."

Michael Clem, Eddie from Ohio

"It was the sound of the Birchmere that made us successful. That kept us in business. Billy Wolf is responsible for bringing us that sound."   Gary Oelze

Gary initially started Birchmere shows as the hands-on sound engineer—announcing the acts and running the soundboard for performances—until he was introduced to

Billy Wolf by Tony Rice in 1988. Gary says, "I learned from Tony that Billy had worked with Jerry Garcia, and was in big demand by California musicians like Maria Muldaur."

Born in New York City and once the bass player for the legendary group The Fugs, Wolf had worked as a mixer for Jerry Garcia, engineer for David Grisman, and producer for Tony Rice.

"My background as a musician, and my musical taste, was very much R&B. That's what I liked," Billy says. "I wanted to be James Jamerson. That would be my idea of heaven. [Jamerson was the bassist on most of the Motown Records.

"One of the reasons that Gary hired me to run the sound and why he and I hit it off is that he was in charge of the music, the kitchen, and everything else. He was overwhelmed, and things were a bit frantic. I was an introverted sort of fellow, but I tried to bring a studio kind of attitude with me into the Birchmere.

"The sound system was ready for some maintenance when I came on. We changed some of the drivers in the speakers and generally elevated the level of sound quality. Gary didn't have a lot of funds to spend on equipment. He paid the artists well, but he wasn't going to make a lot of money back on the size of the second place.

"When I came, the monitors were above the heads of the artists on the stage and were all run from the house position [soundboard at the rear of the stage] The second Birchmere was made from two stores (rooms). The mixer was in the back of the second room next to the kitchen. There was no separate monitor system [for the performers to hear]. This worked with the Seldom Scene and other acoustic artists. But with a jazz or country band, especially with a drummer, we needed bigger, louder, and a real monitor system.

In 1996 certain acts began bringing their own engineers, and I would assist. One country star, Clint Black, told me 'I'm deaf. I need the monitor to sound so loud it pushes my hair back.'

"Before we moved to the third location, we purchased a great monitor system from Mick Fleetwood when his Alexandria

450

waterfront club closed, just as I was leaving the hall." Gary continues this story: "The Clinton campaign chose Fleetwood Mac's "Don't Stop Thinking About Tomorrow" as a campaign song. Mick's earlier music club attempt, "Fleetwood's," opened in West Hollywood in 1991 but closed soon. At a Clinton event, somebody thought it would be good for Mick to open a music place in Alexandria. Some investors got him to put his name on this bar, and they opened it in 1994.

"Just in time, when we were planning to equip the third Gary and Jimmy Mathews attended the auction and sat quietly while everything was auctioned off. Kitchen equipment, bathroom doors, table, sound equipment, et cetera. However, the auctioneer totaled everything that was "sold," came up with the bid totals, and offered a second auction for everything if you could top the total bids. The Birchmere did just that, and all of Fleetwood's furnishings are now in the third Birchmere."

Two acts that Wolf fondly remembers are Steve Earle and Vince Gill. "Earle came in quite early (before the separate monitor system) when I put compression on his voice and he was happy. I really related to his music. I've been told by people that he went back to Nashville and told his friends, 'You really need to go play the Birchmere. They know what they're doing.' Working with Vince Gill and seeing him play solo was very exciting."

Wolf remembers when his old friend and musical associate, David Grisman, was scheduled to play the Birchmere and Alexandria was hit with a heavy snowstorm, closing the airports. "However, the place was packed anyway. I was elected to go on stage and let people know that they'd have to come back to see Grisman. However, I looked a bit like Grisman back then, and they thought I was him when I took the stage. So, I first had to tell them, "No, I'm not David Grisman."

"And I do like to think that people came back in the second Birchmere not because the sound was so great, but because it could have been really bad given how open that place was. You were sitting in the place in the audience's lap. The sound could have been terrible. It was sort of a smoke and mirrors to make it sound good in there. It was a trick. And, it took me a while to figure out how to do it

451

The artist has to be able to hear what they're doing. It was a big step adding the Fleetwood's monitor system."

Gary(left) Vince Gill (top), Billy (middle) with Quarterback Mark Rypien and other Washington Redskins. The team was 11-0 when this picture was taken in 1991 and they went on to win the Superbowl. © Oelze

Bluegrass, blues, and jazz mandolinist, David Grisman as he looks today. Jerry Garcia nicknamed him "Dawg."   *© Oelze*

Not a Cash Fan

Another artist Wolf discussed is Johnny Cash: "My criticism of Johnny Cash was that he wasn't a good technical singer. I was kind of a pitch sensitive engineer back then. I wanted everything in tune and all that crap. I didn't buy his records, so I didn't pay much attention to him.

"Before his one show, I was in my little tech room doing some soldering. There was a knock on the door. It's Johnny in his undershirt with his clothes in his hand. He asked, 'Could I change in here? There are too many women in the dressing room.'

"He was right. He had a huge entourage with him: his wife, her sisters, his daughters. So, he changed while I was there soldering. We talked. He was a warm person. I saw music in his eyes. He understood music. I really listened to him after that, and I became a fan."

"Billy Wolf is so good at what he does," says Gary. "But he started to have some problems when some acts brought in their own sound people. They weren't as experienced as he is, and there were disagreements. I told him that we can't argue with them. And then one day, he turned in his keys."

"There were definitely issues," says Wolf today. "I don't remember that I cared that much about the outside engineers to make me quit. I also don't remember any arguments. I would say that the reason I left was less professional than that, but I tried to be helpful with the external sound engineers. The rest of what Gary says is accurate. Sometimes they didn't know what they were doing. Sometimes they did. "There were definitely issues," says Wolf today. "I don't remember that I cared that much about the outside engineers to make me quit. I would say that the reason I left was less professional than that, but I tried to be helpful with the external sound engineers.

"For example, before Natalie Maines joined the Dixie Chicks and they became famous, they were doing a showcase to interest record companies. Their road manager asked me to do the sound because I think they had liked the sound at an earlier show. Gary likes to say that the Dixie Chicks played nine years at the Birchmere before they *became* the Dixie Chicks. My leaving was more personal, a churning in my deep heart that made me want to leave the Birchmere. I do appreciate Gary, what he has accomplished, and the good things he says about me."

Today, Billy heads Wolf Productions, which offers a wide array of audio services, specializing in mastering—the last stage of producing a record—and production, which includes all facets of recording. Today, Billy heads Wolf Productions, which offers a wide array of audio services, specializing in mastering—the last stage of producing a record—and production, which includes all facets of recording.

Harold "Bud" Gardner

Bud Gardner, the Director of Sound Production, at his soundboard.
© *S. Moore*

Bud Gardner grew up in Evansville, Indiana. He tells his story: "I played drums in bar bands and started hauling and running the PA system behind my drumkit. Married and divorced and came to Virginia where my Mom was living in Alexandria. I took a crash sound engineering course at Omega studios, and got a job at Jaxx music club in Springfield, Virginia.

"I interned at first, tended bar, and eventually ran the sound for three years, where I learned the importance of problem-solving live music. Later I met Tim Kidwell who was sound engineer at the Birchmere. He gave me a job helping load stage gear and tearing it down. This was 2000. There was an opportunity to try out as stage monitor sound engineer.

"One of the reasons I got that job is when I first mixed a Hal Ketchum show. After his show, Ketchum told me it was the best show of his life. Gary was standing there and Hal turned to him and said 'You better hire him right away.' Then we all went to the Rock It Grill and sang karaoke. Hal sang one of his own songs and nobody there knew it was him.

"Who would have thought I'd come from Indiana and one day be on first name basis with so many artists? One was the late jazz pianist George Duke. I've been a huge Frank Zappa fan, and I knew Duke's involvement on his recordings. I was still green when Duke came to play the Birchmere. He noticed how starstruck I was. He said 'Relax, man. You know, we're all the same. I'm no better than you. You're no better than me.' I was still nervous about what I was doing He made me feel comfortable and instilled a sense of calm in me. All of a sudden all the pressure was off. Everybody I've talked to that's played with George Duke all said that he had a way of bringing things out of them that they never knew they had. That's the same feeling he gave me.

Challenging Parts

Bud explains "Mixing sound isn't difficult. There are many ways to approach it. However, some vocalists sing in falsetto which sometimes gives different softer levels to the mix. Some bands are playing at a volume of 11. And I can't get their vocals loud enough because their microphones start picking up everything behind them. Or they might not want drums in their mix but we often have microphone bleed where there is nothing I can do about.

"There are challenges every night. Yet I prefer to do the stage monitors because the front of the house sound bores me. I like being the band's lifeline. It is exhilarating. You're in the trenches. You are you're part of the show. That's what gets my juices flowing."

Another shining moment for Gardner was mixing sound for Herbie Hancock, accompanied by Frank Zappa's drummer Vinnie Colaiuta. And Chick Corea was "the nicest guy on the planet, with Stanley Clarke on bass for him that night. One would imagine that Stanley Clarke would have an enormous bass pedal rig, but he doesn't. He used two amps. One for his upright bass, and another for his electric bass, with a sole tuner pedal."

Other standouts for Gardner:

Marcus Miller: "As a kid Miller started out playing with Miles Davis."

Brand X: "I loved mixing them because I knew every drum solo and every lick."

Larry Graham: "He started with Sly Stone and is another great guy who comes through with an amazing show.

Steve Gadd: ""Every drummer loves Steve Gadd. Steve has a beat that others try a copy. He's known for his session work with Paul Simon's "Late in the Evening" and "Fifty Ways to Leave Your Lover," and Steely Dan's "Aja." He kept me busy. He told me 'Keep an eye on me' and I did."

Tim Kidwell

One of the sound engineers at the club that followed Billy Wolf was Tim Kidwell. He was Mary Chapin Carpenter's sound engineer in 1989, two years after she got her CBS contract, when he came to work at the hall. Kidwell has been an arena sound engineer for 48 years.

Kidwell says "I'm a very loyal Birchmere person. I believe in what Gary's done and he has a lot of people who owe their careers to him. The second Birchmere was about acoustic music. With acoustic music you don't want to hear a sound system. It needs to sound natural. The sound system is part of the band sound with electric music. However, ideally you should be able to run all of a band sound through the PA system. But the small size of the second Birchmere made that impossible.

Gary, Tim Kidwell, and Justin Kidwell. © *S. Moore*

"One example of a challenge was Junior Brown. He could weld with the volume of his amplifier. He's a great act. Don't get me wrong. But he could be blistering loud in the second hall."

"Interestingly though, some of the bigger acts like Peter Frampton can get a good mix because they keep everything in the PA. Steve Vai, who is a guitar hero, walked in the Birchmere and was immediately on my side. He turned around and said to his crew, 'Okay, guys, only half the gear comes off the truck. We're going to keep it down tonight. This isn't that big of a room. We don't want to blow the walls out.'"

Kidwell cites another act, Chris Botti, a jazz trumpeter who earned acclaim playing with Sting. "Botti came in for a one-night gig and was so impressed with the sound he asked Gary if he could do a four-night residency. Unfortunately, it didn't work out because of scheduling."

Today, Tim's son, Justin Kidwell runs the house sound.

Justin Kidwell

Tim Kidwell always brought wife, Valerie and son, Justin, along on his music work travels. Justin says, "I remember climbing tall mixing towers in fields and sitting on stools next to him the whole night watching the bands play. So, when he became the Production Manager/Front of House Engineer at the Birchmere, it was natural to me to come and see shows. The first standout was when Asia came in after releasing their Phoenix album in 2008. This was a supergroup with original members guitarist Steve Howe and keyboardist Geoff Downes [Yes], lead vocalist and bassist John Wetton [King Crimson], and drummer Carl Palmer [Emerson, Lake, and Palmer

"I helped my Dad with the breakdown afterward, which led me to pick music as my career. I was then 18 and signed up to work for Arlington County and mix shows around the area.

"My very first job mixing the sound for the Birchmere was Riders in the Sky in 2016. I knew them from *Toy Story* and a few of the shows my father let me attend. To say I was nervous was an understatement. They had also just upgraded to the new digital Soundcraft boards, so while I was relieved to not deal with the immense Heritage 3000, I was still walking in relatively blind

Dad had worked the hall for a few years then, but everyone knew and respected him. Stepping into his old boots and working the room he worked is a feeling that still makes me smile.

"One group, Here Come the Mummies, was an incredible sight to behold. Every member of the band dressed up like 10,000-year-old mummies and was a big party band of jazz and visual wonders. But what I essentially remember is the confetti--we found it for months after—and the fact that the whole backline and upstage of the band was set up on these massive boxes they'd brought all the gear in. The poor drummer was basically head level with the lights! I had to applaud their lighting engineer for keeping him well-lit the whole show. Pip the Magic Dragon, too, was fantastic, mainly because I enjoy his stage humor and because I got to really see how professionals can pull off amazing feats of magic."

Chapter 32 – Fanfare

There wouldn't be a Birchmere music hall without loyal audiences. The Birchmere has earned a remarkable fan base over 55 years and maintains a club mailing list of over 150,000 names. Here is a small selection of photos and stories of staff and fan celebrity memories from years of special evenings. Our thanks to all contributors and we look forward to seeing you at the Birchmere.

Teresa, Lacie, and Vince.   © *E. Milner*

In his 25 years keeping the Birchmere parking lot in order, Officer Ed Milner's favorite memory isn't related to his job but rather to his daughter, Lacie.

Lacie, and his wife Teresa, are huge Vince Gill fans. However, Lacie is disabled with cerebral palsy. Officer Milner explains, "She also can't tolerate loud music. Once when Vince Gill was doing an acoustic performance in 1985, Gary arranged for his wife and Lacie, then 18 years old, to come to the show." Bridgett brought a friend, who helped her with Lacie's wheelchair. When Vince found out it was my family," says

Milner, "he invited them to have dinner with him in the dressing room before the show."

"A half-hour into the show, Lacie needed the ladies' room. As Bridgett wheeled her up the aisle, Vince stopped the show.

"Lacie, are you leaving?" Vince called from the stage.

"No, we'll be right back," Bridgett assured Vince, and the show continued.

Lacie eventually did have to go home early, and again, Vince stopped the show to bid her farewell.

"That was pretty cool," acknowledged Ed, looking back on Vince Gill's kindness and how it created a treasured family story. When reminded of this story in 2020, Vince appeared a little embarrassed about taking much credit for this gesture, explaining it away as, "When you do something nice for the kids of parents, you make a lot of fans who remember it."

Rosanne Cash   © *B. Gardner*

Rosanne Cash's Fan Memories

"I've met people there who I remember from years later," Rosanne Cash told us. "People who really touched me, like a woman who was in the military and in the Pentagon building on 9/11 when the plane crashed into it. And she came into this show and I met her afterwards and spoke to her. And I remember another military veteran who was suffering from

PTSD really badly. And music was the way he stayed grounded. It was his therapy. His parents brought him and I met him. I start tearing up thinking about that guy and so many people who've been so humble and open. So non-judgmental and who come and you can give them music.

"And that's been an honor. It really has. It makes you feel so humbled to know them. Hey, it's not about me. These people come to the show to give me something and for me to give them something. That is what the world runs on."

Alison and Art in 1988.   © *The Horns*

Horn Sonata

Alison Adams arrived in Falls Church, Virginia in 1984 and fell in with a new group of friends who went to the Birchmere regularly. Today Alison tells her story: "We went every week to see the Seldom Scene on Thursdays. On weekends we saw Johnson Mountain Boys, Doyle Lawson, Quicksilver, New Grass Revival, Doc Watson, and Tony Rice, when he started up there. The biggies (Monroe, Stanley, Country Gentlemen) played less often, but we were always there for them, too."

"I met a guy named Art Horn and we started to sit together close to the stage. Another couple, Bruce and Merle Harrison, were there almost every time we were and they sat in the upper level directly behind us.

"Today, its Alison Adams Horn. I married Art in 1988. Bruce and Merle say they watched our courtship from a front row seat."

Journalist Charles David Young recalls "The first time I saw **Susan Tedeschi** in concert was March 15, 2000 in her Birchmere debut. That show convinced me she was one of the best new artists I'd seen in many years, and I saw her again at the in early 2003..

"Then on Saturday November 4, 2006, she and her band joined her husband **Derek Trucks** and his band in the bigger space of the Birchmere Flex stage for a standing room sellout show that felt like the start of something big. Of course, it was, with the Tedeschi-Trucks band growing out of those early twin-bill shows, and now they're one of the biggest concert draws around. Thanks to the Birchmere, I was able to see Susan in those early intimate solo shows, meet her a few times, then see her share the stage with Derek and meet him as well. It's a great example of the sort of historic musical collaboration testing ground the hall always provided for both artists and fans."

Dance, Dance, Dance

Takoma Park, Maryland resident Kenneth Davis recalls this happy memory: "My wife, Julie, and I had met doing Contra Dancing at Glen Echo Park, but when it was time to get married, May 18, 2002, we held our reception at the Birchmere. We did not use the Music Hall but instead used the outer room to set up a stage with a contra dance band and caller and celebrated by teaching all our guests to Contra Dance. The chef at the time was a gourmet chef who welcomed the opportunity to show off finer things than the usual Birchmere fare."

(l to r) Jackie Wheelock, Jim Starkey, Julie Miller, Phip Wheelock
© Jay Pulli

The Greatest Fan

When Hamilton Smith moved to Alexandria from his Richmond, VA home in 1980, his new friends told him about the Birchmere. "My first show was "Guitars and Saxes" with Jefferson Airplane guitarist Craig Chaquiro and guitarist Peter White, who collaborated for years with Al Stewart, another Birchmere perennial favorite. After that, I began showing up every time I could." says Smith. "And Gary and the staff became my *Cheers* bar buddies ever since

You can spot Ham, as he's known, sitting at the table nearest the bar. He's usually there with a friend. Linda Kennedy, who Ham calls "my Birchmere wife."

"Ham and Linda usually come two or three times a week, and sometimes more," Gary says.

Ham with Mindy Abair.   © Oelze

Best memory: "Being invited on stage to dance with saxophonist **Mindy Abair**." Greatest show: "**Greg Allman** in 2006."

"I'm WET, man."

Bethesda, Maryland resident Rob Olausen remembers: "I went to see Buddy Guy in 1993. Gritty bluesman John Campbell opened up for him, and my friend, Scott MacLaren, and I wanted to meet him and get one of his free cassettes signed. So, we wandered back and somehow ended up in the dressing room and saw John on the sofa to the right. He was happy that we dug his opening set, so we chatted, and he graciously signed my cassette cover.

"All the while, Buddy Guy was sitting on the sofa to Scott's left, and we didn't even recognize him initially. We knew we weren't supposed to be in the green room to begin with, so we just said, "What's up, Buddy?" and got the hell outta there."

After the show, we tried to find Buddy again to get him to sign one of his cassettes for us. He was nearly out the door waiting for his car [Maryland tagged], but he was gracious enough to sign it after saying, 'I'm WET, man, I'm WET!' He was sweating profusely. We said that was OK. He got into his ride and disappeared into the Alexandria night.

"To this day, me and Scott, my concert-going friend of 35 years, say jokingly to each other, 'I'm WET, man, I'm WET!'"

© K. Roseman

Journalist Ken Roseman with **Madelaine Edith Prior, MBE** (b. 14 Aug. 1947, Blackpool, UK). The English folk singer Maddy Prior is best known as the lead vocalist of Steeleye Span.

Buzz with Carla Bruni   *Photo by Leslie Aun*

Buzz McClain recalls this story: "My wife, Leslie Aun, is a fan of Carla Bruni's music but I only knew her as the former first lady of France (she's married to Nicolas Sarkozy), so when she

465

saw she was bringing a band to the Birchmere, we (me) took a chance on whatever we were going to see. Carla was utterly charming throughout the show, sincerely thanking the audience after each song in a set that included the unlikely cover of an AC/DC hit ("Highway to Hell"). We did the post-show "lurking by the green room door" in the hopes of saying hi—and she was very gracious. We talked about her music and how much she enjoyed the venue; this photo captures the expression of a smitten fan who finds a supermodel, singer, songwriter, former first lady's arm around him. Just another example of Birchmere magic."

© *S. Moore*

I've got your number

At six o'clock Gary takes the microphone and begins calling out the line numbers for entry into the music hall. "The evening begins when the staff and audience hear my voice," explains Gary. "I feel they know we are all a team when we open the inner doors for seating. I enjoy the personal meet and greet with everybody. I know many people by name or nicknames and also by face over the years. I get a sense of how the night is going to go depending on the crowd. A folkie turnout will probably keep the kitchen busy and a rock show will keep the bar staff hustling.

"Calling the numbers also gives me the opportunity to show how grateful I am that they come out for the show."

Chapter 33 ~ Encore

The 2020 pandemic shut the Birchmere down. The last act to play before this unprecedented, sudden closure was the High Kings. Guitarist-songwriter-singer Tommy Emmanuel was the first performer to do a virtual streaming performance was This event on August 15, 2020, was a benefit for the Birchmere, with Rob Ickes and Trey Hensley supporting him.

"Without some support, we are in danger of losing some of the independent venues that are a part of our culture and our local communities," said Emmanuel.

Tommy has been a Birchmere favorite since his first show in 2005, returning 16 times and typically selling out.

William Thomas Emmanuel, AM
(b. May 31, 1955, Muswellbrook, Australia)

Tommy Emmanuel is known for his complex guitar technique. One of his standout performances is his rendition of the Rogers and Hart tune, "Blue Moon." It starts off with a steady bass line for four measures, and then the drums kick in. A brisk rhythm guitar joins the mix, followed by clean jazzy lead notes. It definitely swings.

What makes this so special is that he does all this alone on stage playing an acoustic guitar.

"The Birchmere is honored to be the first venue to have Tommy Emmanuel do a streaming concert for us," said Gary in a Birchmere message. "Tommy has been one of our favorite and most valued artists to perform at the club in its 54-year existence. Tommy's musical prowess as performer and composer is only exceeded by his kind and generous spirit. He brings that to our stage and audiences, every time he is here. Though we may not be together in body for this special show, we are certainly together again in spirit."

Open For Business

"John Lennon once used a 1957 *Readers Digest* quote in a song: "Life is what happens to you while you're busy making other plans." Gary agrees that the quote applies to this book project. "The COVID-19 pandemic struck a few months after we began our research and writing. It temporarily shut the place down in April and we followed the city of Alexandria's occupancy restrictions.

The COVID-19 pandemic struck a few months after we began our research and writing of this book. We followed the city of Alexandria's occupancy restrictions when we reopened in July 2020. I'm proud of the fact that we were able to keep most of our staff together throughout this crisis. The Alexandria health department was very helpful and we worked hard to meet their guidelines.

"The decision of the staff to continue working at the hall was difficult and personal. We didn't have full shifts to offer. Some of our loyal waitresses like Katherine and Karen had been with us for years but had to now stay home to care for family. Our longtime general manager, John Brinegar, also decided to leave. He will be missed me, staff and performers."

We reopened on July 10, 2020 with the soul-blues music of The Billy Price Charm City Rhythm Band. Billy is a familiar friend to the hall, especially for his Tribute to Roy Buchanan shows.

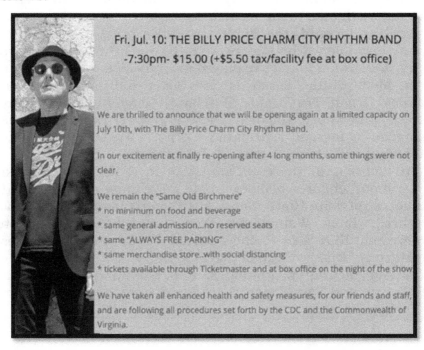

Fri. Jul. 10: THE BILLY PRICE CHARM CITY RHYTHM BAND
-7:30pm- $15.00 (+$5.50 tax/facility fee at box office)

We are thrilled to announce that we will be opening again at a limited capacity on July 10th, with The Billy Price Charm City Rhythm Band.

In our excitement at finally re-opening after 4 long months, some things were not clear.

We remain the "Same Old Birchmere"
* no minimum on food and beverage
* same general admission...no reserved seats
* same "ALWAYS FREE PARKING"
* same merchandise store..with social distancing
* tickets available through Ticketmaster and at box office on the night of the show

We have taken all enhanced health and safety measures, for our friends and staff, and are following all procedures set forth by the CDC and the Commonwealth of Virginia.

Jorma Kaukonan played a solo show during the COVID-19 pandemic in 2020. © Oelze

Subsequent acts who braved the pandemic include Daryl Davis, The Allman-Betts Band, Paula Poundstone, Robert Earle Keen, Tab Benoit, Marty Stuart, and Jorma Kaukonen. Birchmere thanks them for their loyalty.

Looking forward, the Birchmere takes pride in presenting young new talent who may prove to be our future stars," says Gary. A short list that we've played recently includes Samantha Fish, Molly Tuttle, Sarah Jarosz, Sierra Indications, Delvon Lamarr Organ Trio, John Moreland, Gene Noble, Anthony Brown, and Robert Glasper. There are many Hull, Christone "Kingfish" Ingram, Brandon "Taz" Niederauer, Jake Shimabukuro, Durand Jones & The others.

In addition to these artists, here is a list of the "next generation," children of older artists we've presented: Lily Hiatt (daughter of John Hiatt), Sarah Lee Guthrie (daughter of Arlo Guthrie), Lucy Wainwright Roche (daughter of Loudon Wainwright III & Suzy Roche), Curtis McMurtry (son of James McMurtry), Django Walker (son of Jerry Jeff Walker), The Traveling' McCourys (Ronnie & Rob McCoury, sons of Del McCoury), and The Allman Betts Band (sons of Gregg Allman & Dickey Betts).

We estimate there have been 13,000 discrete performances over the years with an approximate audience of three million people.Recognizing it would be impossible to present a *complete* history of the hall in one volume, we had to be selective when compiling this book. We've tried to be as inclusive as possible. Our enormous gratitude to every single one of the performers and their fans, whether or not we were able to mention them by name, who together created the alchemy of so many magical nights at the Birchmere.

Samantha Fish in 2021. © *S. Moore*

"Every night is different," says Gary. "Every audience is a special crowd. Every band has a distinct personality. It's almost 57 years. I've always wanted to come to work. I'm lucky."

Sincere thanks for reading this history. We will add to this Birchmere legacy effort in the future; there are exciting conversations taking place for future projects, perhaps the release of soundboard recordings, certainly the posting of more photos and performance information on our "All Roads Lead to the Birchmere" Facebook page. Who knows what lies ahead on these new roads? Please stay tuned and join us on the ride.

To be continued...

Afterword

by

Bob Schieffer

Country music was a big part of my life growing up. We just called it music back then. We could get the Grand Ole Opry's WSM radio broadcast on Saturday nights in my hometown of Fort Worth, Texas. In 1957 I went to the Grand Ole Opry with two of my college fraternity brothers. We saw Ernest Tubb and "Cousin" Minnie Pearl. It was the first time I had ever been away from home on a trip without my parents.

It's funny that all through the years, and all the political stories I've covered, my two favorite pieces were my country music interviews with Willie Nelson and Tanya Tucker.

Bob Schieffer's band album.

While at CBS, I had a country music band for 10 years called *Honky Tonk Confidential*. We played just about every place from the Grand Ole Opry to the Smithsonian Museum in Washington DC to Bass Hall in my hometown, Fort Worth. One place missing from our credits—and which I always regretted—is that we never got invited to play at the Birchmere. I'll tell you that you've got the mother church of country music in Nashville's Ryman Auditorium, and my feeling is next to that is the Birchmere. It is such a great venue.

When I had the opportunity to do the Tanya Tucker profile on *CBS Sunday,* I was so happy that she was coming to perform at the Birchmere. I thought it was the perfect place to see her. I had never met Tanya before and she was something. We did some of the interviewing in Nashville and then came to the Birchmere for her show. In her element there and totally outrageous, she was sitting on stage on a stool, charming the audience. At one point, she noticed that her pants were unzipped. "Oh well, open for business," she quipped. She would have won the audience over even if she didn't sing a song. Tanya was up for Grammy awards when we did the piece, and she won two of them by the time it aired.

So, you know you have arrived when you've played the Birchmere. The Birchmere has a reputation all to itself. I started to hear about the place from my music friends like Vince Gill. They've all played there. Again, I never did, and I regret it.

Oh well, that's the breaks. I really don't think of myself as a musician. I play some guitar chords and sing a little. I wrote some of our band songs like "TV Anchor Man" for our band's *Road Kill Stew* album. We played the Ryman Auditorium in 2008, which was an election year. I was coming to Tennessee's Belmont University to cover the Presidential debate, but I was still absolutely stunned when the Ryman asked the band to perform.

Trisha Yearwood went on before us, and she was standing next to me while I was almost ready to go on. She calmed my nerves by saying, 'Just go out there and have some fun.' I was still more nervous when I stepped onto the Opry stage than I was the following week when I moderated the next presidential debate. Trisha's advice was more easily said than done.

Another country music experience comes to mind. The first book I wrote was *The Acting President*. It was about President Reagan and the Bush campaign in 1988. I was doing a book signing and got a tap on the shoulder. I turned, and it was Johnny Cash. He couldn't have been nicer but what impressed me was how gracious he was with everyone. He acted like he was so interested in *you*, meaning everyone he met. I've written five books, and I did tours with every book. I look back at that moment, meeting Johnny Cash, as the highlight of my book tours. I imagine many audience members have similar unforgettable memories meeting their favorite performers at the Birchmere.

I'm so glad this book was done to summarize the Birchmere's remarkable run and to honor the performers who "arrived" by playing the legendary hall. If not on stage, my thanks for including me in the story.

Acknowledgements

It's evident from this history that teamwork is an essential ingredient for the success of the Birchmere. Our thanks to everyone who helped us document the story.

We begin with gratitude to Michael Jaworek for sharing his adventures. Rapid communications with all the artists who contributed to this history was also made possible by Michael.

We thank Buzz McClain for our Foreword. He began covering Birchmere acts in 1983 as the entertainment editor for the *Journal Newspapers*, a local daily, and later served a ten-year tenure as a music reviewer for the *Washington Post*.

Our appreciation to Bob Schieffer for contributing our Afterword, and to Susan Oelze for arranging our interview.

We thank our editor, Patty Johnson Cooper for project supervision, and devotion. Patty's enthusiasm, wit, and music expertise was essential to the project. Our sincere thanks to music writer Richard Harrington for invaluable insight and ardent suggestions. Appreciation also to writers Steve Lorenz and Charles David Young for their editorial input and backing.

The Birchmere's value was achieved and is maintained by its sound. We thank Billy Wolf, Bud Gardner, Tim Kidwell, and Justin Kidwell for their sonic memories.

We sincerely thank present and past Birchmere staff for their stories and advice. These include Jimmy Mathews, Dawn Williams, David Beebe, Bud Gardner, John Brinegar, Ben Finkelstein, Stuart Wodlinger, K.C. Alexandria, Chris Adams, John Meadows, Jorge Escalier, Officers Ed Milner and Mark Uzell, Eminiah "Fly" Shinar and Clarence "Shoe" Shumacher, John Longbottom, Peggy Mai, Marlize Mason, Mary Beth Aungier, Teresa O'Brien, Connie Brandt Smith, Neva Warnock, and Sesi Warnock Miller.

We are grateful to our friend and talented artist, Stilson Greene for designing our book cover, and to Angela Hoy and her excellent Booklocker crew for publishing our book with flair and expertise.

Our thanks to Arlo Guthrie for helping us develop the "Birchmere celebrity interview" approach we used for subsequent performer discussions. We appreciate the time and effort the following Birchmere players and professional associates provided: Adele Abrams, Randy Ashkraft, Elise Auldridge, Kevin and Michael Bacon, Janie Barnett, Dick and Linda Bangham, Matt Bogert, Peter Bonta, Mark Benson, Ray Benson, Bryan Bowers, Junior Brown, James Burton, Mary Chapin Carpenter, Rosanne Cash, Jon Carroll, Tom Carrico, Jack Cassady, Don Chapman, Michael Clem, T. Michael Coleman, Cerphe Colwell, Shawn Colvin, Dudley and Sally Love Connell, Robert Cray, Rodney Crowell, Katy Daley, Daryl Davis, Lee Michael Demsey, Cliff Eberhardt, Ben and Barbara Eldridge, Bill Emerson, Tim Finch, Savannah Finch, Cathy Fink, Carl Fleischhauer, Cleve Francis, Rick Frank, Danny Flowers, Erten Fuller, Julie Gold, John Gorka, Vince Gill, Tom Gray, Tommy Hannum, Chris Hillman, Seth Hurwitz, Janis Ian, Jorma Kaukonen, Robert Earle Keen, Lucy Kaplansky, Pete and Maura Kennedy, Bill Kirchen, Patty Larkin, Christine Lavin, Maysa Leaks, Nils Lofgren, Ottmar Liebert, John Longbottom, Lyle Lovett, Kathy Mattea, Marcy Marxer, Akira Otsuka, Tom Paxton, Rich Pagano, David Pomeroy, Al Petteway, Paula Poundstone, Phil Rosenthal, Mark Segraves, Ron Thomason, Debi Smith, Ricky Skaggs, Fred Travers, Kenny Vaughan, John Waters, Susan Westenhoefer, Cheryl Wheeler, Dar Williams, and Dave Williamson.

Our thanks to other journalists and photographers including Mark Engleson, Joe Heim, Mike Joyce, Geoffrey Himes, Nick Kalivretenos, Keith Loria, Dave McKenna, Michael Oberman, Ken Roseman, Joe Sasfy, David Segal, Tim Stafford, and *Michael G. Stewart* for their published work, comments and photos. Finally, our sincerest thanks to the fans and friends of the Birchmere who contributed memories, research, photos, and enthusiasm to this project.

Sincerely, Gary and Steve

Index

D

T